W9-CUI-504

I WAS A HORSE
IN BRYANSK

GEORGE V. GEMER

Illustrations by

Tamas Nagyreti

© 1995 by George Gemer
3rd printing

All rights reserved

No part of this book may be reproduced or utilized in any form or by
any means, electronic or mechanical, including photocopying and
recording, or by any information storage and retrieval system, without
permission in writing from the publisher.

ISBN # 0-919555-95-0

Produced by Printing Services, The University of Lethbridge

*To my daughters Robin and Tara
and my dear wife Carole*

ACKNOWLEDGMENTS

Although the idea to write my story was born in my heart along time ago, it took many years of encouragement and persuasion over many glasses of beer with terrific friends like Tom Golden and George Kuhl to finally make me lift my pen. Thanks to both of you for your support!

For their gratuitously reading of the manuscript when it was in its infancy, the time they spent making corrections and suggestions, and the encouragement they provided, I am thankful to Katy and Peter Letkeman. Their critiques and assistance was invaluable.

The illustrations and cover page were done by the talented Hungarian graphic artist, Tamas Nagyreti, my school chum and soccer buddy from Felsogod. His humor, friendship and good heart saved my life in the initial days of my prison life. No one could have captured the images better than one who had also lived through the dreadful times. Thank you, Tamas, not only for your fine artwork, but for your genuine friendship.

To my oldest daughter Robin, I thank you for your love and encouragement, and to my youngest daughter, Tara, who made a tremendous contribution by carefully going through the text correcting and moulding it without changing the thoughts or the ideas of the writing, thank you. I would like to believe that besides my gratitude, you will draw some benefit from your work by knowing me better.

Finally, credit for what seemed to be endless labour goes to my dear wife, Carole, for transferring my long hand to the 'magical computer'. The numerous changes and corrections of corrections certainly tested her patience and sentenced her to over two years of long days in front of the computer which often stretched into the wee hours of the morning. I am forever thankful for your tireless work and your love and understanding, Carole.

TABLE OF CONTENTS

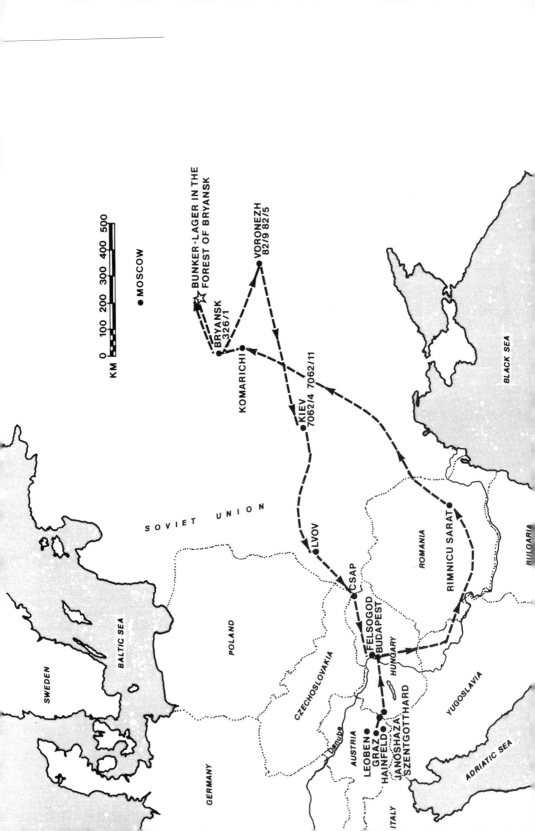

PROLOGUE

What you are about to read is a true story. It is a story of the events of my youth and the struggles and hardships I endured during the years I spent in captivity in Russian prisoner-of-war camps. It may seem to be an insignificant story when compared to the suffering and tragedy experienced by millions of Jews during the Holocaust or when compared to the destruction of entire cities and deaths of thousands which occurred in many parts of Europe during W.W.II. Indeed, this story, a story of one man's life, is but a paragraph relative to the magnitude of the Great War and the harsh conditions to which millions were exposed; nonetheless, the years of this era are filled with countless such paragraphs from others who endured the atrocities of war. Together, each small paragraph records a slice of time and gives volume and perspective to the larger story of the second world war. This is a short chapter in the book of history.

What are written here are my experiences. They have served as great lessons for me in the school of life and have included a curriculum of subjects such as human behaviour, tolerance, understanding, patience, self control, and determination. These lessons have formed my philosophy and instilled my values, making me the person I am today. I have learned not to take for granted all the good things I enjoy, and thus I appreciate everything I have. Now, when I 'roast' myself in front of my fireplace on crisp winter evenings, I think back to the miserable cold I felt in Bryansk, and I savour the warmth of a fire immensely. When I take a steaming shower each day, I recall the times when, for weeks, I did not have an opportunity to clean my filthy, lice-infected body. When I eat a good meal, I am thankful for the bounties I have. No longer must I live each day with the pain of hunger.

I do regret that I could not complete my formal education, but the wisdom and perspective I have gained from the events of my life, I feel, are worth more. These lessons cannot be taught in any school; they must be experienced. I have experienced them, and thus have recognized the importance of cultivating basic human qualities which would enable people to make this world better, and reduce the human suffering and misery that currently runs so rampant. I learned that when we struggle it gives meaning and substance to our lives, and happiness as we progress. I remember the great Hungarian writer Imre Madach's masterpiece, The Tragedy of Man. In the conclusion of his drama the Lord said to Adam "Man, I have spoken; strive on, trust, have faith!" It seemed to give some explanation and direction to the questions of our existence and future in this world and this is all we need to know. I learned to dream and to set goals, for if you do not, you have nothing to aim for nor can anything be achieved.

IN-FLIGHT REFLECTIONS

The 747 jumbo jet's engines roared like thunder as the giant bird took off from the runway of the Calgary airport. I was sitting in a window seat among the affluent and experienced passengers as it reached cruising altitude in the brilliant sunshine above the silver clouds. As a representative from Alberta to the Sports Minister's National Advisory Council on Fitness and Amateur Sport, I was on my way to Montreal for a regular meeting. "Sir, red or white wine"? asked the flight attendant. I replied, "White, please."

Enjoying Gerschwin melodies through the headphones, sipping the wine, I remembered a dear old friend's words, "You poor Hungarian refugee; you're doing just fine!" Yes, I escaped from communist Hungary during the 1956 Revolution, and as a political refugee came to build my nest in Canada via Austria, Germany and England. All my worldly possessions were in a suitcase filled with clothes that I had received from the Austrian and German Red Cross, but in my heart I carried a wealth of memories from Hungary and from my prison life in Russia. My mind held valuable experiences in athletics as well as my never-diminishing love and enthusiasm for coaching.

As I soared through the blue sky at the zenith of my life, I couldn't avoid looking back and remembering its nadir. Pictures kept popping into my mind like colorful kaleidoscopes from the past. Although enjoying the royal treatment, the delicious meal, and the beautiful sights, I could not help remembering my earlier years filled with difficult times. It had all begun far below the silver clouds and thousands of miles to the east in my homeland - Hungary.

MY YOUTH

I was born in the small town of Felsogod, north of Budapest on the bank of the blue Danube. It was, and remains, a peaceful little village with red-tiled roofs, dirt roads, flower gardens and fruit trees. Behind a variety of fences which embraced tiny parcels of land, lay each owner's pride and joy - well-cultivated rows of vegetables and, in some cases, grapevines. As the sun fell behind the Pilis mountain range, cut shrubs, lilac bushes and acacia trees spread their sweet scents in summer's evening air. My family lived contentedly in this tranquil summer resort. I was the youngest of five children.

My oldest sister Eszter spent most of her early school years away from the family. We saw her only occasionally when she came home to Felsogod during the summer vacation. With the help of a relief organization, she was granted the opportunity to receive a proper education and to live a comfortable life. This also meant my mother had one less mouth to feed and one less body to clothe, but Mama's caring thoughts and love traveled the distance with Eszter, over the Alps to the Swiss village where she grew up as an accepted member of another family. My other sister Olga, my brothers Tibor and Laszlo, my mother and I lived in my uncle's large brick house. It had a steep red roof of ceramic tiles and a yellow stucco exterior. This old house served all

our needs and we lived out our dreams within its walls. The trees behind the house provided us with plenty of fruit, and also shaded our backyard playground where summer tenting adventures and endless battles between cowboys and Indians unfolded. My brothers and I shared a spacious bedroom, and during the winter months, large ceramic heaters radiated soothing comfort which warmed our toes. It was Mama's dear care and love, though, which warmed our hearts year round throughout our childhood.

My father had left the family when I was very young. One of my few memories of him is a time when he took my brothers and me to the countryside to visit his relatives. I could not have been more than three or four years old, but I recall the great excitement that captured my young heart as I took my first train ride. This is the only time I remember spending with him until many years later when I was in high school. He served his compulsory army years in the Hungarian cavalry, and a photograph of him in his army officer's uniform sat on the desk in my mother's room. His sword hung on the wall. These were the only reminders we had of him. Ten years after that first train ride with him, he appeared at my school, much to my surprise. Emotionally, the meeting seemed to affect him the most. He saw his three sons had grown up. We had managed without him, and he could see that Mama's love and Uncle Gyula's care had provided us with everything we needed. We had not missed father; nevertheless, we accepted his occasional invitation to a fancy restaurant for dinner. We walked by these places on the way to school, but never, even in our wildest dreams, did we think we would see the inside of those buildings. I remember him as a tall, well dressed, handsome man with affectionate brown eyes. After his army service, he found

15

work in a law office, and so was able to give us some money. He seemed to hope this would gain our affection, but after so many years of living without him, our feelings for him never grew to resemble those of a normal father-son relationship.

After our meetings with father, we were always anxious to go home to Mama and tell her about where we had been and give her the money father had granted us. I never knew why he left us, and my mother never spoke ill of him. The years separated us further, and I never saw him again.

It was Uncle Gyula who, upon seeing my mother left with five kids and no support, inherited us and took responsibility for us. He shared his home with us and encouraged us to complete our education. His support and care was extended to my beloved grandmother and my aunt Sarolta, my mother's older sister who also lived in the house. My family had found refuge with Uncle Gyula. So, my brothers and sister and I grew up in Felsogod, attending the local elementary school. We completed our high school education in Budapest, commuting daily via the only transportation system that was available - the train pulled by a steam engine.

Uncle Gyula, in effect, became a more-than-adequate substitute for our father. He was a proud, handsome man who was very strict, but deep down he was also very warm-hearted. He was in good physical condition - his medium sized frame stocked with strong muscles. His complexion was dark, and black curly hair accentuated his light blue eyes. He soon became our role model. Each spring, when April's sun cast its blessed warmth on the countryside and colored it green, Gyula was the first to swim in the cold waters of the Danube. He taught us to be disciplined, and thus we obeyed Mama's every word without question. We never skipped school, and we learned to perform our duties of cleaning the yard, shoveling snow or chopping fire wood.

Uncle Gyula never did marry. He already had a family larger than he had bargained for. Mama, in turn, took good care of him, and a warm supper always awaited him no matter how late he came home. Occasionally she helped him to bed when his equilibrium was affected by a few glasses of wine. He was well liked by his friends, whom he met regularly. They would often celebrate their camaraderie over a few glasses of wine, singing traditional Hungarian folk songs, accompanied by gypsy musicians. Gyula was never short of female friends due to his flamboyant nature and noble conduct. He lived the life of a bachelor, but his feelings of obligation always put the family first. At the end of each month, Gyula would give Mama a small allowance. He also brought home sweets to share in celebration of his pay day. He spent all of his working years as an employee in the Hungarian travel agency, where he earned a fair income. His position provided us with some welcome security as well. I felt he deserved all the good things in life because of his extraordinary generosity and the respect and kindness he demonstrated toward other people. He was proud of his heritage and he lived each day of his life proving it.

As far as I can remember, Mama's life was an endless struggle. She endured long years of lonely nights and often awoke upon a tear-soaked pillow. Her days were filled with the demanding task of caring for four children, cooking daily meals on a shoe-string budget, and washing dishes and clothes. Above all, she made peace and ensured justice amongst us, her three fighting boys who were so full of vigor and mischief. She accepted God in her heart, and I strongly believe that because of her faith she managed to go through life without breaking down or leaving to find another man. In her early thirties, she was small-framed with lush, brunette hair which framed her delicately-cut face and her blue eyes. I believe the eye is the mirror of the soul, and her eyes certainly reflected her warm character and genuine goodness. I remember times when wandering beggars came to the house for a few pennies that she could not spare. Instead, she offered them a bowl of steaming soup. Her devotion and love for us, as children, was extraordinary, and the feeling was mutual. Everyone in the village respected her for her gallant fight to provide for her children. My brothers, my sister and I clung to her like burs to a wanderer's pants.

One of the most delightful pastimes of my early childhood was to go with Mama to the local marketplace twice a week in the summertime. Fruits and vegetables were brought in abundance to the market from nearby small holdings where people made their living growing agricultural products. Horses pulling loaded wagons were lined up in neat rows, and customers walked between them, comparing prices, meeting friends, and bargaining for the best deals. The scent of fresh fruit and vegetables mixed with the smell of live ducks, chickens, and horses, gave the place a distinct aroma that was lively and exciting - a treat for the nose. After a glorious hour or two of shopping, we returned home, carrying baskets full of goodies. Happy grins spread across our faces, and great anticipation of the upcoming feast of delicious juicy fruits and crisp vegetables filled our hearts.

Aside from preparing regular meals, Mama made bread for the family with tender care. Not having enough space in our wood-burning kitchen stove, we put Mama's bread dough in two big containers and took it to a nearby bakery to be baked. The end product was two round, wheel-sized loaves of bread weighing approximately five kilograms each. The bread was made of whole-grain flour, a mixture of wheat and rye, and mashed potatoes that helped to keep the bread from drying out too fast. Two loaves lasted us a week, and we loved its thick, crunchy crust and rich flavor, accentuated with caraway seeds. With the same joy and anticipation as our visit to the marketplace, we looked forward to those days when we would collect a new batch of bread.

On weekends, Mama took us for walks in the country-side through the pine forest where we picked mushrooms and wild flowers. We laughed and ran playfully and tried to out-sing the meadowlarks. As we returned home after these long walks, we were tired but happy. These weekend excursions kept our family together and moulded our strength.

The carefree tranquility of these early years was disturbed by the death of my grandmother whom we adored very much. I was ten years old. My family was shocked and deeply saddened. She had added great joy to our lives and we missed her kindness, understanding and warmth from the moment she was gone. The other member of the family, or as far as we were concerned, the other occupant of the house, was our Aunt Sarolta, my mother's older sister. The house was physically divided to provide her with separate quarters. She also had a private entrance and fenced yard. She was a widow, without children, alone in her isolated world. She had very little tolerance for my brothers and sisters and me, and she displayed more affection to her variety of house pets than she ever did to us. When our ball would accidentally fly over the picket fence into her territory, we would not get it back for days. Even then, it was returned with words so harsh, they could only come from a 'house dragon'. Perhaps, deep down, she was jealous of my mother who had her problems but also had our love. At any rate, we did not like Aunt Sarolta much, and the feeling was mutual. We avoided her as much as possible.

Olga was a very sensitive girl, with a terrific sense of humor and a pure heart. She quickly became Mama's right hand and a second mother to my brothers and me. Doing work around the house and helping Mama take care of the rest of the family was a labour of love for her. Besides the household chores and her school studies, she played the violin. She was a young member of the local symphony orchestra for a number of years. As she grew more mature, she became more like a friend to Mama than a dependent.

Tibor, my oldest brother, was a blond, blue-eyed, very masculine guy. He loved horses, dogs, and animals of any kind. His ambition was to go through agricultural college, which he did. He spent a couple of years in Switzerland where he grew as strong as a bull. The change of climate and other conditions were certainly of benefit to him. He spoke two languages fluently.

Laszlo was just two years my senior. He was a small-framed boy, quiet and withdrawn, but he had inquisitive deep brown eyes. He was the typical science-oriented individual, and he showed great interest in the world of electronics. By the time he was in junior high school, he had already built himself a primitive but functional radio. All of his free time was spent reading, playing with gadgets, or constructing things.

I look back at my youth and consider it a very precious period of my life, especially the summer vacations when we roamed around our village barefoot, playing endless games of soccer and swimming in the Danube. I recall the quiet summer evenings when I sat on the bank of the river and soaked in the warmth of the blessed sun. I loved to watch the gold-

en rays dance on the water as the sun dipped into its shim-
mering surface. I can remember times when my friends, my
brothers and I committed our greatest crimes, jumping
fences and raiding fruit trees and gardens. Early summer
meant cherries, apricots and green apples. Autumn's gifts
were tomatoes, plums, grapes, pears and kohlrabis. Fruit
was plentiful throughout the village and in the nearby vineyards and orchards. What excitement! These raids presented a challenge, and our mild feelings of guilt were overcome
by mischievous delight. On some occasions, we were caught
by the owners of the yards and our embarrassment was enor-
mous. Still, we continued to creep through gardens like
thieves, nabbing any fruits and vegetables in our path.

I was nine years old when the 1936 Olympic Games
were staged in Berlin. My brothers and I eagerly read the
newspaper reports to learn about the great sport events. We
were happy and proud of the achievements of our Hungarian
athletes who won ten gold medals, and thus brought home
ten little living oak trees to honor our land. All of the neighbourhood kids kept a close watch on the athletes' performances, and we adopted Jesse Owens as our hero. We
decided to host our own Olympic Games, staging the events
on an empty lot, and adopting the identities of the athletes
who actually participated in the Games. At that time, my
greatest enjoyment came from participating in sport. When I
was ten, I played soccer with the sixteen-year olds, and quite
successfully, I might add. I was soon named by the coach as
one of the most valuable players. One day he said, "Boys,
instead of our regular training session, we will organize a little Olympics." So, we did the long jump, the 100-metre
sprint, the high jump, and a ball toss. I enjoyed the afternoon immensely, perhaps because I managed to match the

performances of my older counterparts and, in some events, performed even better than they. From that day on, I began to organize my own little Olympics in the nearby empty lot. I invited all the kids who lived close by. It became a regular event, satisfying our great appetite for running and jumping competitions. My love for physical activity and competition found a new dimension and gave me much pleasure. By the time I went to high school, my mind was set to pursue track and field, despite the fact that I could outplay my comrades anytime on the soccer field.

On one occasion in school, we were instructed not to change into our physical education uniforms. Instead, we were ordered to stay in our classroom and wait. After a few minutes, a very handsome, well-built young man came into our class and announced he would be our new physical education teacher. He wrote his name on the blackboard - Jozsef Varszegi - then turned to the class and asked, "Does anyone know this name?" A few seconds of silence passed. Then I blurted out with great enthusiasm, "You're the Hungarian National Champion and record holder in the javelin!" His eyes lit up, and with a surprised smile on his face he asked, "How did you know?" I told him I was very interested in track and field, and I knew every accomplished athlete's name, event and performance. Indeed, I was a walking sport lexicon, cutting sport-related pictures and stories from magazines and newspapers and pasting them into my album. I spent my last pennies on track and field books that I found in second-hand book stores.

Mr. Varszegi became my idol, and I watched him perform in Budapest in various competitions and international dual meets. He became a source of inspiration and encouragement to me in my teenage years. During our physical education hours, I tried to do the utmost to please him. As a result, I gained his respect, and frequently he requested that I demonstrate some elements to the class. He expected me to do everything well and above standard. On one unforgettable occasion, we had to set up two box horses with the proper mats in the gymnasium. "Today," he said, "we will learn the tiger jump." This involved a run to the box, a two-foot take off and dive over the length of the horse. After breaking one's fall with his hands and arms, one was to do a forward roll and stand up. Before I could say anything, Mr. Varszegi pointed to me and said, "Little Gemer - you demonstrate." I stood there in a cold panic. I had never done this before. I did not wish to reveal my fear, nor did I want to disappoint Mr. Varszegi, so I decided to go for it. With butterflies in my stomach, my heart pounding in my ears, and my legs shaking, I ran toward the horse which was taller than I, jumped as hard as I could, and flew spread eagle over the box. I reached out desperately with my hands for the ground, then tucked and rolled. I landed a bit roughly but without injury on the other side. As I stood, my eyes met the admiring gaze of Mr. Varszegi, and his look of amazement and pride seemed to hang an Olympic medal around my neck. The ringing applause of my classmates snapped me out of my focused concentration. A proud grin swept across my face, and I tried to conceal my own amazement.

THE LAST FREE SUMMER

After finishing my high school education in Budapest, my mother sent me to further my education at the teaching college in Marosvasarhely. This city, which had been part of Transylvania, had been returned to Hungary from Romanian rule in 1940. Mama's rationale behind the move was that if I could not stay home, I should be in a place where we had relatives. So I continued my college education in this lovely city. After one year of college I enjoyed my summer vacation away from the teaching college. During the hot summer days I found carefree contentment with my friends by the refreshing waters of the old Danube. We practically lived by the river, laughing and joking the days away. Sometimes, we would sail on the water under the brilliant stars and bright moonlight. We danced when our hearts desired, and sipped slowly at our beer - it tasted rather bitter compared to our usual drink of raspberry syrup mixed with soda water. Deep in our hearts, each of us felt he was in love but did not have the courage to admit it to that special girl. So, with carefree happiness, sweet freedom, and excellent camaraderie, our last innocent summer passed.

Subconsciously, I felt this was a farewell to all the things that were good in the years of my youth. It was good-bye to my old friend the Danube, my pals, and the dear girls. Good-bye to the old willow tree which provided shade for the garden tables, to the songs and the dances, to the sparkling sunshine that danced on the water, and the dark-blue silhouettes of the familiar mountain range of Pilis. Good-bye to the unforgettable student life, the midnight serenades and my never-returning youth. Throughout that last wonderful summer, we ignored the tragedies of the raging war and cruel bombing raids which were part of our life. We read the reports, and when we were at the movies we watched the news releases that were played, concerning war, but Russia and Germany seemed so far away from us. Our attention was focused upon our regular meetings at the bank of the Danube and our soccer games, rendezvous and garden parties. Even the frequent jolts of bombing raids failed to alter our youthful, carefree attitudes. The adults of the village were much more wary. They sensed impending tragedy as the Russian army advanced and bombs crippled the factories and disrupted communication. We, on the other hand, did not recognize the seriousness of what was happening around us at the time.

During this time of youth and innocence, characterized by schoolbooks and sports, my friends and I began to witness some discrimination against the Jewish people, fueled by the Hungarian Nazi party, the Arrow-Cross. Jews were required to wear a yellow star on their chest. Some of our soccer buddies and their parents were affected, but it seemed there was nothing we could do about it. These events were a prelude to the storm which would be created by the war, a storm that was gaining more turbulence, becoming ever more threatening and ominous on the horizon.

In July of 1944, my brother Tibor arrived home from the Murmansk front for a short holiday. He had been fighting for the Germans against the Russians. We were ecstatic to see him and enjoyed his company during the hot summer days which we spent on the river bank and in our family home. He was the center of attention amongst my school friends, and all of us were anxious to hear of his experiences on the front. He spoke of frozen bodies in the snow, bloody battles, hunger, and human suffering. It was the first time I had heard a first-hand description of the war, and I found it frightening, cold, and cruel. His stories were quite the contrast to the pleasant days of summer which we were experiencing. Our playful summer days rolled by quickly though, and as Tibor's departure date grew closer, the smile on his face began to fade, and his feelings of uncertainty and worry began to show. Before we knew it, we were saying good-bye to him again.

Autumn arrived quickly, and with its cool, easterly breath came disturbing news from the front line. The Russian army had traversed the Carpathian mountain range and had entered Hungarian territory. For the first time, the school doors did not open in September for the students to start a new academic year. I was heavily engaged in athletics, so I was not so disappointed about spending my days outside the walls of the school. Instead, I spent a lot of time walking in a nearby open field throwing the javelin religiously.

One day, my coach said he would take me to Szekszard[1] to compete at the Hungarian National Junior Pentathlon Championships. My mother was not very happy about my request to participate. I did not know why she was so against it, but after much begging she reluctantly let me go. We bought watermelon at the train station for a snack

---

[1]   A city in the South.

during our journey and happily boarded the train. The enjoyment of the train ride and the excitement and anticipation of the competition quickly turned to fear as we heard the wailing of a nearby village's sirens warning of an impending bombing raid. The train stopped on the open line, and we ran to a nearby cornfield for cover. The evening sky lit up with hundreds of 'Stalin-candles'[2] which enabled the bombers to gain a clearer view of their targets. Seconds later, the whistling sounds of falling bombs and the thunderous roar of their explosions surrounded us. We lay close together on our stomachs, in the cornfield. My heart was pounding as if I had just finished a 400 metre run, and my throat was dry. I broke out in a cold sweat and prayed for my life. The raid seemed to go on for an eternity, but finally ended. We were safe. We went back to the train on shaky legs, found the watermelons, and with silent relief enjoyed their succulence.

Eventually, as our hearts slowed and the train rocked away our fears like a mother with her child, we laughed about our close encounter and stuck our heads out the window of the train. The feeling of the evening air rushing through my hair and over my face, pacified me. Once in Szekszard, I had a very enjoyable competition and a memorable weekend with my cousin, Robi, and friend, Miki, who had come along with me.

When I arrived home, I was in the railway station when I heard the news that our village Felsogod had been bombed by the Russians. Cold panic grabbed at my heart as, with shaking knees, I ran from the station to my street. I turned

---

2   A light which was hung on a small parachute, thrown out of Russian planes.

the corner, and there I stopped. I could just see a glimpse of my beloved home in ruins. I could also see my mother and sisters in tears. Sympathy reached out from the faces of onlooking bystanders. It was difficult for me to control myself and hold back my tears. I ran to my mother.

My 19-year old brother Laszlo was dead. He had been killed almost instantly when he was struck in the heart by fragments of the bomb that had exploded in our backyard. The explosion had blown numerous holes in the utility shed where my mother and sisters were hiding with Eszter's young baby. Miraculously, they were not injured. The beautiful trees that once surrounded the yard had been uprooted. Parts of the heavy brick walls of the house were demolished, and a segment of the roof had been blown away. Thick dust now blanketed my family's dream and the lifetime that had been spent building our nest. It was a grim welcome home from a competition that had perhaps saved my life. Suddenly, I understood my mother's strange and nervous behavior when I had asked her to let me go to compete. Deep down, she must have sensed the danger. Perhaps she had premonitions of the horrific event which had hit our lives with such a devastating blow on that fourteenth day of September.

Felsogod, a small holiday village, certainly did not have any military importance. Why the hell it was hit twice by the Russians during the fall of 1944 still remains a mystery to me. Rumor had it that Russian sympathizers had signaled to the bombers with white lights from the otherwise dark and sleepy village. We never believed such tragedy would hit us.

The days following the bombing were full of sorrow. The reality of the war had finally struck me personally. Again, on the unbearable day of my brother's funeral,

Russian planes disturbed his service by flying overhead and spraying bullets over the congregation. I felt a savage rage and fury. That day, I swore over my brother's grave that I would fight the enemy of my family. The Russians would pay for Laszlo's death and the destruction of my home! I would fight those who had killed my brother. I would fight the enemy of my beloved homeland, Hungary.

The schools remained closed, and I was thankful. Day after day, I sweated and struggled to clean up the debris and repair the damaged section of the house. We continued to live in the part that was left standing. I grew up quickly, and tried to be a source of comfort to my mother and sisters, calming them during the ensuing nightly bombing raids.

From our home in Felsogod, the sky over Budapest looked like fireworks during the holiday season. Because Gyula was in the reserve, I was the only male left in the house. I had to remain strong and appear in control, despite my overwhelming emotional despair.

Throughout the country, every single boy over the age of 16 was required to participate in a para-military organization program twice a week. This program provided sports training and taught combat drills, and emphasized physical fitness and discipline. Most important, it promoted a devotion to our country. Parallel to the volunteer boy scout groups, which had a positive influence on the Hungarian youth, the compulsory Levente[3] organization also gave direction and structured programs within and outside the school system.

One foggy mist-covered morning, all the young boys of the village were instructed to assemble on the local soccer

---

[3] The name of a young warrior in Hungarian history.

field for a briefing. During the summer, we had played soccer there from dawn until dusk, returning home with empty stomachs and exhausted bodies but happy souls. This time, the soccer field served as the site for the delivery of a somber message by the local commandant of the Levente organization. His message held words that gripped my heart forever;

"Our reconnaissance planes have seen long columns of hungry and depressed Hungarians, marching under heavy guard in the direction of Siberia from a part of our country which has fallen into enemy hands. Are we going to let them do this to our blood? This is the time when your country calls upon you, so, step forward if you feel Hungarian!"

A cold shiver ran up and down my spine. The dryness of my throat nearly choked me, and I could hear my own heartbeat. I stepped forward. I was seventeen and shaking in my boots. That cool November morning, I made one of the most important decisions of my life. I returned home with mixed feelings. I was proud because I had the courage to volunteer, but frightened of the uncertainty of my future. When I told my mother I was going to fight, tears rolled down her cheeks, but her reply was strong. "Go. If I could, I would go too!" she said. If ever there was a heroic and noble gesture, it was this reply from my dear mother, a woman who had just lost one of her sons, was terrified of the daily bombing raids, and knew that only grim days lay ahead. I knew it was difficult and painful for her to let her third son go.

With nothing but a piece of bread in my bag and the clothes on my back, I left by train the next day with my cousin Robi to join the army. The time we spent on the train allowed us to talk extensively about our new adventure, and to enjoy the beautiful countryside which was still dressed in the gold and rust colors of fall. We felt somewhat smug in our courage to volunteer, and we scorned the other boys who had failed to demonstrate their patriotism in a similar manner.

Gazing out the window of the train, I envisioned the warm welcome we would receive upon our arrival at the army base. I was excited to meet the many other young boys who would be arriving from various parts of the country with the same eagerness to serve their country. We were headed for a place called Varpalota, a city which lay in the western part of the country close to Lake Balaton.[4] Shortly after we walked through the military's guarded gates, the last drop of our innocence was swallowed by soldiers of the regular army. Their attitude and behavior certainly did not resemble the image that had been imprinted in our minds throughout our patriotic upbringing in the school system. I remembered the Latin words engraved on the medals that I had received for my efforts in high school sports competitions: "Dulce et decorum est pro patria mori." Translated, this meant: "It is sweet and honorable to die for one's country." These were my thoughts when I entered the army; however, the battle-weary soldiers I saw before me now made every effort to discourage us from joining the army by not giving us any food or a place to stay. We were told to stay with the horses in their stalls. Perhaps they sensed the end of the war was near and did not want us to get involved in a lost cause. Eventually, a corporal came and led us through the gate. He told us to go home. So, there we were. After coming all this way with courage and excitement in our hearts, we found ourselves out on the street, disillusioned, hungry and confused, but secretly a bit relieved. We turned and headed home again.

---

4   A wonderful summer holiday retreat, often referred to as the Hungarian Sea, about 120 km southwest of Budapest.

Upon reaching the highway by foot, we jumped into the back of a truck filled with people headed for Budapest. From there we took the train back to Felsogod, which was only 27 kilometres from the capital. The relief I saw in my mother's eyes when she saw I had returned home stirred my heart. During my few days away from home, another bombing raid had hit our town, and three bombs had fallen on our street. Our home had suffered damage yet again. Uncle Gyula was at work in Budapest, and my mother and sisters were alone and terrified. After all that had happened, it was clear they were overjoyed to see me again.

THE FORTUNE TELLER

It was during this disturbing time of uncertainty and upheaval that my friend Fabian came from Budapest to visit me in Felsogod. He had also come to see a fortune teller he knew - one who lived in a tiny house on the outskirts of our village. He begged me to accompany him. "I don't think so," I replied, "I don't believe in that mumbo-jumbo." Still, he coerced me, insisting that it would be good to know, in these uncertain times, what she may predict, so that we might find some direction. Finally, after lengthy discussions of the pros and cons, I agreed to go along.

When we arrived at the fortune teller's house, she met us at the gate and asked what we wanted. When Fabian told her we wished to know our future, her immediate response was that she was very busy and didn't want to waste any time on us. "Especially with you," she said, pointing to me. "You don't believe in my powers." Fabian pleaded with her, telling her that he had come a long way to see her. Finally, she gave in and let us pass through the gate into the little house.

She was a petite woman that the pressure of the years had taken their toll on. Her stature was stooped and her face crisscrossed with deep furrows. A testimony of her age pressed on her physical being. A large back shawl blanketed her back. Her straight gray hair cut bluntly at her neck gave her a distinguished look. We sat down at a crudely-hewn table, and she shuffled a deck of cards. Her green eyes initially showed slight anger and reluctance, but as she began her predictions they seemed to reflect understanding and wisdom. After placing the cards down in front of me, she told me to split the deck into three piles, which I did. She picked up the cards, again looking at them, and as she spoke she was calm, dignified and unthreatening in her approach. "You have a blond brother on the front line fighting, and he has just been wounded." I will never forget those shocking words. I tried to figure out how the hell she could know all this.[5] The fortune teller continued, "The authorities will force you to leave your village, and eventually you will go to Germany. After that, you will go on a long, long journey, but you will return. Upon your return, you will have difficult times, and your future in your birthplace will not be good. In time though, you will cross a big body of water and will be very happy and content. You will have a family and you will be rich." At first sight I greeted her with skepticism, but by the end of the session I was questioning my judgment. She had definitely not done this for financial gain, and that shed a different light on our meeting.

Fabian received her predictions and warning of a great sickness which he would go through; however, she told him that he, too, would travel to the other side of a big body of water and would live a happy life in great wealth.[6] We sep-

---

5 Shortly after that, my mother received a letter stating that Tibor was in an army hospital, wounded. Later, contact was lost, and he never returned home.

6 Six years later I learned he had gone to Australia and was the head of a manufacturing company. He was living a very comfortable life in good health.

arated after that event. He returned to Budapest, and I never saw him again.

As time went by and events occurred, I had to realize that the old lady's predictions were coming true and her references and descriptions fit the happenings.

I stayed home patching our damaged home, boarding up the broken windows, cleaning the debris, and keeping an eye on my mother and sisters. The sunless, rainy days and the fog-covered evening increased our growing desperation. The grim news flowing from the occupied territories had, indeed, painted a vulgar picture of the Russian troops. Rape, looting, murder and destruction were reported from the so-called 'liberation' army's path. We could visualize the terror and, after long debates and daily discussions, the women decided to flee from the Russians' path and go into Budapest. The consensus was that in small places like Felsogod no one could stop the Russians and they would dictate their own laws without mercy. It would be more difficult to hide, and impossible to avoid the atrocities they inflicted. It made us sad to leave behind our beloved home which had always been our refuge and protection, but now it could no longer provide us with any security. The day came when we woke up to the Russian guns' rumble at Vac - a city only ten kilometres away - and in the panic we gathered our few belongings to leave. It was heartbreaking to say good-bye to my dear mother and sister, and in those dreadful days we held little hope of a reunion. Only the thought that they would be safer in Budapest made our separation easier. My neighbourhood friends and I did not want to fall into Russian hands either, and so, under the command of a local officer, we joined a group of young students and also left Felsogod. We were quite willing to leave our hometown to flee from the Russians and take part in a strategy which would transport the youth to the western part of the country – all this with the hope that the Russians would be stopped along the Danube, then driven back and out of our country. It was ludicrous to even dream of the success of such a plan, especially at that stage of the war, but we were young and naive and wanted with all our hearts to believe it was possible. The most important thing, though, was trying to survive this dreadful time.

Our first stop was Budapest, where we spent the night sleeping on the gymnasium floor of a school. The piece of bread that my mother had given me disappeared in a hurry as I shared it with my dear friend Tamas who had nothing to eat. The next day we traveled in the box car of a cargo train to Gyor, an industrial city located in the western part of Hungary. The officer who was with us arranged accommodation and meals for us with local army units. More often than not, we missed meals. We drifted from one village to the next in a group, asking the peasants for help. The reception from each household was different.

During this time, we learned to share and help each other as we spent day after day begging for food and accommodation. Sometimes we ended up in a warm peasant home, sleeping in a spare room. Other times, we spent the night in a haystack in someone's yard. The Christmas of 1944 was the first I spent away from my family. This night, our host was a school teacher who shared his food and allowed us to sleep in his home. Here we met a Russian war prisoner named Ahmed. He worked for the school teacher, cleaning the yard and feeding the pigs and chickens. He was well looked after, and his slanted Mongolian eyes showed contentment. We were curious about his background, so, through sign language and broken Hungarian, we communicated with him and discovered he was a Mohammedan. "Why are you eating pork?" I asked. "Isn't that against your religion?" He replied with a grin, "Allah cannot see me through the roof of the house." We had a good chuckle about his comment. It was evident that he accepted life without complications.

When the last days of 1944 arrived, we were drifting from village to village and house to house. Szani, my comrade, obtained a small piglet from one of the peasants. With a glowing face and a squealing little pig under his arm, he announced that our New Year's celebration was secured. He planned to make a "hell of a feast" for us. We spent the long winter evening in the warmth of a small peasant house, by the brick oven, waiting for the piglet to roast. Swooning in the delicious aroma of roasting meat, we waited for what seemed an eternity to have our New Year's feast. By three o'clock in the morning, struggling with tiredness and heavy eyelids, we finally ate the tender, young roasted pig. This proved to be our last good meal for the next few months. The chill of the harsh winter froze the generosity of many peasants as they themselves struggled to survive. Accommodations and meals grew increasingly difficult to find. On top of this, a chance to wash our clothes or to take regular baths had become impossible. My comrades and I discussed our situation which had deteriorated drastically. The clothes on our backs were becoming very worn and dirty, and our personal hygiene was certainly lacking. We decided it would be best to join the army where we would at least have food, clean clothes, and a roof over our heads. By that time, the battle for Budapest was over, and half of Hungary was occupied by the Red Army. Joining the army resulted in an organized, structured lifestyle. As we had hoped, we received clean uniforms, warm showers and regular meals; and notably, yet another of the fortune teller's predictions had come true, I found myself in a place called Neuhammer, in the eastern part of Germany.

NADIR

FROM SCHOOLBOY TO SOLDIER

It was January 1945, and thousands of Hungarian boys between the ages of 15 and 18, including myself, volunteered for the army. Members of athletic clubs, school pals, and work colleagues from various villages signed up to become soldiers. Once enlisted, we were concentrated in a huge camp called Neuhammer. My close-knit group of friends from Felsogod and I were to become part of a ski battalion. We were assigned to the same platoons and companies to play an extremely different role than we were used to in civilian life. Upon hearing my assignment, I remembered the fortune teller's conjecture that I would go to Germany, and the laughter my friends and I had shared regarding her prediction. Now it had become reality.

Our time in boot camp was short, but extremely intense. Daily combat drills, harsh discipline, long winter marches, and the seemingly unreasonable conduct of our corporals, certainly made our life difficult. The corporals were seasoned soldiers from the conscripted army, and it was obvious they reveled in their authority over young volunteers. The corporal in charge of our unit expected us to jump to light his cigarette the moment he put it to his mouth. When we did not respond quickly enough, he made each of us hold the edge of an outstretched blanket in the centre of which we had placed a match. We then had to run from the far end of the barrack to him, with one person grabbing the match to light his cigarette. This way all of us were punished, and all participated in serving the needs of the corporal. As a result of this, and many other humiliating incidents, a deep-rooted malevolence developed within the group, and some of the boys swore revenge against our corporal; nevertheless, we managed to regain our pride and dignity as we became stronger and wiser soldiers. We skied the Alps and hustled through obstacle courses and combat drills in our camp near the city of Leoben. Each morning we marched through the city, singing army songs to lift our spirits and restore our pride which at times had shrunk under the command of our corporal. As we marched by the bakery shop, our noses inhaled the delicious aroma of freshly baked bread, causing our stomachs to grumble. We were at an age when we were always hungry, so the army meals seemed small and too far between. Even though they gave those under 21 years of age extra rations, and more still to those under 17, the provisions were never enough to satisfy one's hunger.

Our sergeant-major Vawrick was an old soldier who had served in every war that had been fought in his lifetime since he was 16 years old. He was a survivor of the First World War, the Spanish Civil War, the Italian - Abyssinian War, the Finnish War, and five years in the French Foreign Legion. Thus, my comrades and I were in the hands of a seasoned army dog. Vawrick was short, but he was a strong, stocky man. A two-inch scar had been carved from his right eye down his ragged face and seemed to provide visual testimony of his ferocity. When he smiled, which was a rare occasion, his facial muscles pulled his lower eyelid down to expose the white surrounding the cold, green iris of his eye. His voice was coarse and harsh, and it was impossible to know whether he was angry or happy as his face was without expression. Still, behind his stony outward appearance, I figured there must have been some goodness for he seemed to care about us as soldiers like an austere father. He led us effectively and when he blew his whistle at six o'clock on cold winter mornings, we scrambled out of our barracks in a panic, naked from the waist up. We lined up hurriedly and waited motionless like obedient children for further commands. We then went through the routine morning exercises and running drills. Afterward we broke the ice on the creek and washed ourselves in it. It certainly was a rude awakening each morning. Later on, we marched through the city, up into the hills where we spent the day performing combat drills and skiing until the final downhill run. The long march back to the base served as the finale to each exhausting day.

In time, we learned to dismantle and reassemble our machine guns in minutes. We practiced in the evenings in our barracks as part of our recovery from the tiresome drills of the day. The guns were the fastest used in W.W.II. They weighed 26 kilograms, which was relatively light in comparison with some of the other guns used previously, and were designed so that overheated barrels could be changed in seconds with a few quick hand movements. These guns became a part of our being, well respected and cared for since they were our protection as well as our weapons. We cleaned, oiled and memorized each piece of them.

On occasion, German officers inspected our unit while we performed our exercises over the obstacle course. One of the officers who visited us was very young and eager to flaunt his physical abilities. At one point in the course, we had to do dive rolls over six of our comrades who were lying on the ground side by side. The young officer saw this as an opportunity for pageantry and instructed two more soldiers to lie down with the others. He then ran and dove gracefully over them, and as he triumphantly replaced his hat on his head, an arrogant grin slid over his face. His pretentiousness was disturbing, and his haughty smile provoked a challenge. I motioned to our Hungarian officer that I would like to try diving over nine soldiers. A picture of the demonstration I did for my physical education class years prior flashed through my mind. Without further delay, I began to run. Fueled by a touch of anger in my heart and with the most speed I could muster, I jumped and soared majestically over the soldiers and rolled out with apparent ease. A victorious ovation from my comrades followed my successful dive. I was proud to have met the challenge, and my Hungarian officer was equally thrilled behind his mask of sternness while the German officer reluctantly smiled.

On the outskirts of Leoben, I managed to 'shuss'[7] down from the slope of Mugel Kup on my skis, with all the equipment I had to carry. I also had the fastest time in the battalion for running through the obstacle course. The rewards I received for my efforts came in different forms. Sometimes I was granted a free ticket to the movies in the city, or an extra meal ticket. Meal tickets were most welcome since I was always hungry. One afternoon, our marching drills were performed in a field close to the river Mur. I was the youngest, as well as the shortest in the unit, marching in the back row, up and down, turning left and right to the commands of the drill officer. On one occasion, I was at the front of the group and was approaching the river. I listened for the

---

7   German word meaning to slide straight down the hill.

command to turn. It did not come. We marched closer and closer to the water until it splashed beneath our boots. Still, the command did not come. Finally, the command came to turn. We properly executed a turn in unison, and when we reached the dry ground, the officer halted the group. He said, "Now you are beginning to act like soldiers." Then he chased us through the field until we had dripped dry. We were exposed to harsh discipline, and we learned to respect each other as we became effective soldiers. The positive thing was that we, the soccer buddies and school chums from the village of Felsogod, were in this together.

The warm spring sunshine melted the snow, and the undulating terrain became greener each day. By this time, our battalion was thrown onto the Russian front near Feldbach and Riegersburg, Austria. We could not use our skis anymore, and from dusk to dawn we reinforced the front line, taking up positions among the other soldiers. Our eyes pierced the dark, endless nights. Our closest comrade was 50 metres away in the next hole. I felt very alone as I hid in my foxhole by the edge of the deep forest, only a short distance away from the Russian Army. The slightest noise in the dark brought a cold terror to my heart. Each day, as the welcome dawn brightened the morning sky and pushed back the trepidation of the night, a wave of relief swept over me. Days were more jovial as we moved a short distance back from the front line. We prepared our meals with food we had retrieved from the pantries of abandoned farmhouses, and for meat we killed some of the livestock left behind. Each group decided what they wanted to cook; with great enjoyment, the day was spent preparing hearty meals that burst with zesty flavour, unlike the typically bland army meals.

For now, the days of hunger and famine had ceased

temporarily, and we were rather content with our situation. We sat on a relatively quiet, stationary front line, without any major battles or offensive movements. The spring weather gradually grew warmer, and except for the night duties in the holes when our company had to reinforce the line, life was good. We were unaware of the overall developments of the war, that is, the battle for Berlin and such, and we were not participating in any of the historical battles. We received daily rations of cigarettes or cigars, and weekly rations of wine or champagne. As a non-smoker, I gave my portions of tobacco to my comrades, and in return they invited me to share in their group feasts. So I was relatively content ... for the time being.

It seemed our officers were not especially keen to engage the Russians. They avoided confrontation and refrained from giving us assignments that would disturb the quiet front line which lay along the newly dressed forest and the lush pasture lands. We occupied abandoned farmhouses which sat on hills and were surrounded by orchards of apple trees.

On May 7, 1945, at 11:00 p.m. while on duty in my foxhole, I heard a strange noise. I aimed my machine gun in the direction of the sound ready for action. "Halt!" I shouted to the dark silhouette of a person. He stopped. "Who's there? Password!" The password was given. "Come closer!" I shouted. He came closer. "Halt," I ordered. He asked me for the counter password, which I gave. Then he gave me the latest order that we were moving off the line. "Come," he said. So I left the hole, and he went to collect the other comrades. I moved back to the farmhouse that had become our headquarters, and found the rest of the group in the feverish action of gathering their equipment and moving out. Our young officer came and asked for some volunteers to fall behind to protect the battalion from behind so we would be able to move to the American side, about 40 kilometres from our present position.

"The war is over," he said, "We have 25 hours until midnight, May 9, when the guns will finally fall quiet. We must reach the American forces. We don't want to fall into Russian hands." He pointed to me and to my friends Szani, Tamas, Paul, and some of my other pals from the unit. "You, you, you. Fall behind, and slow the Russians down, but keep moving toward the American front lines." So began a twenty-five-hour marathon.

By the time daybreak came, my friends and I were exhausted. We had been carrying our equipment, machine guns, ammunition and food all night. We adopted a routine of running, stopping, looking back, fearful of spotting the Russians, then running again. We even ate on the run, and as we became more fatigued, we began to throw away some of our equipment and food. Blankets, gas masks, helmets and extra food were left in heaps by the roadside. We kept our weapons, belts of cartridges and a little food, which together were not too much weight. As evening approached, we needed progressively longer breaks for rest during our grueling trek.

We seemed to gain distance on the Russians and therefore, began to relax a bit, at least mentally. By 11:00 p.m., one hour before the war was officially over, we spotted a large haystack in an opening near a forestry road. My friends and I decided that we would take a longer break since we did not expect that the Russians could catch us within the next hour. We made holes in the hay, climbed in, and within minutes we were sound asleep. When we came to life again, it was 4:00

a.m. on May 9, 1945. We threw our weapons in a pile, went back to the road and began to march, relieved that the war was over. We had survived to the end in good health, without any problems. The group numbered 15 soldiers and one young Hungarian officer. As we marched along, we suddenly heard the noise of engines behind us. Looking back, we saw a jeep and a truck loaded with Russian soldiers approaching. They stopped, and a Russian officer stood up beside the driver of the jeep. On his trousers we saw two wide red stripes. These symbolized his status of General.

The soldiers surrounded us, pointing their guns in our direction. Other than the prisoner I had met in Hungary, and a few prisoners we had caught during our action, this was my first close encounter with Russians. The General spoke up, using his limited German. "Krieg kaput. Gitler kaput,"[8] he said. We stood motionless. He asked for our officer. Our young leader stepped forward and saluted, lifting his arm German style. It was an automatic reaction, but I wondered if this action was wise. The General asked for our weapons. Our officer told him we had left them behind. He motioned for us to go back and get them. He also gave our officer a note with instructions to collect our weapons, then continue along the road. So, back we went for our guns. We then followed the beautiful, winding forest road. Our apprehension was dispelled, and I was somehow relieved.

Shortly after this, we heard another engine roar behind us, and an army truck packed with Russians pulled up. They were hostile upon seeing us with weapons. We were close to having a confrontation, but we quickly threw our weapons down and peace was established. They then lined

---

8   The Russian pronunciation of 'g' is similar to the English 'h'.

us up and took whatever watches, binoculars, pocket knives, and other tools we had, and left us with whatever they did not want. Their uniforms were ragged, and their faces revealed a variety of ethnic origins. Finally they left, and we continued on our journey. As each wave of troops passed us at regular intervals, they frisked us, taking anything we still had that they fancied, but they never harmed us. Later on in the morning, a Cossack group came on horseback. The leader of the group was a vicious bastard, swinging his whip as he directed us off the road. I felt very uncomfortable and believed he would just as soon line us up and shoot every third person as look at us. By this time, we did not have anything left for him to take. I reminded my officer that he should show the leader the note from the General, which he did. The officer, after reading the note, cussed, and reluctantly motioned us back to the road. He definitely had some unpleasant plans for us, but we were saved by the note.

It was nearly midday when we reached the outskirts of the Austrian city of Graz. The victorious Red Army of the Soviet Union, with all its hordes of drunken soldiers, had just moved into this lovely Austrian city. Some of them were bareback on horses, some rode bicycles without tires, and some drove army trucks. Disorganization caused accidents at intersections. It was quite a display of the Russian army.

Amidst this total chaos, we sent one of our comrades to ask a group of Hungarian soldiers what was going on, what we should do, and what the latest news was. I can still clearly remember his solemn words. "They will hang the volunteers," he said in a low, resigned voice. I looked up to the cloudless May sky and pleaded with God. "Not now!" I cried. "After all I have been through, the long years of misery, the bombing raids, now I have to die?" My feelings of relief and anticipation of returning home were replaced by confusion and heavy fear. We marched as inconspicuously as possible down the cobblestone street, while the Russian liberation army continued to terrorize the city like a bunch of rebels. As we walked, I pictured myself on the end of a rope. My friends and I talked and tried to make a decision about what we should do. I proposed that we change into civilian clothes, go up into the hills, find a place where we could work for the farmers, and wait until the situation became clearer or at least, more settled. My comrades had different opinions; thus we followed the crowd to the center of the city where columns of soldiers, as wide as the road, marched in the same direction. Although I felt we should seek refuge in the hills, I trusted my friends and did not wish to leave them. They believed that so many people - all those travelling to get a 'document' from the Russians that would supposedly allow them to go home - could not be wrong. The majority had to be right. With this belief in my heart, I became one of a huge flock of sheep that travelled to doom by the promise of freedom. It was the biggest mistake I ever made, right to this day!

IN RUSSIAN HANDS

From the city centre, we followed the masses until we ended up on the outskirts of the city by a huge building that looked like a palace. It was Schloss Hainfeld[9], a privately owned property, occupied and vandalized by the Red Army, then used as a military prison camp. By the gate, a Russian soldier informed us that anyone under 18 years of age was not required to enter the camp and could leave. I was under 18, but my comrades were just over the age limit. Although we had no documents to provide proof of our age, my friends had been taught to be honest and did not realize that it would have been beneficial to lie about their ages. They walked through the gate.

Tamas, a red-headed, talented comic and a true friend whose instinctive humour brought smiles to our faces in the most tense situations, was a selfless, trustworthy and very dear companion. His graphic artistry turned blank sheets of paper into vivid portraits of people within minutes. In unpredictable times, his friendship was the only sure thing. Szani was a distant friend, and the other two comrades came from our same village. We had been trained to follow orders, and when the opportunity came to act independently, we were incapable of thinking for ourselves or acting as individuals

---

9   Castle Hainfeld located on the outskirts of Feldbach, Austria.

for our own benefit. I hesitated, but not knowing what lay inside those gates, I decided to stick with my friends, no matter what the outcome. So I accompanied them.

In retrospect, I realize this mistake cost me five years of my youth, but in that given minute, a decision had to be made, and I chose to stick with my comrades. Hundreds of people were collected in this compound, and the courtyard was packed with bodies, side by side, like sardines in a can, uncertain of the future and hopeful for the promised document which never came. The building with its architectural splendor, lovely arcades and numerous rooms, served as the headquarters of the occupying Soviet forces. That occupation certainly left its imprint. A so-called 'liberation' had taken place, destroying the delicate furniture, systematically slashing beautiful paintings with knives, and herding horses over the exquisite hardwood floors. They built fires for cooking, using century-old codices of the Schloss library as firewood. It was difficult to understand their motives for this deliberate destruction. I questioned how these people would be capable of creating the new order for millions of liberated people. How would this army and these soldiers, who held no remorse for the treasures they had destroyed, construct the future? What kind of future could we hope to have? Questions like this could not escape my mind. I was a student whose education had been temporarily interrupted by the war, but I did not forget my respect for books and their value. Rather than seeing the priceless books go up in smoke, I took two of them with the hope of keeping them from the Russians and selling them to a museum. One of the books was printed in 1472. Entitled "The History of the Jews", it was written in Latin. The other was a 13th century hand-written book of poems by the Dutch poet, Cornelius

Boon. During the few short days I spent in this camp, I visited the library often to read and admire the books. I planned to preserve a few for the future, if I could.

A large number of people flowed through the camp. While we were there, we were stripped of our hair. We were also 'disinfected' with a solution which was sprinkled on our bald heads, under our arms and around our genitals to prevent possible epidemics. We slept under the sky in the courtyard, with barely enough room to walk between the tightly packed bodies.

The next day we left the camp, walking in wide columns under the direction of an old Russian soldier who rode ahead of us on a frail and weary horse. Had there been more guards surrounding us, we would have had some doubts as to our destiny, but as it was, we were walking toward Hungary with the promise that there we would be receiving the document. There seemed to be no reason for worry. Two days on the road and one overnight sleep in the roadside ditch certainly gave us ample opportunity to split from the column and make our way home individually or in small groups. Still, the apparent necessity to obtain the document, coupled with the reassurance provided by the huge numbers of people who were also travelling to obtain their papers, kept us in line. When we reached some small villages along the way, we questioned the civilians. They told us that the radio had reported that we would all go home. Unfortunately, we were unaware that the radio was now controlled by the Soviet forces, and the broadcast messages of freedom were untruths. We heard from some women that they would hide themselves each night as they heard the Russian soldiers were indiscriminately raping women, from very young girls to elderly women.

After passing through Szentgotthard, our destination was Janoshaza, a small town with a large camp fenced in with barbed wire. We still hoped that perhaps this would be the place where we would receive documents. When we passed through the gate, five at a time, some young boys donning Russian army hats with red stars on them frisked us. Still, I managed to save the books I was carrying and passed by the control guards without problem.

Inside, the food rations were not yet organized. Hungry as we were, we scrounged around the yard and utility buildings where animals were once raised until we found some corn pushed into the ground under the feet of men and animals. It was some relief to find something to nibble on; however, I am unsure whether it really helped our starving systems to eat the raw, hard corn. Finally we were herded out of this camp, five people abreast with guards and dogs on both sides, and five metres between each of us. It was then that we realized that we would not be getting any documents, and we certainly would not be going home. Under heavy guard, 50 people were jammed into a boxcar which had only one small window protected by barbed wire.

We were trapped. The war was over. The Western world celebrated their victory while millions lost their freedom in the lands occupied by the Red Army. Like animals, we were locked in boxcars and were travelling to an unknown destination.

THE FIRST FREE MAY IN BUDAPEST

We stopped in Budapest, and for two days remained locked in our boxcar in the Ferencvarosi railway station. Hours of anxious waiting turned to days, and with passing time, my hope grew that we may soon be freed. Perhaps some incomplete administration was holding us here, but once this had been taken care of, we would surely be on the way home. In this, our capital city, where figures of authority made influential decisions, we could hope for some assistance. I visualized a government delegation approaching the train, throwing open the doors, and setting us free on the road to our families. After all, the war was over and we had not fallen into Russian hands during battle. My comrades and I let our imaginations fly high and verbalized our expectations of heading home, unaware of the pacts which had been made by the powers above and which now stamped our future.

The days spent like animals locked in the boxcar were stifling, and with each minute, the walls seemed to inch closer together. The daily food rations consisted of a bucket of salted fish, to be shared amongst 50 people, along with a slice of bread and a cup of water for each of us. When we tried to look outside through the little window of the boxcar, Russian soldiers on the other side threw rocks at us. From what we could see, the situation outside was very grim. The once beautiful bridges which arched over the Danube had been blown up. Frightened people in rags scrambled about, trying desperately to identify their husbands or sons in the transport. It suddenly became clear that we were not going home, but rather were destined to be sent to the Soviet Union. Thousands of Hungarians, Austrians, Germans, Yugoslavians, Romanians, Poles and Czechs would be heading to the Soviet Union for a malinki robot.[10] The realization of what was happening was heartbreaking. Locked in the boxcar, hungry, thirsty, angry and humiliated, we tried to peek through the little window to see what remained of our beloved city of Budapest. We saw hungry people staggering beside the railway cars, looking for their relatives, and being laughed at and chased by Soviet soldiers. At one point, a young boy appeared with a stack of newspapers under his arm. I will never forget the headline, printed in large red letters on the front page. It read, "The First Free May in Budapest". I could have burst with anger as I read the words. They implied that Hungarians had never experienced freedom throughout their existence in the Carpathian basin over the last thousand years. Now, in May 1945, we were granted our first taste of 'freedom' courtesy of the Soviet army. Realizing that my 'freedom' would grant me a free trip to the Soviet Union on board this train, with departure possible at any moment, I was frantic to contact my family to let them know I was alive and to make certain they were too.

One of my prison comrades had managed to hide a tiny note book in his shoe, and it had not yet been discovered during the numerous frisks we had undergone. I pleaded with him for some time before he finally gave me a piece of paper,

---

[10] Russian words meaning 'little work.'

and another prisoner allowed me to use his small piece of pencil. In a hurried panic, I scribbled my mother's address on the paper, and when the soldiers were not looking, I slipped it out of the window. Thoughts of the possible fate of my note rushed through my mind as I sank back into a dark corner of the boxcar. Would anyone find it, or would the wind steal it and land it somewhere where only the sun would gaze upon its letters? Still, if someone did find it, would they make an effort to deliver it? Would they find my mother alive? Would she come to find me in time? Would I ever see her sweet face again? So many thoughts and questions raced through my head and, time after time, I fought through the crowded boxcar to position myself by the window so that I could look for my mother. The chance of seeing her was remote; still, I maintained my vigil.

I ignored my thirst and growling stomach as I waited through the agonizing day, praying Mama would appear, like an angel from the heavens, but my optimism slowly disappeared with the setting sun. As dusk spread its orange blanket over the city, the commotion in the railway yards subsided, as did my hopes of seeing my mother tonight. Emotionally exhausted, I collapsed to the floor and squeezed in between my comrades. Soon I was asleep.

With the arrival of morning came new anticipation which was strengthened by the discovery that we were still in Budapest, but as the day progressed without event, my soul felt great torment as a tide of doubt flowed in and washed over my hope in waves. The misery of being locked up without enough food and water made my destiny clear. Nevertheless, I regularly peered through the window, hoping my fate would change. Later that afternoon, as we sat in silence, the train suddenly lurched into motion. Terror gripped my heart. The journey was about to begin, and I had not seen my mother, nor did I know if she was all right. In a panic, I jumped to my feet and leaped over bodies as I scurried to the window to take one final look. As we began to pull slowly out of the station, like a vision - a dream - I saw my dear mother, running alongside the train, looking for me. I shouted out the window, "Mama! Itt! Itt vagyok!"[11] She heard my cries and, with wide eyes, turned and raced toward me. I tried in vain to hold back the tears which now welled up in my eyes. A wave of relief swept over me to see she had survived the battle of Budapest. She asked me if I was hungry. I told her "No", though my stomach pained with hunger. She asked me if I was thirsty. "No", I said, though my throat was parched. It had been many hours since I had received my daily ration, but I did not want her to worry, nor did it seem to matter now. It was difficult to see through my tears, but I detected the panic in her eyes and her fear of what the future held.

We were destined to separation at a time when we needed each other's support the most. I felt helpless to do anything but watch in agony as she struggled and tumbled, out of breath beside the train cars, tears streaming down her face. As the train pulled out, this was my last glimpse of her for many years. Frantic and grief stricken, I stuck my hand through the barbed wire grate which protected the window. I cut my hand badly, but managed to wave my farewell. The train gained momentum, but I stood with my hand outstretched until I could no longer stand. Miles outside the city by now, I staggered back to my space, dodging the bodies of my sleeping comrades. I was heart broken. (Forty five years

---

[11] "Mama! Here! Here I am!"

later, I discovered that Fabian, the same friend who had taken me to the fortune teller, had found my note and delivered it to the address in Budapest.)

Outside, the bright sun warmed the earth, but the only light I could see from my spot on the dark, overheated floor of the boxcar, was that which came through the tiny window and through a small hole which had been cut in the floor for sanitary purposes. Hay was strewn over the floor, and the stinking, sweaty bodies of the prisoners lay upon it, side by side, like sardines. Panic, vicious threats and heated arguments about our future broke out between the prisoners. Meanwhile, the monotonous clicking of the train wheels reminded us that we were rolling further and further from our country, advancing through unfamiliar landscapes.

At each stop, the guards went through the transport with big hammers, knocking on the boxcars, looking for loose boards - a sign of possible attempts at escape. My close friends from Felsogod and I often spoke of planning an escape. It might have been possible, providing all fifty people in the wagon had agreed to it; however, we were far from agreement. The only way we could see to escape would be to enlarge the hole in the floor of the wagon with some sharp object. Surely, someone in the wagon possessed something we could use. Then, during the night, when the train was travelling at a slower speed, as it often did, we would slip through the hole, one by one, and drop between the rail lines beneath the wagon. Once the train had passed over, providing no serious injury was incurred, we would be free to flee. Many were eager to carry out this scheme, but some of the older fellows were afraid to participate in this rather dangerous plan. Still others believed that we would spend no more than six months in the Soviet Union, and felt that a few months lost was better than to risk losing their life. Thus, there was a sharp division between the prisoners over the issue of escape. Many who did not wish to take the risk of escaping were afraid of being beaten and punished by the Soviets in unthinkable ways for letting others break free. So, they kept a watchful, unblinking eye on us, the younger ones who were willing to make a move for freedom. Their guard was tighter than that of the Soviet soldiers. Under these circumstances, a chance for escape was impossible.

As time went by and the train continued to speed forward, laying endless miles between us and our home, we grew increasingly more uncomfortable from the heat and lack of water and food. Some cried out for water, oblivious to the reality that no one but those of us in the wagon could hear them. Others drank their own urine, in a desperate attempt to relieve their thirst. When it rained, people would crowd to the small window to try to collect a few drops of water in the palm of their outstretched hands.

Thirsty, cramped, heated with frustration and anger, we travelled parallel to the Danube through Hungarian borders toward a Romanian camp, Rimnicu Serat. Upon arrival, another disinfecting procedure and frisking took place. After a few days in this camp which accommodated thousands of prisoners, we discovered we would be transported further along to a destination yet unknown to us. So, on a bright summer afternoon, we were forced to march out of this camp to the sound of a military band, as though we were in some grisly parade. Guard was heavy, leaving no chance for escape. One hundred and five people were jammed once again into the large, Russian-made boxcars. As before, barbed wire lined the windows, hay was thrown across the bottom of the car, and a small hole was cut in the floor.

Thankfully, the five boys from Felsogod - Tamas, Szani, Paul, Bandi, and I - were still together. It seemed to be the only positive thing that had happened to us thus far, other than remaining alive. The long journey had begun. Throughout the trip, which lasted ten days, the door of the wagon opened only ten times and just long enough at that to dish out a ration of water, a piece of bread and a bowl of luke-warm soup to each of us. The soup was nothing but a thin, salty brew that differed from a bowl of water only in that it contained some bits of fish (which were more decoration than substance). The salty soup, combined with the stale heat in the wagon, caused unending thirst, and water was a precious commodity. On top of this, the incessant pushing and shoving landed me close to the little hole cut in the floor. Here there was constant urinating and shitting as the 105 members of my instant family struggled with dysentery. My stomach wretched with the sights, sounds and smells which smothered me throughout those days, making me unable to eat the little food that was provided. By the end of the journey, I had very little energy and spirit left.

When the train finally jerked to a halt, I was on the floor, feeling weak and miserable, nearly unconscious of the things going on around me, but as the guards yanked open the boxcar doors and shouted, "Davaj! Davaj!",[12] we realized the dreadful journey had ended at last. Hardly able to get to my feet, the bright sun momentarily blinding me, I nevertheless took a deep Schluck[13] of the fresh air and attempted to exit the vile mobile prison cell. My effort fell short, for the next thing I knew I was on the ground, flat on my face, until

---

[12] A Russian word meaning 'Move! Move!'

[13] A German word meaning 'gulp.'

Tamas and Szani pulled me up onto my feet. It was July 12, 1945, and the past ten days of physical inactivity and mental apathy, combined with a lack of eating, had taken their toll on me, as sure as hell. My friends supported me on either side, but the world began spinning around me as though I were riding a merry-go-round. I did not hear a sound, and a strange numbness spread over my entire body. We had to line up 'po piat'[14] so that the officer could count us. "Raz, dva, tre, chetiri, piat,..."[15] he barked as he started the count at the beginning of the column. By the time he reached the rear of the group, I could stand no longer and collapsed like a sack of potatoes. He saw this and asked what was wrong. At that instant, my friends pulled me up again, pretending everything was in order. The officer grunted and turned to resume his count, but could not continue for he had forgotten what number he was at. Angrily he went back to the head of the column, cursing all the way, and initiated a new count. "Raz, dva, tre, chetiri, piat, ..." he growled. He numbered us all until he had counted nearly 600 people. He approached where I stood, and again I collapsed upon his arrival. There was some commotion and, of course, he forgot the number a second time. For causing him such embarrassment, he dragged me out of the line-up and kicked the hell out of me. By then I was unconscious, and thrown onto a wagon pulled by three horses. Once awake and able to focus on the space around me, I found myself in a large, woven, willow basket with numerous other sick people, all lying against and on top of one another. When the officer succeeded in completing his count, the column began to

---

[14] 'Five in a row' in Russian.

[15] 'One, two, three, four, five,....' in Russian.

march. The prisoners were escorted by dozens of barefooted Russian peasant women, whom the local authorities had called upon to aid the soldiers. Stern and merciless, they pointed and waved rusty, 1896 rifles complete with long bayonets, seemingly ever ready to strike out if so ordered. The women's heads were covered with white scarves, and their narrow, serious eyes, deep set in their sunburned faces, seemed to pierce us with their gaze of mistrust and hatred. They seemed feminine enough, outfitted in their colorful blouses with simple skirts tied at their waists, but they were strong, and obviously accustomed to hard work in the fields of nearby collective farms.

The officers wore their typical Russian gimnastorka,[16] cinched around their waists with tight belts. Their pants were tucked into black, knee-high boots, and a round hat, pulled down to barely reveal their eyes, completed their uniform. The hat bore the symbol of communism - the red star, within which was the hammer and sickle. A tall, serious looking major was our Lager commandant. His icy, gray eyes showed no warmth or hint of humanity, but rather revealed only hostility toward the prisoners. Another short officer, who always had a pipe hanging from his mouth (thus known as 'pipas' - 'the piper'), was a simple soul who showed signs of kindness. Pipas eventually became responsible for our welfare and supplies. A third person, a sergeant, was a most miserable bastard, and his abhorrence for us was evident in his every move. Beneath his ragged complexion lay a dark, inner soul, flooded with contempt and black with hatred, and we instinctively knew this man, in charge of the guards, was a person to stay clear of at all costs. The officers and the

---

[16] A khaki colored shirt-like top with a high neckline.

peasant women were our reception committee, and as they walked the column along the dirt road, the other sick prisoners and I rode in the rickety wagon behind the group. A blur of colors floated before my weary eyes as the cart bumped and rolled by the green grasses which swayed in the breeze alongside the dirt road. The clear, blue sky, the fresh, sweet scent of hay, and the warmth of the summer sun made for a perfect day; how could it be that I was here, frail and heart sick, in the powerful grasp of the Soviet army? How I ached to be running barefoot in the velvety green grass with my friends, blowing reed whistles and laughing merrily. It seemed like only yesterday that our hearts were light and our days were playful and carefree, not unlike the little Soviet children who now followed our procession. The children, showing natural curiosity of the young, followed the parade of zombies, and showed hostility as they threw dry 'horse lemons' at us, shouting "Fritz-Fritz!" (a derogatory nickname for German soldiers).

We were now being escorted into captivity as though we were criminals responsible for all the events and horrors of the war. At least, we were free of the stinking boxcar, but, despite the bright sunshine, my mind was clouded with thoughts of my uncertain future. "Where was I going? What was to be my fate? What did the future hold?" Only a few kilometres down that long, dusty, hot, unfamiliar road, would the answers, at least partially, be offered. We reached yet another camp, and this would become 'home' for a longer period than the previous Lagers.[17]

---

[17] German and Russian word for 'camps.'

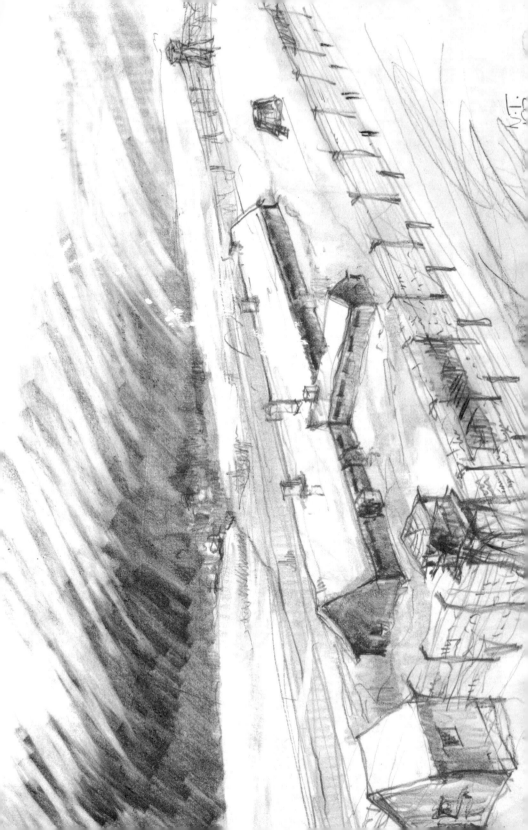

KOMARICHI

During the reign of the Czars, the place we were in had been a large pig barn. Constructed of wood, this weathered, old building now became our shelter - our first Lager. The fence surrounding the compound was not yet completed; so, the guards and the peasant women, in turn, sat watch through the night and into the next day until the prisoners finished putting up the fence.

Upon arrival, we sat on the ground waiting for orders, hoping for food and water; and while sitting, hungry and hopeless, we heard an officer asking if a doctor was present. Three hands went up from the crowd, the hands of men claiming they were doctors. Calling them forward, the officers then fitted each of them with a white armband which had a red cross painted on it. Instantly, they had become our camp's medical staff with the responsibility of looking after 600 people. Adding to their burden, supplies and sanitary conditions were almost non-existent.

My deteriorated condition landed me in a separate room with the rest of the ill prisoners under the care of the three 'doctors,' and over time these three men became very close to me. I am ever thankful to them for saving my skin in this early but critical time of my prison life. The youngest of the doctors, named Ali, was a first-year medical student with little experience who, in spite of this, became the surgeon. Dr. Leganyi was actually a lawyer, obviously well taught in legal matters, great in philosophical discussions, but rather ineffective when medical attention was required. The third member of this distinguished staff was a veterinarian whose knowledge and experience formed the nucleus of the medical trio. He diagnosed the problems and gave sound advice, even though it was based on his experience with animals. He was a kind man full of good, caring feelings. (How sad it is to know that he never made it back home to his loving wife and young children.) During those early days in camp the four of us became good friends. After learning that I was the youngest person in the Lager and barely out of school, they kept an eye out for me in the infirmary. The genuine concern and the friendship extended to me was good medicine, healing the open wound in my heart and my mind. They accepted me as an intellectual equal and friend, and from them I learned much that strengthened me. I cherished their great spiritual support during the initial time of my prison life.

This, my first Soviet camp, was 96 kilometres south of Bryansk in a place called Komarichi. I never did see the town. We lived on the outskirts of it and were kept isolated from the civilian population. Our only contact with the towns people was at the work place, an old sugar factory that had been bombed to the ground. Our assignment was to rebuild it.

The camp slowly but surely began to take shape. Men were divided into six companies and each company was split into brigades. The size of the working brigades varied according to the task they were assigned to do, and even here, behind the prison fence, we began again to feel as a unit.

The dirt floor of the pig barn was covered with hay.

There were no blankets of any sort to use for cover, so, total-
ly exhausted after twelve hours of work, we simply collapsed
onto the hay each evening. The camp's water source was a
swamp-like water hole situated four kilometres away. Water
was continuously transported in a big wooden keg which was
fastened on two wheels and pulled by the frail skeleton of a
donkey. Although that poor donkey was driven back and
forth to the water hole from early morning until the midnight
moon, the water supply at the camp remained perilously
insufficient. The overworked mule was as much a victim to
the unbearable conditions as were we, and one day he finally collapsed, like so many prisoners had before him. One
could not help but feel that prisoner and mule alike finally
gave in to misery, but at the same time each had finally freed
himself from any further pain this life could give. With the
mule gone, the water wagon was pulled by the only substitute
for the donkey - six prisoners, just as bony and weak and
near their end. Each time the water wagon arrived at the
camp when we were in the Lager, it was a fight to get some of
the water into our containers. If we were fortunate enough to
get some, we had to wait until the black particles of soil in the
water settled to the bottom, and then drank carefully from
the top.

A daily ration of seven decilitres of soup was given to
each prisoner twice a day, with one litre of warm water in the
evening. The two bowls of soup and the warm water were
dished to each brigade from a big gasoline drum that sat out
in the open, rain or shine. After everyone had received his
portion, there was always a desperate fight for the remaining
few litres of leftovers. There were more black eyes and blood
than full stomachs after each daily 'wrestling match'.

Our brigade of seventeen men was also required to

share one loaf of black Russian bread which had to be cut into equal pieces. The daily bread-cutting ceremony became the most important ritual in our lives as seventeen pairs of hungry eyes peered at the shaking hands of the cutter. His skill was impaired by the object that he had to use as a knife - nothing more than the handle of a spoon sharpened on a rock. It was truly a primitive tool, but the only thing that was available. A slip of the knife, an imperfect cut, the slightest difference between the pieces, caused heated arguments and recurring vicious fist fights amount the angry and starving prisoners. The bread was the only thing we could bite into and chew for a few precious moments, allowing our starving bodies momentary relief from the pain of hunger. The bread was more precious than the soup because it was the only solid food we received. After completion of the cutting of the loaf, the pieces were numbered and displayed on a wooden board. Then we pulled a numbered wooden block out of a hat. The first draw was just to establish the order of the second draw determining which slice of bread each prisoner would receive. If lady luck smiled on you on that given day you would pull the number for the corner piece of bread with the thickest crust. If you pulled a number which was attached to a smaller piece, much time was spent just contemplating your fate.

Thank God I never smoked, for, in addition to the unending hunger, the craving for tobacco experienced by those who smoked added an extra burden to their life. Initially, the lack of tobacco in the camp forced prisoners to collect leaves from the trees along with grass or wild flowers from the fields to use as a filling for their 'cigarettes'. Getting paper in which to roll the tobacco and, of course, obtaining something with which to light the cigarettes were the next obstacles as there simply was no paper nor matches available. It became obvious to me that the fate of the codices I had saved from the first camp at Schloss Hainfeld was written on the wall. So far, I had managed to smuggle them through several controls and frisks, but my friends began to lobby and plead for my books, after having made cigarettes from the ones they had saved. They argued, "We are never going to make it home, and, as long as we are still kicking, we should make our miserable life as bearable as possible".

Indeed, the condition of the Lager, the hard work, inadequate food supply and lack of hygiene, certainly took an increasing number of victims each day. Dysentery, typhoid, tuberculosis, malaria and edema cut wide rows from the prison population. The grim outlook for the future was impossible to ignore. Finally, I could no longer refute the arguments of my smoking friends, and slowly, page by page, the books I had treasured went up in smoke.

How to light the cigarette was another story. The needs justify the means, so, with a quick return to the stone age the problem was solved. A piece of pipe (1 cm. in diameter), a woven piece of cotton, a suitable rock and a chunk of iron were necessary for the task. The cotton was stuck into the pipe; then, by hitting the rock with the iron, a spark was created which lit the cotton. By blowing quickly but gently on the cotton caused it to smoulder and the cigarettes could be lit. It was called 'pitchki', certainly a very primitive method. Under the circumstances, however, it was a valued gadget which was used not only by the deprived prisoners but by the Russian civilians and army officers as well. One of the officers was a daily visitor in our camp. He was a step above as he proudly lit his pipe with a lens taken from Bandi's camera. He thought he was quite brilliant using the lens to magnify the sun's rays for lighting his cigarette, in place of the widely used pitchki. It was more effective, but on cloudy days he was in trouble.

During these days, I was still under the care of the three doctors. I lay on the bunk bed in the infirmary where the sick prisoners came and sometimes went, but sometimes never made it out again. Ali, the young medical student, performed minor operations, cutting open boils by using razor blades disinfected with garlic. I watched as he knelt on one patient's chest to perform minor surgery. The poor bastard's arms and legs were held down by other prisoners. There was no anaesthetic, so the procedures really tested a patient's tolerance of pain. While watching, I prayed I would never have to experience such torture. I witnessed the suffering and slow death of many of my fellow prisoners, victims of various illnesses or simple starvation.

Regardless of the weather - rain or shine, hot or cold - each morning, and every evening, everyone was herded into the courtyard to stand five in a row by companies for the poverka.[18] Usually, several unsuccessful attempts were made to account for and balance the numbers of dead and alive prisoners before the task was finally completed. The exception was in the infirmary where we just lay as the officer did his count. Every morning, he came in shouting "Drastvujte! Skolko kaput?"[19] The bodies of the unfortunate, or were they the lucky ones, were dragged from the infirmary and buried outside the camp in unmarked graves.

The chance to wash our clothes or ourselves was rare, so our filthy bodies were infested with lice feasting on our

---

[18] Roll call in Russian.

[19] "Good Morning, how many are dead?" in Russian.

undernourished skeletons. Of the original 600 taken to this camp, the number of survivors dropped day by day.

The Russian doctor occasionally visited the infirmary to check on the sick prisoners. Upon Ali's advice, I would pretend that nature had called me and would hobble out to the latrine whenever the doctor came. At that time, I did not have any problems, but I was certainly undernourished and weak, and managed only to walk with a cane. I was still under the care of the Hungarian doctors, who were trying to save my strength and my life by not sending me out with the working brigades.

The latrine was nothing but a large hole, measuring about five metres wide, ten metres long, and six metres deep. A few wooden beams had been laid across the hole, and heavy planks were placed over them with spaces in between. Of course, the open air facility lacked the luxury of toilet paper. Surrounding grass was used instead, but before long, what little grass there was, was soon either picked or trampled down.

The barbed-wire fence which enclosed the Lager was reinforced with another row of wire, and watch towers were built at each corner to house the newly-arrived soldiers who replaced the peasant women. They did not appear to be much better off than the prisoners. Some of their boot soles were completely worn out, revealing blackened, curled toes. These people were Uzbeks[20] who knew little Russian in spite of the fact that they had served in the army for five to six years without any leaves or holidays. Indeed, they were a sad-looking bunch. At times, I would hear gunshots from one of the towers and would know that another had made his own ending to a dull and hopeless life.

---

[20] People of the State of Uzbekistan, located by the Ural mountains.

The majority of the camp's working force slaved away the days to rebuild the sugar factory. Tamas, my friend and a fine graphic artist, drew portraits of the officers and their wives and thus escaped the grueling work. In addition to our inadequate food rations, he often received a few cucumbers or potatoes for his effort and these he shared with me. I was in sad physical condition. My teeth were loose, just hanging in my mouth - the signs of scurvy.

One night I struggled from the barrack to the latrine to relieve my dysentery-ridden body. As I squatted down beneath the blanket of stars above, my feet spread apart on the planks, I felt all my remaining energy leaving me. Panic struck me, and my mind raced with thoughts of my inevitable conclusion. Death was so close, I could feel its finger gripping me. "Please, not here. Not like this. Not now!" I thought. "My finale should be more honourable than falling into a pool of shit." With one last summons of strength, I managed to straighten my shaking knees and lunge to the edge of the cesspool. As I lay by the brim of the latrine I sensed that I would soon be gone unless someone helped me. No one was near, but the kitchen was not far off. Surely, someone would be there. I attempted to crawl, but my legs failed to respond. I called, but my dry throat and empty lungs could produce only a muffled moan in the night. I was fading quickly. Finally I grabbed my cane, and with all my might tossed it weakly at the door of the kitchen. Darkness blanketed my mind. One of the cooks heard the clamour, and thankfully, emerged to pick me up and carry me to my quarters. When I came to, I was in the barrack, lying on the hay. Recalling the event, I realize how near I was to the end of my life. This was a close call, but God must have decided to let me carry on. The cook who had rescued me was from

Vac, a city close to Felsogod. We became close friends, and from time to time he smuggled food from the kitchen for me in an effort to help me regain some strength. In addition, I crushed the charcoal from burnt wood and ate it with the hope that it would cure my dysentery. With time, I slowly recovered from this dreadful illness which claimed the lives of many of my comrades. Some of them did actually fall into the latrine to die a horrible death. No effort was ever made to retrieve them.

The days which followed were spent clinging to a bare existence, fighting just to stay alive. By this time, the clothes we wore had slowly deteriorated or had been exchanged with the civilians for food. The hot summer days and the growling of our stomachs dictated our decision to trade. We did not think of the future, nor did we consider the cold weather which lay ahead. We were forced to live day to day, not knowing if we would ever see another winter. To prepare for conditions which we might endure months from now was ridiculous, considering that to see the next day often seemed an unattainable goal.

One day, during the evening poverka, after long hours of waiting and several repetitions of the count, the Russian officer discovered five prisoners were missing. The guards and camp officers were disturbed and confused. Personally, I was pleased to know that someone still had the energy and courage to attempt an escape, even though thousands of kilometres from our homeland and most likely unable to speak any Russian. These prisoners had exercised the only right a prisoner has according to international law - the right to escape. My prayers were with them and I hoped that on behalf of all of us who remained behind, they found a path to freedom.

One week passed. We had heard nothing more about them, until finally we were ordered to assemble in the court-yard. Waiting there in columns, we watched curiously as an American Studebaker army truck crawled up the road toward the camp gate. When the truck came to a halt, four prisoners, clothed in only their underwear, were kicked from the back of the truck by the Russian guards. It was obvious they had been severely beaten. Their faces were bloody and swollen, and their eyes black. The sergeant, who was a noted 'wild animal', waited for them at the gate. He instantly released his fury on them, beating them with the butt of his rifle. With anger and frustration tearing at us, we could do nothing except stand motionless in silence as we heard the blows and curses being delivered on our groaning fellow prisoners. I had never wished more for my machine gun so I could shoot the bastard, even though it would have meant my own end.

When the sergeant was finished with his welcome-back reception, the four prisoners lay near death on the ground beside a fifth prisoner who had died by the bullets of the guards' automatic gun. His jaw was dangling, held to his skull only by a piece of skin. The horror and fear he had felt in his last moments was frozen in his face, in his unblinking eyes. The four badly-beaten prisoners were forced to drag the lifeless body of their comrade to the front of our column. They were then ordered to lie down beside their dead friend while the Lager commandant informed us that the fifth prisoner had tried to jump from the truck and that was the reason the guards had killed him. It was a warning to us all, and the picture of it certainly needed no accompanying words. I was angry for days after that cruel and unfair display from the members of the so-called 'liberation army', but life went on, and so did our daily struggle, and that tempered my emotions.

Later on, when I was transported to another camp, I found out that the prisoner had been forced to jump from the truck so the guards would have the satisfaction of killing him after such a gruelling manhunt. He had pleaded for his life, and as tears streamed down his face he told the guards about his children and wife, but they had no mercy. They emptied their guns on him. They felt it necessary to set an example to discourage any further attempts at escape - a right we, as prisoners, were supposed to have.

On a few occasions during the summer, we were herded to a natural lake where we had much-needed baths. The cool water was soothing as it slid over my sweaty, filthy body. As I splashed about in the lake, I felt refreshed and invigorated, but a certain feeling of melancholy flooded my heart as I watched the sunshine shimmer on the surface of the water. The sight brought back old memories of wonderful, carefree summers spent in the silky waters of my beloved Danube.

The food for the camp was transported periodically from a central camp located in Bryansk. It took the convoy two days to complete the journey by rail. Pipas, the officer, and three prisoners, including my pal Szani, were assigned to join the convoy. Compared to the daily robot, travelling on a train was an adventure for them. They loaded bags of grain, salt and other staples onto the train and guarded the cargo throughout its journey back to the camp. During the sojourn they feasted heartily, using some of the stores in the shipment to cook their meals. When the opportunity arose, Pipas would often sell or swap some of the guarded items with the civilians for other more delectable food items or vodka. Of course, he would then live it up, savouring his prizes. All of the prisoners assigned to this detail were guilty of stealing, and were silenced by their personal gain. Pipas let the prisoners stuff themselves with food. In return, they overlooked the business deals he struck with his acquaintances. The kilograms of grain that went missing from the bags were 'recovered' by dipping the bags in water. This ensured the weight was the same as what was stamped on the bag. Of course, the receiving officer would also receive a 'gift' for overlooking any weight discrepancies. The daily 1200-calorie standard never did reach those of us who did not enjoy the food-retrieval detail.

Starvation drove many prisoners to eat grass and various types of wild plants picked from the roadside. We usually received one piece of bread each day. It was made of whole, untreated and unrefined flour, and was the only substantial food we were given. Sometimes, though, there were periods when we were given two pieces of dry bread called 'suhary'. These pieces of stale, dusty bread were too difficult to chew with my loose teeth, so I soaked them in water. This also chased the lice out of the pores. In spite of my ravenous hunger, I chewed the bread cautiously to ensure the number of teeth I had was the same after the meal as before.

One day, I looked about me and gazed at the deteriorating bodies of my comrades. They appeared to be walking, living skeletons. No trace of the spark that once lit up their eyes could be found. Instead, they stared out of dull eyes, sunken within their hollow faces. My head dropped in despair at the sight of what surrounded me. I looked at my own scaly, frail hands and could plainly see each bone beneath my papery skin. I realized that I must be the mirror image of my comrades.

Time after time, I was called from the infirmary to perform some camp duties, which, most of the time, meant digging graves for my prison comrades. I was still among the lucky ones who dug the graves for someone else. Twice a day, the poverka continued to be executed with clock-like regularity, but as the days and weeks crawled by, it took less and less time. By the end of the summer of 1945, when the autumn winds blew their first cool breath across the vast Russian steppe, only 200 of the 600 prisoners still lived. The rest had been buried in unmarked graves outside the fence of the camp. Freed from the misery that the last few months of their lives had seen, they finally ceased to suffer the ever-present hunger, the bite and crawling torment of lice, the physical fatigue of their weak, stricken bodies, and the mental agony which bowed the soul to dust.

One cloudy day, as an icy, swirling wind swept throughout the camp courtyard, the remaining prison population was ordered to parade in front of a delegation that had arrived from Moscow. The eight-member commission included a high ranking officer and two female members who sat beside a table in the open air. Naked from the waist up, despite the bitter, stinging cold, we were instructed to line up, single file, like a long snake. As we approached the table, we had to drop our pants. Humiliation fell over me as we displayed our filthy, skeleton-like bodies to this audience which inspected us like animals at a slaughter house. The two lady doctors pinched our buttocks to assess our 'fitness level'. It was an exercise to determine our percentage of fat, using fingers as calipers. Of course, instead of finding our gluteal muscles, they pinched into the floppy skin which now hung from our backs like two empty leather purses. Our pathetic bodies were seemingly devoid of any ounce of body fat or significant muscle tissue for that matter. After examining approximately half of the lifeless prisoners, the head of the delegation angrily jumped from his chair and stopped the parade. After a heated exchange of words between him and our camp officers, the delegation left, obviously disgusted by the conditions they found among the prisoners. Within a few months, two-thirds of the prison population had perished. The remaining one-third was barely alive, and the delegates held the officers responsible for this appalling situation

A few days later, we each received a set of fresh under-wear, a cuffless, collarless shirt, and long pants with a draw-string. These basic clothes were welcomed with relief. The original shirt we had received and had since worn all summer was now rotten, rank, and lice-infested. Some of the prison-ers' shirts had nearly disintegrated, leaving them to walk around most of the summer with only the cuffs and the col-lar of the shirt fastened to their naked upper bodies. It actu-ally looked rather comical, but was necessary to prove that the prisoner had not sold his shirt, a practice which was against the rules.

The day finally came when I was to leave with a select-ed group of prisoners who were in very poor physical condi-tion, and consequently had become ineffective at work. When the officer read my name at the early morning poverka as one of the people destined to leave Komarichi for another camp, I felt extreme relief. My optimistic heart hoped for bet-ter days ahead, and I was excited to think of leaving this God-forsaken place behind me. Suddenly, cruel reality struck me as the officer completed reading the names on his list. None of the names of my friends had been called. My heart raced with panic. My weak body began to tremble. This meant sep-aration from my friends, my school chums and soccer bud-dies from Felsogod. Until now, we had always been together, enduring the hardships and hunger as a group. We found our strength in one another. It was a heartbreaking and frightening moment to depart from Tamas, Szani, Paul and Bandi; their support had provided such great comfort, especially in very difficult times. Bandi, the photographer whose camera lens was taken by one of the Russian officers, stayed in Komarichi. This was the last time I would see him. (Five years later, I learned that he died in this camp a few months after I left.)

I fought back my tears when the moment came to say good-bye to the three doctors. Their consideration, understanding and help had saved my life at a time when I was too weak to walk. Ali, the tall blue-eyed medical student with the big smile, gave me a friendly slap on my shoulder and said, "Hang on, young man. Don't give up." Dr. Leganyi, the lawyer, shook my hand. "Good-bye," he said, and that was all. Gyula, the veterinarian, gave me an affectionate hug until I could only see their blurred silhouettes through my tear-filled eyes. He held me in his arms and whispered into my ear, "God be with you." I could say little with the lump in my throat except a short 'thank you' for all that they had done for me and for their friendship which had been so important. A deep sorrow stabbed through my gut as I walked through the gate amongst the sad-looking bunch of prisoners. My friends stood silently, watching me through the barbed-wire fence, waving farewell until we could no longer see one another.

As the kilometres between my friends and me grew, and the outline of the Lager faded into the horizon, a strong feeling of loneliness came over me. I was really alone now, walking among strangers. The future was colored with uncertainty, and my thoughts were plagued by apprehension. We were destined to travel to the city of Bryansk, the location of the central Lager. I kept looking back as I stumbled along the dirt road. Drained emotionally as well as physically, I could still picture the watchtowers of the camp against the morning sky - the symbol of my first summer in captivity.

It seemed to be a long hike to the railway station, and I had a hard time making it. Some of the prisoners collapsed during the march, but were able to get up and struggle on. One failed to stand again, and the guards became upset when this one lifeless body remained on the ground. A soldier asked me what was wrong with him. I told him the dying prisoner simply did not have the energy to walk anymore and that he was hungry. The soldier, showing a rare display of compassion, reached into his side bag and tore a piece from his own bread. He then shoved it into the poor soul's mouth. The prisoner tried desperately to bite into the solid black Russian bread, but his effort was in vain. His glassy eyes showed no sign of life. The dry yellowish skin on his bony face contracted into a final grotesque grimace as his soul left his miserable, filthy corpse and death took him. We gazed at him with blank expressions on our faces, powerless to save him.

The soldier looked at me, asking, "Konyec?"[21] I nodded my head, acknowledging his end and replied, "Da."[22] The soldier motioned to the group to pick him up and go on "Birom - davaj - davaj,"[23] he ordered. We hardly had enough energy

---

[21] "The end?" in Russian.

[22] "Yes" in Russian.

[23] "Bring him - move - move" in Russian.

to walk, and now we had to drag the dead prisoner behind us, not being able to carry him. Four of us held onto his arms and legs and pulled him down the dusty dirt road. The guards were responsible for the number of prisoners, dead or alive, so we had no choice but to take him with us. As we staggered down the road in the middle of the vast pasture land, the pleasant scent of dried hay mixed with fine dust lingered in the air. Everyone was silent and withdrawn in their own world of thought. After marching a few kilometres, we finally reached the railway station. It seemed as though we had walked for hours. We lifted our dead comrade on an open platform car and climbed on ourselves in preparation to travel.

Clinging together for warmth, we travelled about one hundred kilometres on the flat-deck railway car until we reached our destination. As the train sped toward Bryansk, a collage of landscapes whisked by. Grassy pasture lands, undulating hills and magnificent forests, all dressed in splendid autumn costumes, floated before me and eased my heart. The crisp morning air lured tears from my eyes, and the blurred kaleidoscope of colors, mixed with hazy images of the camp, lingered in my mind. The memories of the past and the emotions of the present were intoxicating. The train ride gave us a welcome rest for our bodies and an opportunity for our souls to soar through the beautiful countryside. To jump from the train was no longer a viable option. In our poor physical shape it would have been suicide. We were victims of circumstance, unable to plan or command our own lives.

LAGER NO. 326/1 BRYANSK

It was October 1945. We were cold, miserable and hungry. Lacking adequate clothing, we had travelled on an open platform of the train for the entire day. Finally, the train halted at a central Lager in Bryansk which at any one time held a few thousand prisoners. The city was located approximately 350 kilometres southwest of Moscow. The camp housed prisoners from many nations, but was comprised mostly of Germans who had been captured during the war. They had already survived incredibly harsh conditions, but would face many more years of hardship if they remained alive. As we approached the confines of this new camp, the hope I had carried of returning home after a malinki robot disappeared, and was replaced in my heart by a foreboding fear of the Russian winter which soon would set in. It was well known that the German army's greatest enemy during the war had been the incredibly cruel Russian winter. I pictured the frozen bodies buried in the deep snow and the human suffering which my dear brother had described to me when we had last spoken.

As we walked through the gate, five abreast, the officer on duty kept count of the distraught-looking bunch. The numbers had to be correct, so the dead were dragged into the compound by fellow comrades at the end of the column. The guards were responsible for a precise number of prisoners and so, dead or alive, each one must be accounted for. When inside the camp, I noticed a few large buildings. Painted on them in bold red letters were the following words: "BROTH-ERHOOD AND EQUALITY", "PROLETARIAT OF THE WORLD UNITE". The irony of these words made my skin crawl. As we were herded into the compound like animals, I lacked any sense of equality with anyone but the animals and my fellow comrades. I certainly could not consider establishing any sort of brotherhood with the Besarabs who enjoyed the trust of the Russians and were the ruling society of the Lager. They worked as guards, or in the kitchen, the warehouse, the bath house, or the tailor shop. Still others worked only as stool pigeons or served as interpreters for the interrogators.

We quickly discovered that our food rations, compared with the first camp at Komarichi, would be better. We each received three pieces of bread per day - a total of about 600 grams - along with three servings of soup (seven decilitres per serving) and one ladle of "Kasha", a thick stew-like substance which varied in content from time to time according to what was available. It often contained barley, corn or millet. In addition to these daily rations, we each received a level spoonful of sugar and three cigarettes worth of mahorka. Mahorka was the stem of the tobacco plant ground into small pieces. Since we could not have the leaves of the tobacco, this was considered the next best alternative. Once the difficult task of lighting these cigarettes was accomplished, a most unpleasant putrid-smelling smoke billowed up. Occasionally, someone would blow this smoke in my face causing my eyes to fill with tears and forcing me to burst into a coughing spell.

It seemed that the conditions in this camp would be more bearable, and our future here seemed a bit brighter. As

I looked back over the past few months, I came to the conclusion, with some degree of satisfaction, that I had managed to clear the first hurdle and survive Komarichi the first camp in Russia. This had been one of the most primitive camps I had experienced up to this time. God had mercy on my soul, and I felt fortunate to have the Hungarian doctors, as well as Tamas' support and friendship, near. Tamas had nursed and guided me through these very rough times. I was often but a breath away from the end, so close I could smell the smothering presence of death, but I succeeded in staying alive by believing in God. The religious tutoring given to me by my mother, and the positive influence of my education which taught me to respect and love God, certainly granted me strength and courage when I needed it most. I managed to stay calm when other prisoners panicked. I said, and I believed, that the Russians could take me anywhere they wanted, but they could not hide me from God. He would always be with me. I believed He would never test me beyond the strength which He provided me, strength which was fortified through my prayers. Through my faith I made it to the end of each day, and I was able to encourage and inspire others who were twice as old as I.

I met some officers in the Lager and, in the evenings after a long day of work, was a welcome guest in their quarters. It was interesting to talk with them, especially with one who had been in the 1936 Olympic Games in Berlin. For me, his tales of the events and details of the Games brought as much wide-eyed amazement and dreamy imaginings as a bedtime story did to a child.

These conversations with different people lifted my spirits and helped me to escape from the barbed-wire fences and reach new heights. For at least a moment, my soul was free. Although my body was locked behind a fence, my soul remained unchained as long as I did not let the Russians rule me by forcing my mind to accept their twisted dogmas.

The working brigade to which I was assigned was made up of 60 people. We marched in rows, five abreast, on a dirt road which wound through golden fields. Guards traced our every move intently with the barrels of their guns. We hiked somberly to the railway station which had been nearly levelled during the war. Here we were sent to clean up the debris from the area. Part of our duties entailed cleaning the bricks with a piece of iron bar and then stacking them into square piles, measuring one cubic metre. The working site was quite a distance from our camp; therefore, we had to get up at six o'clock to down our daily cabbage soup and a piece of bread. Hurriedly, we would fall into line and march through the gate, five abreast, to be counted and received by the guard so we could meet the eight o'clock starting time at the railway station. The daily working hours eventually shrank from twelve consecutive hours to eight; however, we did not receive any lunch because they could not transport the soup. We would work straight until 4:00 p.m.

For cleaning bricks, we were spread over an area the size of a football field. The endless hours and the cold breath of the blowing wind made our lives miserable. It was here, one day, we met a large group of approximately 50 to 60 soldiers who were interested in exchanging tobacco for bread. Unfortunately, we too, had no bread, and we were just as hungry as they. We found out that they were young Latvian boys who had not heard anything of their parents for years. They were herded out of their Russian-occupied land and were forced to work in the labour camps. Unfit, and not trusted enough to be drafted into the Red Army, they were now living under conditions similar to ours. This was in spite of the fact that many of their parents had been well-to-do, industrious people working as farmers or factory owners or high-ranking officers in free Latvia. Since the Russians had occupied their land, they had lost their freedom and lived their lives like so many millions now under Red rule.

We were instructed not to leave the column, and knew that trouble was assuredly in store for anyone who did. One day, as we marched across a harvested potato field, one of the prisoners spotted a green potato lying just five steps off the road. He was in front of me, and I could see his steps hesitate, but finally he decided to go for it. By the time he reached the potato, the guard was standing over him. The prisoner was trapped. He realized that he would face harsh consequences anyway, so he stuffed the small potato into his mouth. The guard grabbed the prisoner's throat with one hand, and with the fingers of his other hand tried to fish the potato out from the boy's mouth. The starving prisoner, in a desperate effort, managed to bite the potato in half and swallow. With a slight grin on his face, he endured the guard's anger delivered to him through a rifle butt. I could sense his feeling of triumph, combined with an understanding that nothing one achieves comes without a price.

One Sunday morning, rows of army trucks stopped outside the camp gate. Again, we were ordered to line up in columns of five to be counted as we marched through the gate to the trucks. With three guards on each truck, we headed to a collective farm located approximately 50 kilometres from the camp. When we arrived, we could see on the horizon a vast field of unharvested cabbage covered with fresh snow. The instant the trucks stopped in the middle of the field, which was intersected by the dirt road, the starving prisoners disregarded all the rules, jumped from the trucks, and ran into the cabbage field in every direction. The panicked guards shouted "Stoj, stoj"[24] and began shooting into the air, hoping to stop the prisoners; but this was not an attempt to escape - it was a mad rush to fill our empty bellies with cabbage. I told the guard beside me that we did not want to escape, but only to eat before the work started. Finally, the guards gave in.

A short while later, we stood before the guards with full stomachs and content smiles, somewhat more ready to work. The job was to pick the cabbage. Normally, the procedure involved cutting the cabbage away from its base, but because we were not allowed knives, we did not know how to start. One of the Russian officers provided the answer to our questioning faces by muttering "Ya Pokazsu"[25], and proceeded to kick violently with his boot, causing the half frozen cabbage to separate from the stem and roll in the snow. "All right, boys!" we exclaimed, "Let's play soccer!" We began booting the cabbages left and right. As our game progressed into midday, the snowy field became littered with green cabbage leaves. Seeing the smiles on my comrades faces was an exhilarating experience. Now that everyone's belly was stuffed with cabbage, this carefree moment allowed our eyes to light up with contentment. Suddenly, the long, painful, hunger-stricken days had turned, momentarily, into a day of plenty as we found ourselves surrounded by cabbage. Everything looked good, and even the dumbfounded guards somber faces looked more relaxed. Our mood had been elevated, and we were now eager to work.

---

[24] "Stop, stop."

[25] "I'll show you."

Now we were told to collect the cabbage into piles. I had never seen such hills of cabbage, lying on the ground exposed to the inclement weather. The Soviet collective farm workers were not concerned with the early snowfall and cold weather. They did not try to rescue the crop since their shares or wages would not increase, whether they hustled or not. Incentive and pride in their work had been killed by long years of Communist rule. We prisoners wondered what Marx and Engels would say upon witnessing the peoples' apathy in "The Peoples' State." The overnight frost took another toll on the harvest. Most of the crop was frozen and rotten because there was inadequate storage space. It was sad to witness such waste from one of the earth's most fertile areas - the so-called chornaja zemlja.[26] This unsuccessful effort to reap the yields of such crops was the result of an ineffective system and an irresponsible and lethargic effort by a whole culture comprised of people who simply did not care.

Visits to the farm came frequently during the harvest season. On one visit, we were assigned to make up for civilian apathy by helping pick potatoes. The early frost created crust on the ground surface below which was hidden the potato crop. In order to break the crust and turn the soil over to expose the potatoes, an ordinary plow was used. We followed behind the plow, picking potatoes in the field. A chilly wind swept through the field as we worked diligently through to midday. Finally, we stopped for a quick lunch break, which brought us anger and frustration rather than a full stomach. A big barrel, filled with water from the nearby collective farm, sat over an open fire and the guards boiled potatoes. We each received two. We had hoped that since we

---

[26] Black soil.

were surrounded by thousands of potatoes we would receive enough food so we would not have to go back to work hungry, but this was not the case. In the midst of plenty, we were sent back to work with our stomachs still growling fiercely. Of course, our reaction to this ridiculous situation drastically affected the harvest. The potatoes that were exposed by the plow were stomped back into the ground rather than picked up. Dirt was kicked over them or they were kicked away. Perhaps one-third of the crop was harvested and bagged, while two-thirds remained underground because of a lack of proper machinery and the discontent of hungry prisoners.

On still another occasion, we picked beets and, again, collected them into large piles. This time, we managed to eat enough during our efforts. We wiped the dirt off and ate the beets like apples. Short-lived panic resulted when we saw our own urine turn red like blood. We thought we had finally been called up; however, we soon realized that the beets themselves had created the discoloration.

One cold November day, as the breath of winter enveloped the terrain with thick fog, a pleasant surprise was in store for us when we returned to the Lager after work. In addition to the welcome of warm soup and bread, we were each given a Red Cross postcard and now, at long last, I would be able to let Mama know I was still alive.

The picture to be painted for her on that card was not very colorful, and my outlook for the coming winter was grim. The odds were less than 50:50 that I would survive the winter, but regardless, I tried to keep an optimistic outlook, although I did have some doubt as to whether I could keep fighting.

Since the postcard would likely be read by the authorities, I knew better than to write anything negative about our situation for fear it might jeopardize the chances of it reaching my mother. I also did not want to destroy the possibility of being granted another card in the future. Besides, my mother could do nothing to change the conditions with which I had to cope. Learning the truth about my situation would only hurt her and make her life more difficult because she would be even more concerned about me.

My hands were swollen, rough and blistered from the hard work, and it was quite an effort to hold a pencil and write, but with the indelible pencil that was passed from one prisoner to the next, I managed to scribble on the card, dated November 8, 1945, the following message:

"Dear Mother! God has been with me through this time and has saved me. Now, I am waiting for Him to give me back my freedom, but in case we don't see each other, there is another place where we will meet for sure. Thank Uncle Gyula for everything, God bless him. Until we meet, with love: Gyuri."[27]

I honestly had doubts that my card would ever reach its destination.

The weather turned cold, and an overnight snowfall blanketed the ground with an icy cover, two feet thick. We eventually received this camp's issue of winter clothes, which were second-hand rejects from the Red Army. The individual allotments consisted of a three-quarter length coat, pants which were lined with cotton batting, and a set of long cotton underwear. We each also received the traditional Russian winter hat with ear flaps on each side, and even though we

---

[27] That original card is still in my possession. Mama had saved it and others I had written and returned them to me before she died.

1.)

СОЮЗ ОБЩЕСТВ КРАСНОГО КРЕСТА и КРАСНОГО ПОЛУМЕСЯЦА
СССР

Почтовая карточка военнопленного
Carte postale au prisonnier de guerre

Бесплатно
Franc de port

Кому (Destinataire) *Gemer Vincené*

Куда (Adresse) *Venes Jozán, A'non* ВЕНГЕРИЯ/*Magyarország:/Felsögö*
Pest megye
(страна, город, улица, № дома, округ, село, деревня)

Отправитель (Expéditeur)
Фамилия и имя военнопленного
Nom du prisonnier de guerre

Gemer György, Vin

Почтовый адрес военнопленного
Adresse du prisonnier de guerre

Vöröskereszt: Moszk
326/I.

Тип. «Красное знамя», Москва, Сущевская, 21. Заказ 1922

Kedves Édesanyám! 1945. XI.

A jó Isten eddig mindig velem volt és mindenen keresztül megőrizet. Most is csak kö-nörgöm a szabadulásért ami remélem eljön a... Nagyon örülök, hogy a jó Isten megőrizte az egész családot. Éljenek boldogan kedves Jáim, esetleg nem is látjuk többé egymást, maj-jan egy hely még ahol találkozunk. A jó Isten velem van. Gyula bácsinak mindent köszön a jó Isten áldja meg. Mindenkit rokon csókolok. Édesanyám mindent köszönök... hogy ... megháláljatni... Milliomos csókok mindenkit a vizont... tásig Gyurka hated the sight of these hats, they protected our heads from the cold. Finally, a crude pair of mitts, sewn from old army coats, offered protection for our hands. My original ski and mountain boots were still holding together, but having no socks, a thin layer of rags was used to provide my feet with a little protection against the cold. A piece of wire around my waist held my pants up, and another outside my coat kept the wind from racing up my body.

Then, one crisp cold day I nearly burst with joy when I finally heard my name among the lucky ones who had received the standard Red Cross reply card from home. With a shaking hand and tear-filled eyes, I tried to read my dear mother's delicately formed words. It took a bit of time before I could make out the short message and her acknowledgment of my existence. Finally, I found comfort in knowing that someone at home knew I was still alive. I was relieved to know that with the exception of my brothers, the family was together in Uncle Gyula's house. There were no details of their lives, but the most important thing was to know that we were all still alive even though separated by vast distances. I read the card over and over again while lying on my bunk bed at evening until I finally fell asleep. I kept the card with me when we went out to work and I re-read it at every opportunity. It gave me extra strength to fight on and was cherished until the writing faded and the card disintegrated.

The work became more miserable. We now had to dig deep under the snow to recover bricks, and the frozen mortar just did not want to separate from them; nevertheless, we cleaned and stacked one cubic metre of bricks each day. This was set as our task which had to be completed in order for us to receive the evening portion of our daily ration. To keep my feet from freezing, I forced myself to keep moving.

This reduced the time I had left to complete my task. So, I built four walls from clean bricks measuring one metre wide by close to one metre high to form the outside of the cube. I then collected some scrap pieces of lumber, covered the top of the cube with them and camouflaged them with the last two rows of bricks. It certainly took fewer bricks, and it appeared as a solid cubic metre when the Russian yard master came at the end of the day and checked our production. These were the types of games we had to play in order to survive. The next day, I used the same bricks to build a similar pile in another location. So, in this way, I survived each day until we neared the end of the year.

During the hard winter, the conditions undoubtedly were very difficult. Every day seemed like an eternity, and to fight the elements while working outside tested our health and physical endurance. This was trying, to say the least, but to face each day, not knowing when our strife would end was a tougher test of our mental strength. My friend Attila was the only child of a high-ranking officer and, until now, his life had been relatively easy. Now, facing these extraordinary hardships, he lost his desire to go on and take life as it came. Despite my daily words of encouragement, he argued with me. One day, as we were heading out to the field, he said, "I'm going to die. I will never go home." "Don't say that," I retorted. "We will go home, but right now we just have to take this and work and fight to stay alive." "No," he replied, "I will die here. I have only a few days left." He was not sick, but he was run down and weak. Eventually, he began to run a fever and was allowed to stay in the Lager. He lay all day on his stale bunk bed, counting the days to his predicted death. He soon stopped eating his food and gave up completely. He had lost his will to live and, as the days went by, his weakness grew more recognizable through his voice. My sermons were in vain. At the end of one particularly grueling day, I went to visit him in the evening. He kept whispering, "Tomorrow, tomorrow..." The next evening, I found his bunk bed empty. His body had been taken during the day to the wooden shack where they piled the naked bodies on top of each other until the next burial occurred. I could only hope that God had taken his soul.

"SILENT NIGHT"

We felt every day, every hour, every minute of our lives as we fought the elements in the ever-present state of hunger, but the time clock just kept ticking and Christmas day had arrived. The Godless communist state did not recognize the birthday of Christ celebrated world wide. This sacred day was to pass like any other. It was a great relief to finish our work that day. We rushed from the cold to receive our soup and bread and to withdraw to our bunk beds to rest in the relative warmth of our barracks. The Hungarian officers initiated a low-key Christmas celebration by sneaking in a pine tree branch. Staring at this twig green with life, we sang 'Silent Night'. I remembered past Christmas nights with my family spent around a brightly colored tree with branches bending from the weight of the candies wrapped in glittering paper.   There was plenty of food, particularly my favourite, the traditional Hungarian poppy seed rolls. In the quiet of the night, with the peaceful singing soothing my soul, my thoughts travelled far away. As waves of memories of childhood Christmases lapped over me, tears welled up in my eyes and trickled down my cheeks. My mind wandered dreamily amongst visions of my family, my mother, the warmth and cheer of my home. Suddenly reality came crashing in and my thoughts were interrupted by the German barrack commandant's harsh order "Antreten!"[28] We had a new order to march to the railway line to unload a train full of frozen sugar beets from the boxcars. We were reluctant to leave the relative comfort of the barracks in the middle of the night; however, it was more upsetting to be so harshly pulled from the refuge in my mind back out into the hopeless situation I had found myself in.

Out at the railway line, being hungry like always, I tried on occasion to bite into a beet, however, with the beets frozen solid and my teeth dangling in my mouth like piano keys, it was much like trying to chew a bowling ball. Fortunately, opportunity provided us with a chance to steal some beets after finishing the task. I took only one beet though, knowing that we would be frisked. If we were found guilty of stealing we would surely have to bear violent consequences. Some of the other prisoners tied their pant legs at their ankles and desperately filled their pants with beets to the point where they could barely walk. Later, we reached the camp, and the big barbed wire and wood gate swung open. Inevitably, we were instructed to step forward from our line, five abreast, stop under the dim light, and be searched. I hid my beet under my arm and when the sergeant began to frisk my comrades, I discreetly dropped the beet behind my heels and stood motionless as my heart pounded with great anxiety. Discovering the treasures stored in the bulging pants of the other soldiers, the sergeant became quite busy kicking the hell out of my greedy comrades and forcing them to unload their booty. Finally, he stepped toward me and frisked me roughly. Not finding anything, he sneered and stepped over to examine the next soldier in the row.

---

28 German word for 'Assemble!'

Meanwhile, I managed to work the beet in between my feet. When the five of us were cleared, he shouted "Shago, marsh"[29]. On command, we moved forward and with the skill of a pro soccer player I kicked my beet in front of me and out of the light into the safety of the dark unnoticed. Then I quickly picked it up and, with a happy heart, ran into the barracks and disappeared into my bunk bed. My Christmas celebration began when the beet finally thawed out and I was able to eat it slowly. I thanked God that although it was not a sweet, delicious candy wrapped in fancy tin foil, I had received something to replace the traditional Hungarian Christmas candy. This was my first Christmas in Russia, and everything being relative, I found contentment after all. The rats, our every present companions who scampered frequently under the lowest row of bunk beds, observed my silent celebration to the last bite, but did not receive even the smallest morsel.

The rats were unwanted, hated companions, but they shared camp life with us, skittering about the compound with empty stomachs in search of food. In this sense we shared the commonalty of hunger and the struggle for survival. One of the large barracks housed more than five hundred prisoners, and the high ceiling allowed the building of three-storey-high bunk beds in rows with narrow walking spaces between them. Occasionally the evening entertainment for those of us who slept on the lowest row - a foot from the floor - was to sit on the edge of the bed and try to drop rocks on the rats as they ran by. For some reason they came to life in the evening, and there was quite a bit of traffic before everything would finally quieten down. We

---

[29] "Forward, march."

made a desperate effort to get rid of them, but without great success. From time to time we managed to catch one alive. We would poke their eyes out, then turn them loose again. They would run around in a frenzy, and their squealing would spook the other rats keeping them away temporarily; however, after awhile they were back again as part of our community.

The long winter's evening activities included a variety of things. One popular pastime, besides bombing the rats, was lice races. These were organized by folding a piece of paper like an accordion, with each crease numbered. Paper was scarce, so these racetracks were carefully preserved. The competitors came from our underarms - well fed, trained and eager to run. Each trainer placed his bet - his two hundred gram piece of bread - in the pot. These were high stakes, as a loss would extend the hunger pangs until morning, but a win would mean a feast was in store. The lice were guided into their respective creases and the races were on. Of course, in lice circles the race was a slow crawl, but the prolonged event made it more exciting. By tapping the edge of the paper, the competitors were urged onto the designated finish line and a blade of grass kept them moving in the right direction. The race was rather slow, interrupted by some unexpected stops, but tension among the spectators grew, as well as among the participants. The pre-selected jury members, upon completion of the race, declared the finishing order and the winner. Of course, some of the contenders, after performing well, were placed back inside the owner's shirt; but the losers were given an immediate death sentence of being squeezed between the nails of the angry owners.

Our unsuccessful struggle with our tiny friends, the lice, went on for years. From time to time we would make an

effort to execute them by turning our shirts inside out, examining the creases, and exercising no mercy over any lice we could find; however, after such a raid, we sure as hell, would not find the peace to allow a wink of sleep that night. Somehow, from somewhere, a new herd would arrive, and one's body would become the battleground for a war over territorial claims. This period when the existing tribe of lice was fighting to hold their position against a new army of hungry intruders created a very uncomfortable situation for the host. Eventually, we learned that any individual effort to kill them was in vain. We grudgingly accepted them as part of our big happy family, which had come to include the rats, bedbugs, scabies, mice, mosquitoes, flies, and now, the lice. The saying: "let nature take its course" became our accepted position, until years later when we were finally able to get rid of them for good.

The latrine in this camp was a huge pit covered with lumber which had holes cut at regular intervals. The large population in the camp forced the maintenance crew to empty the latrine pit quite often. It was a regular occurrence to see the shit wagon, a large wooden keg on wheels, being pulled across the yard by some pathetic-looking prisoners. During the cold winter months the cleaning process became rather irregular and the shit pile often grew to become almost level with the openings in the boards. At times like this, our friends, the rats, would frequently run just beneath the boards and interrupt our squatting position. It would be rather undesirable to have one's nuts bitten by a naughty rat with a sense of humour. So, we were rather alert when answering Mother Nature's calls. Those prisoners whose weakened physical condition did not allow them to work outside the camp at the regular places were assigned to the latrine crew. They were still able to walk, but staggered about with such a slow pace that death followed their every step and gained momentum quickly.

During the regular monthly physical check-ups, the Russian physician with his female nurses determined into what physical category each prisoner fit. The number one and two categories were supposedly in good shape and able to work eight hours a day. Category three had to work only four hours a day. If individuals did not fall into these three categories, they were assigned to camp duties (like the shit brigade). Beyond this was dystrophy No. one, two and three; these subjects were the not-swiftly-but-still-moving skeletons whose future would likely hold little else other than a sub-terranean residence, unless they could somehow gain some weight by not working and by having a little better ration. This monthly examination was performed as before, with each prisoner parading naked from the waist up to a table, then dropping his drawers and showing his bare butt to the nurses for a quick pinch. With the doctor's input, these nurses judged each prisoner, placing him in a category, in effect assigning him his destiny. Some prisoners deliberately ate excess salt to look skinnier, without realizing the drastic consequences to their kidneys and arteries. By appearing thinner, they hoped to fall into a lower category, which meant less or no work at all. This was just one way to avoid the long day outside, working in -35° C weather. Another method was to stage an industrial accident and cut off a finger, so one could spend the winter under a roof.

Many performed these types of self-inflicted wounds, but such an act just did not appeal to me. I was planning to throw the javelin once I returned home, so I did not want to resort to such drastic measures. All I wanted was to have a one-day holiday from the cold. One night I went out into the dark and decided to cut my hand. In a very depressed mood I began to sharpen the handle of my spoon to try to make a cutting edge by rubbing it against a brick. In retrospect, I consider this one of my more shameful and stupid plans - following others to try to escape my fate, but at the time, the thought of just one day inside clouded my better judgment. I grabbed the primitive knife I had made and held it tightly in one hand. After a few breaths I cut through the skin of my other hand, but not deep enough to draw much blood. Having eaten only cabbage soup three times a day for the last four months, I expected more cabbage juice than blood to ooze out of the wound. I realized that it did not work. I made another attempt by putting my hand on a rock and hitting it with a brick, in the hope it would swell up quickly. It did not work either. I had a cut in my hand and it hurt like hell, but I did not even go to the infirmary to try to ask for the day off. It was my first and last attempt to inflict upon myself more pain and discomfort than I already had. I had enough trouble trying to cope with what was dished out by fate. It was the time period when the Russian winter lived up to its reputation, causing lots of frostbite on our faces and toes.

When the six-day work week, with all its shivering and pain finally ended, we hoped to spent Sunday in the camp in the barracks. It was a wish which seldom materialized; instead, we were herded out again to the forest to cut some trees and carry the logs back to camp on our shoulder.

The Sunday walk took all day, out again in the cold in the morning, struggling in the deep snow, fighting the fatigue, and by the time we came back it was dusk. We were always entertained, and we seldom had a day when they would just leave us alone and let us rest.

Another dreadful exercise that we had to go through was the monthly banya.[30]   By brigades we were herded out into the cold and stripped from our stinking lice-riddled clothes in front of an old building.   We had to string our clothes through a metal ring with a small number on it.   We had to remember our number in order to identify our clothes. The piles of clothes were then threaded onto a long pole and placed in the building in rows over the fire.   The objective was to kill the lice by heating the clothes to a temperature of greater than $85^{\circ}C$.   While this procedure took place we rushed, without a stitch of clothing on and with a shrinking blue 'ding-a-ling', to another building for our bath.   In assembly-line style we lined up in single file to let the barber smear some soap from a bucket onto our face, underneath our arms and around our genitals with a big paintbrush, one after the other.   We then had to face the guy with the razor-knife, who, with quick movements shaved our beards, our armpits and our chests.   When he finally grabbed my penis to shave off my pubic hair, I stood motionless in a stiff panic, thinking "if this stupid jerk makes one wrong move while he is swinging his knife, he'll cut off my love life," which had not yet begun. I would have rather died.   (At that time, not having had any experience, I did not know very much about sex except what I deducted from the stories of my comrades.)   It was always a relief to get through this shaving procedure which usually left a cut or two on some part of our bodies.   Next, we each received a cube of soap one inch square and waited for the water.

On the ceiling of the bathhouse a network of two centimetre iron pipes had been installed.   Not having shower

---

[30] Bath.

heads, the Russians had simply punched holes in the pipes so that the water, when turned on centrally, would trickle down on us. Each prisoner tried desperately to locate himself under the tiny holes by pushing and shoving the stinking bodies around him. At a given time, the lukewarm water would start spraying through the holes and quickly, using that little piece of soap, we would hastily attempt to clean ourselves, often with limited success. The water would then suddenly stop - we had run out of time. We would stand there, dirt and soap smeared on our bodies, disgusted and angry, yet we had to move on because the next group of people was right behind us. In this state, we then had to run outside in the snow and cold back to the little house where we had to find our clothes. On the way, we could finish up our baths by throwing snow on ourselves and washing off the dirt.

The clothes were thrown out by the crew onto the snow, and we would look frantically through the stinking steaming piles, until we found our ring with our number on it. Quickly, we would jump into our filthy clothes which were now supposedly free of the lice and run into our barracks, ending this torturous ritual called bathing. After that, everything was back in place; however, we did not feel any cleaner because we were forced to put on the same dirty clothes. They were no cleaner, just a little more baked. The lice were still there, but we were happy knowing that the ordeal was over until the next time. Due to the ineffective nature of this primitive procedure, we had to live with the lice for a long time. This is how the days went by, and when the month of January 1946 arrived with increasingly cold weather, only a handful of people from our company were able to work.

The rest lay frostbitten, too weak from dysentery to

move, and with scabies covering their bodies. I had still managed to go outside and work, but was very close to my limit also, and near the end; but, alas, God's merciful helping hand reached out to help me. I was called to report to the infirmary for a checkup. I had to undress, and the doctor examined me. Because he did not find scabies on me, I was sent to the kitchen for duties. It was like flying from hell to heaven in an instant. I could hardly believe my good fortune. God was on my side after all. My new assignment meant no more cold, no more hunger; these two dominant components which, for so long, had been the cause of so much misery and nearly death, suddenly disappeared from my life. I was assigned to the night shift, and on my first shift I had to stay up all night without a warning. I struggled to stay awake and hustled to live up to the expectations of the chef. The cooks gave me extra food, and after a period of time the work gradually became easier. The hardest task was to stir the 600-litre kettle filled with thick corn (kasha) to keep it from burning. I felt like I was rowing a boat, but instead of water beneath the 'oar' - my spoon - there was this thick substance. After awhile I got used to the work and slowly began to regain my strength. In the morning, when I finished up my work and had cleaned the big kettles and the kitchen, I went to my barrack to sleep. This new job was like walking on 'cloud nine' in comparison with my earlier life of a few hours before. Unfortunately, all good things in life must come to an end, as did my duties in the kitchen.

I WAS A HORSE IN BRYANSK

I was selected along with 39 other prisoners to perform a special task. We had to assemble in the courtyard after gathering together all our worldly possessions. All that I owned was the clothes on my back, a pair of crudely-made cloth mittens, the invaluable spoon in my pocket, and the army dish tied to my waist. We stood in the courtyard in the usual five-abreast formation, ready for our assignment. A quick glance at the Kirgiz sergeant's face told me that some unpleasant duties were in store for us. Ten Besarabs served the Kirgiz as guards and cooks. Their time in camp would be short, lasting only until they were cleared to go home, but for now, they were used by the Russians to boost the number of guards. They escorted us to the railway station where we waited in freezing temperatures for the train. Two hours passed, but it seemed an eternity when, at last, the train arrived. The tiny windows of each car were covered with thick frost except for a small central hole where the breath of the passengers had melted the frost so they could look out. After shivering in the miserable cold for so long, we were finally allowed to board the train. Our great disappointment came when we were forbidden to enter the railway cars. We were forced to travel approximately 150 kilometres standing on the steps of the train while the icy wind sliced through our flesh to our bones. At each station - thank God they came fre-

115

quently - the train stopped, giving us a few minutes to stomp our feet and swing our arms in an effort to warm up and get the circulation going in our limbs again. We also checked each other's faces for the white telltale signs of frostbite, then covered up again with rags we had torn from our big coats so that only our teary, red eyes were peeking out. We travelled like this all day, without food, until finally we reached a train station where we were told to disembark. Numb and stiff, we stumbled from the steps of the train, only to be ordered to start walking down a snow-covered road. With heads down and bodies leaning into the sweeping wind we trudged along, our boots keeping time as they squeaked with each step. We passed a few settlements, and I imagined the heat held within the walls of the houses, but this only made my bones ache more for want of warmth. Finally, we came to the end of our journey at the edge of the forest. Our new home lay before us - three dugout bunkers of wooden construction and covered with roofs of dirt. Deep, virgin snow had piled around them, burying them, almost hiding them completely from view. Forty of us occupied two of the bunkers; the third was reserved for the Kirgiz and the ten Besarabs, and also served as a kitchen. By this time, a hallowed moon shone brightly, casting dark shadows of exhausted prisoners on the snow and signifying a long-awaited end to this miserable day. Despite our weariness, we were anxious to escape from the stabbing cold to the belly of the bunker. Pushing and shoving each other, we scrambled underground out of the howling wind. Inside the bunker, it was pitch dark and still bitterly cold. It took some time before someone could activate their pitchki. Using it, we made a light by burning strips of birch tree bark. This became our source of light throughout our stay. Gradually, as the light burned brighter and our eyes adjusted, the interior of the bunker was revealed. On either side of the dirt floor lay some wooden logs that would have to suffice as beds. The bumpy logs were covered with a thick layer of frost and had obviously not been occupied by anyone recently. As uncomfortable as these frozen, irregular beds may have appeared, fatigue made them a welcome sight for each of us.

Each of these bunkers had an empty gasoline barrel in the middle with a pipe through the roof. This served as the stove. One of the prisoners made a fire, and we each received a small piece of bread which was gone in a few ravenous bites. There was no water, but by melting snow in our army dishes on the stove, we were each able to at least wet our tongues. After the gruelling journey, we each soon claimed a space on the logs. They did not provide any comfort to our bony skeletons but we collapsed on them in the depth of the smoke-filled semi-warm bunker and fell asleep. The breath of the cold Russian night rushed between the planks of the primitively constructed wooden door moaning and whisper-ing to us throughout the night.

Still in our clothes and heavy winter coats, our heads cocooned in our hats, we awoke the next morning to the commanding voice of the Kirgiz. "Davaj - davaj"[31] he yelled. It was pitch dark in the bunker as the fire had died out in the night, and now we were herded out into the cold. We lined up in front of the third bunker where we received half of our daily ration of bread and a cup of cabbage soup. Thankfully, we were allowed to go back to our bunker out of the cold wind to eat. The thin soup did not provide very many calories for our starving bodies, but it was hot, and it

---

[31] "Move - move."

felt good as it went down, warming us up temporarily. Those precious few moments when we ate in peace were soon interrupted by the Kirgiz's command. We were pulled out again into the cold morning air where the moon's face was still visible in the dark blue sky. There we listened to the Kirgiz's briefing.

"The horses are kaput;[32] therefore, you are now the horses. Your work will be to load the sleighs with pre-cut piles of wood and pull them to the railway station. Then you will load the wood from the sleighs into the railway cars."

In accordance with the plan, four of us were harnessed to the crude wooden sleigh with cables. When everyone was in place, the caravan, consisting of ten sleighs with four 'horses' per sleigh and escorted by the Besarab guards, slowly began to pull out into the forest. By the time we reached the spot where the cut and stacked wood awaited us, the sun had begun to show its orange face between the trees. This was the coldest part of the day. We were chilled to the bone and could see the ice crystals in the air as we made our way toward the wood piles. We struggled through waist-deep snow to load the sleigh, log by log, and when all ten sleighs were loaded, we climbed back into our harnesses and began the trek back, past our bunkers and down the road to the railway station ten kilometres away. A water tower on the horizon was a visual marker of our final destination. Upon reaching the station, we unloaded the wood onto the boxcars only to return for another load. On some days we had to make only one trip; on others, two. Each morning, the Kirgiz would come to our bunker to wake us, and as we rubbed the sleep from our eyes and the cold from our limbs, we awaited

---

32 German slang for 'dead.'

his dreaded announcement of the number of trips we would have to make that day.

It was early February 1946. This was the middle of the Russian winter, and it was bitterly cold. The temperature ranged from -35°C to -42°C on some occasions. I covered my face with pieces of rags and pulled down the ear flaps of my hat, tying them under my chin. My breath formed ice on the rag and on my eyebrows. My boots had finally worn out before we left the central camp, so I was forced to exchange them for a much-hated pair of shoes made with wooden soles and canvas tops. I asked for the largest size available. I then tore four square pieces from my topcoat, put a layer of cotton from my pants between them, and wrapped my feet with them. The oversize shoes allowed room for the double layer of material and cotton to be sandwiched between the wooden sole and my feet. They were definitely awkward and slippery on the snow, but at least my blood could circulate. I would discover that these 'home-made' boots saved my feet from freezing in the extreme cold. When harnessed to the sleigh, it must have appeared that I was performing an exotic dance - the carioca - all the way to the railway station. Certainly I felt I was, since the slick, cumbersome, wooden-soled shoes made fine skates, causing me to lose my balance frequently. As I danced and slipped through the snow and over the ice, I struggled to avoid being hit by the sleigh.

I discovered that my partner 'horse' who trudged beside me was a hairdresser from Budapest. During the journey, we decided not to look up and watch the water tower, as it never seemed to move closer, despite our efforts. We decided to just look down and keep talking. He spoke eloquently with a colorful tongue as he described the smallest details of his experiences and love affairs with numerous lady clients. His stories pulled our thoughts away from our present misery, and I listened eagerly to tales I had never imagined could happen.

Our daily 'horse' duty continued for weeks and seemed like eternity. The real horses were kaput and the best substitutes were the war prisoners. It puzzles me to this day how the hell I survived this - the darkest and most inhumane time of my prison years.

At the end of each long day, we pulled the sleighs up by the bunker and lined up to receive the second half of our daily ration of bread and cabbage soup. Someone would always light the stove as soon as we arrived back at our bunker, and we would huddle as close to the stove as possible while we gobbled down our meals. This was the best part of the day, but it lasted only a few minutes. After supper, we looked forward to sleeping as this was our temporary escape from the daily struggle. Sometimes a dream would take us back home, or bring us feasts and songs, wine and dancing and warmth.

Each day brought a new extreme test of our wills and our bodies, and each night, those of us who passed the test collapsed in the bunker without even enough energy to nurse the fire through the night so as to allow the bunker to get warm. No longer were there any organized lice-races, no games, or even arguments amongst the prisoners. Each of us crawled, without words, into our space on top of the logs, to sleep or to dream open-eyed, staring into the dark and fearing tomorrow. During these silent nights, I had ample time to think about life - the past, the future, and the dreadful present. I sought answers to recurring questions, "Why? Why me? Why am I being punished so severely? What did I do to warrant such cruelty?" My mind often worked in high gear. During one of my lowest moods, I came to the somber conclusion that life was a big bucket that hung over my head and was full of warm shit. Sometimes the bucket tipped over and dumped its full blessing. At other times, the shit dripped slowly over the edge of the bucket - these were the happy days. Somehow, this analogy has stayed in my mind and is still with me. When one problem after another occurs, I know that the bucket has tipped over. As a rule, I endure these difficult days with the hope that soon the bucket will turn upright again, and I will see better days. This theory certainly is a bit more harsh that the 'bowl of cherries' analogy of life, nevertheless, the idea has remained in my head, especially during those days in Bryansk.

Despite the hardships, the lice, the pains, the dreaded cold, the hunger that stung my stomach as I trudged through the crisp snow ahead of the sleigh, I felt somewhat relieved to be out of the large, crowded camp and closer to nature. The towering pine trees covered with snow, the undulating white terrain, and the blue winter sky provided a magnificent view. It seemed peaceful and serene, freer and more open without the barbed wire fences around us, but the beautiful snow and the vast winter scene also represented a tremendous threat to our very existence. The fence was an unnecessary thing here on the edge of the forest of Bryansk. The elements, the deep snow, the extreme cold, the great distances, our own deteriorated physical condition, and the lack of food were the obstacles that discouraged thought of escape. We had two choices: endure, fight for our existence, and hope for the best or; die.

The minutes, the hours and the days filled with struggle went by slowly, and at the end of each day I believe that I came closer to the end of my test. Some of the prisoners with views opposite to mine jumped out of the harness to cry out and curse God for their suffering. They shouted to the sky,

called God to come down and look around to see the hell on earth that we were going through. Their spirits were broken, and all hope had gone from their lice-ridden bodies.

The daily fight with the elements and the work drained our bodies. We staggered during work hours, made only cautious movements, and did not do more than we were forced to do. Any extra effort which might serve to improve our personal hygiene took too much energy, so we failed to warm water to wash ourselves or clean ourselves in any way. The result was filthy bodies infested with lice. To urinate or shit became a very painful effort, and then only every second or third day. Again we had to go out onto the vast snow-covered field and leave our mark. Our starving bodies metabolized every ounce of food which was digestible. We could only shit tiny pellets.

The smoke from the burning birch tree bark covered our faces, beards and hair with soot and with no opportunity to shave or cut our hair, we looked like scarecrows. Luckily we could not see our own faces because luxurious items such as mirrors were unknown in that hell hole.

Being alone, without a friend, presented additional problems to the primitive conditions of our camp, the elements and the drudgery of our work. Despite working and living together and the close conditions in the bunker, there were no emotional involvements with each other. No trust, nor friendships were struck. Everybody was on his own; fighting his own fight, with no concern or compassion toward his fellowman. I very much missed my friends from Felsogod, Tamas, Szani, and Paul who were with me in the earlier camps. Their friendship and their presence definitely would have provided much-needed support for me. Here I was alone, surrounded by strange people wearing cold crusts on their unkempt faces, struggling for themselves and not show-ing a speck of kindness toward each other. The hairdresser was with me, but I could not see and feel that he had the slightest concern for me. During the dark nights I was alone with my thoughts and my prayers. 'Ora et labora'[33] stuck in my mind. So I worked the long days and prayed during the lonely nights until I could finally fall asleep. With every new morning I, being a believer in God and an optimist, started my new fight for another day.

As we huddled close to a small fire while we waited for the other prisoners to load their sleigh, I dreamt out loud: "Someday I will wash my filthy body in the Pacific Ocean under blue skies. I will warm my buns as I lie on thick soft sand, laced with palm trees." As I stretched my thoughts to imagine the warmth, the salty scent of the ocean, the vivid colors and the clear water rushing over my body, a coarse, gravely voice shattered the images. "You stupid bastard with all your dreams, you will rot here with us. We will never make it home." I solemnly replied, "Even if no one else makes it, I will." They argued and ridiculed my dreams, but deep down, I think they enjoyed hearing my optimistic outlook of my future. So, although I presently filled the horses' shoes, I had a strong feeling that a brighter future lay ahead. I rou-tinely imagined it as I pulled the loaded sleigh and unloaded the wood, day after day.

I ceremoniously ate the pieces of bread and the cab-bage soup, and crashed on the uncomfortable logs until the next morning came. On one occasion, as we returned from the station, the caravan spread out as the prisoners rushed back to seek shelter from the cold. Thus an opportunity

---

[33] Latin phrase meaning 'Pray and work.'

arose to release myself from the wire harness looped across my shoulder, and dash to a peasant house to ask for food or possibly exchange the mahorka for bread. I made a few quick steps toward the little Russian house and knocked on the door. A woman, her head covered with the typical peasant scarf, opened the door. Her eyes were filled with surprise and alarm. As I stepped in the door I noticed an old gray-bearded man in the background grinding a handful of wheat in the primitive stone handmill to make some flour. He sat on the crude bench which was the only furniture beside the table on the dirt-covered floor of the tiny room. A petroleum lamp gave an eerie atmosphere to the poorly heated place. I greeted them, saying "Drastvujte"[34] showing the fistful of mahorka to them while asking for bread. They stared at me for a few seconds, and without exchanging any further words I walked out of their grim-looking home. I realized that they were not in a position to give me anything. They had their own problems which were probably as great as mine.

I hurried to catch up to my sleigh, swung the wire harness over my head, and fell back into line. As I went down the road the image of the old couple haunted me. I felt sorry for them, the twilight years of their lives were filled with nothing but hardship and struggle. I compared my life to theirs. I was the prisoner, and a prisoner's life was not meant to be easy but I still had hope that my struggle, although unbearable, some day would end. What did they have to look forward to, how many years would go by until they would be a bit more comfortable? Life seemed so unfair. I never made another attempt to ask for help from any of the Russian peasants.

---

[34] A Russian greeting like "Hello."

From time to time our caravan was surprised by strange visitors. A pack of wolves followed on our flank close to the tree line and about fifty metres from the edge of the forest. They were shy, but hungry just like we. We never felt in any danger from them, but their mournful howls in the night made us feel uneasy. They roamed the vast forest in packs, and we were the intruders in their home territory.

With the passing days our strength deteriorated and we became shadows of ourselves, weak and near our end. At times like this the smallest physical disorder or sickness meant certain death. And it happened, one by one. Someone's clock beat its last beat, and the person met his end. It came in different forms and at different times. Someone fell on the road unable to walk any further. He was thrown on the top of the wood and froze to death shortly after. His boots and clothes were taken by the other prisoners - they acted like vultures. The naked yellow skeleton was covered with snow and left in an unmarked icy roadside grave. No prayers, no last respects were given, just empty stares from the survivors who were watching to see what their own fate would probably bring in the end. Another prisoner went out in the night to relieve himself and never came back. He would be found the next morning frozen in the snow when we looked for the missing 'horse'. It was an easy way to end the struggle, just sit for a few minutes and slip into another world without pain.

Some of them did not make the morning, they had died during the night. Usually their death was not reported to the Kirgiz until just before we assembled for work. That way their neighbour could eat an extra portion of bread and soup. The Kirgiz was furious, but there was nothing he could do about it. The caravan would be shorter by two sleighs because seven prisoners departed from the group to the eternal resting place at the edge of the woods under the deep snow.

Time seemed to walk with leaden legs, it passed so slowly; nevertheless, we finally completed our special task at the station, loading the few trains with wood. As I said, these days that I spent in front of the sleigh in Bryansk were the darkest and most difficult days of my prison life, yet I came out of them with only the loss of a lot of weight and strength, but without freezing my feet, nor the breaking of my spirit. I was weathered but still optimistic as we left the bunkers. I walked the last time on the snow-covered familiar road toward the railway station under the bright rays of a March sun, my spirit uplifted and with a feeling of triumph. I did not win any championships nor did I win any medals, but I came out a winner of one of the most difficult contests of my life by just surviving this camp. I looked to the sky without seeing anything and thanked God for his mercy. We reached the railway station and saw the train loaded with some of the wood that had been the fruit of our labour. I said a silent farewell to the place as our train pulled out of the station with 33 unusual passengers hanging on the stairs. The weather was now a bit better than three months ago when we started this task. As I hung on the railway car steps I made eye contact with some of my prison buddies, and I noticed their slight smiles on the ragged faces as they acknowledged me. I knew they now approved of my optimism. Perhaps they remembered my dreams, and as we traveled back to the central camp those dreams became a bit more realistic to them as well.

Upon arrival at the central camp, the ragged, filthy and tired bunch was herded to the banya without delay.

Three months of beards and hair was shaved off, and three months of filth was washed from our undernourished skeletons. Our rag-like clothes were decontaminated of lice and exchanged for somewhat better quality attire. We received warm soup and a piece of bread, and were directed to the barrack where we went to sleep. Like a bad dream, our adventure in the forest of Bryansk was finally over, but it is still vivid in my memory.

NEW SPRING

The sun climbed higher in the sky each day, sculpturing long icicles from the eaves of the houses. This was the first sign of a welcome spring. My heart flooded with new hope and relief as I watched the dreadful Russian winter lose its strength day by day. By the 1st of May, the Communist Workers' Holiday, the radiant sun began to unleash its welcome warmth upon my skin. This was the first holiday that we did not have to work or perform any camp duties. As we basked in the sun, I remembered those who had died in the winter and now lay outside the fence under the melting snow. It had been impossible to dig graves for them in the frozen muskeg. We watched grimly as huge overfed blackbirds pecked at the remains of our dead comrades whose bodies were now exposed beneath the melting snow cover. The shit wagon was also more visible because the milder weather necessitated more frequent trips. An outdoor shower facility was constructed by using a long pipe with holes punched in it to accommodate more people at one time. The outdoor eating area remained the same as last fall. Just outside the kitchen, rows of rough wooden tables still stood chest high. A tradesman had made bowls from the American conserve tins. These had been left on the tables throughout the winter exposed to the weather, so they had rusted and corroded. Nevertheless, at meal times the prisoners used them in relays.

As soon as one finished his soup and wiped every drop out of the bowl with his fingers, he passed it to the next prisoner who was waiting impatiently. The bowls were never washed, just passed to the next one to use. Some lucky prisoners had their own dish that they had managed to smuggle through the search, but they had to guard them between meals.

Strict discipline was maintained in the Lager, comprised mainly of Germans. Cheating on or stealing from fellow prisoners was considered a terrible crime, and the penalty was very severe. A cage had been constructed using a heavy wooden frame, covered with wire. It was just large enough for one person to crouch down in. The bottom was open, and the criminal had to crawl into the cage as one side was lifted by fellow prisoners. The guilty party would have to stay inside this cage for hours or days, depending upon his crime. He was often spat upon or urinated on by other prisoners. Sand and water was thrown on him frequently, and he generally received an array of verbal abuses.

At the working place we mixed with the civilian population. A small wooden shack sold bread to the Russians prior to the celebration of the Workers' Holiday. It seemed to be an effort to boost the morale of the discontented workers. A long line of people waited patiently outside the shack to buy a loaf of the black bread. As soon as the bread was received through the little window, it was gobbled up. Most of the workers were poorly dressed and very somber in appearance. They seemed dissatisfied with their lives, but they worked without complaint. They struggled as much as we did, and seemed to be patiently and passively awaiting better times. I felt sorry for them. They were simple, ordinary people like myself, trapped in a dreadful situation, waiting for some miracle to change the course of their unhappy life.

Up until now, the Russians had never asked us what army unit we had served in during the war, or what role we had played. Now everyone was interrogated - in some cases, repeatedly. They were searching for soldiers from the regular German army who had served in the occupation forces in Russia. Those who were found were systematically beaten and forced to sign a confession. These confessions had been written by Russian officers in the Russian language, which most of the prisoners did not fully understand. In some cases, the charges against the individual were based upon seemingly solid evidence, but others were mere fabrications of crimes. The Russians often used the false testimony of witnesses to send innocent soldiers to 25 years in exile. We would never see them again. There was no defense, nor was there any filing of complaints. The jury was made up of three officers whose decision was final. If the Latin words "Ira impedit animi iuditum"[35] are true, then we could not hope for a fair decision. The anger of the officers was clearly evident. When my turn came to be questioned, I was very apprehensive as I entered the interrogation room. The personal papers that had been taken from me at Schloss Hainfeld, along with my photograph, were now on the desk of a female K.G.B. agent. As she questioned me, she kept hitting me on the head with the butt of her pistol. I tried to reason with her with the aid of the Besarab interpreter, whose knowledge of Hungarian was very limited. She could see from my date of birth that I could not have played an important role during the war. So, after a few more questions, my experience with the K.G.B. ended - thankfully, without trouble.

---

[35] Sober judgment cannot be made with notions.

Aside from information learned in the interrogations, the Russians wanted to know each prisoner's background, as well as what they were thinking. So, with the aid of a network of prisoners who were willing to collaborate with them, they gained the information they desired. The informant prisoners were considered the slime of our prison society, having not a speck of integrity and changing their colors like chameleons. They sold their fellow prisoners for a lousy bowl of soup. We soon learned not to speak freely, or express our opinions with anyone except our most trusted friends. To exchange thoughts, or talk about our past lives outside a close knit group of friends was not wise. It took some time to identify the informants, but once they were discovered, their fate was written on the wall. During work, there was ample opportunity to stage accidents. Penalties were dished out to guilty parties by other prisoners, often with fatal consequences.

The spring not only brought warm weather, but also news about a transport which would take some of us to another location. I was selected to go, and with mixed feelings I made my rounds to say good-bye to some of my comrades. I was especially sad to leave the officer with whom I had spent so much time listening to his Olympic experiences. To leave a camp always made one wonder if the new camp would be better or worse than the present. Trying to be optimistic, I assumed it would be better, and I was pleased to leave this Lager.

I discovered my destination was Voronesh, a city located 450 kilometres south-east of Moscow. It was a substantial trek southward, which gave me hope that I would soon experience warmer weather than I had in the more northerly Lagers. We travelled by train in the familiar boxcars with hay on the floor, a little hole, the door closed, and the window protected with barbed wire. Of course, the heavy guard ensured an 'undisturbed' journey. The time we spent on the train provided us with a few days of savoured rest. My pal, the hairdresser from Budapest, was with me. We were in a relatively good mood and looked forward to life in the new camp.

LAGER NO. 82/9 VORONESH - JUNE 1946

Upon arrival at this central Lager, we went through the usual entrance procedure, including a body search. Everything we might have on us, above the standard issue of clothing, was confiscated. We then waded through the shower which was much better than at any of the earlier Lagers. Next came the physical checkup. Looking over the population of the Lager, we happily acknowledged that the prisoners were in reasonable physical condition - an indicator of the improved camp conditions we would now face.

The physical checkup took place under a warm sky and provided us with a humorous incident. A long line of half-naked bodies approached the table where the delegates waited for us in the usual manner. My pal, the hairdresser, was in front of me in line, looking good with his tanned upper body. As we approached the table, we saw, sitting beside the male doctor, a stunningly beautiful lady doctor. She was dressed in a crisp snow-white uniform. The wide lapel of her dress displayed the rank of major. Beside her sat a female secretary. This time, in addition to the usual 'once over' and pinch, the male doctor checked our heart beats with a stethoscope. Finally, when his turn came, my friend stepped close to the table and dropped his pants. His dark, muscular, lean body was exposed, including his rather good-sized penis. The two women looked at him with wide eyes, and the secretary asked what his occupation was.

He replied, "Hairdresser." With smiles on their faces they looked at each other and back at my pal's exposed manliness. His face flushed red, and in his acute embarrassment, his heart rate jumped so much that, after putting the stethoscope on his chest, the male doctor placed him in the third health category, which meant only four hours of work per day! We laughed for a long time, recalling the incident of how he was saved from working a full day because of the extraordinary size of his instrument. We later searched through the rest of the Lager's population, looking for any familiar faces, but we failed to find anyone we knew.

I was out the next day in the working brigade, digging ditches, shovelling dirt, and doing various construction jobs. Our bread allowance was 600 grams per day, with an extra 100 grams awarded if one completed his outlined working duties. Although the bread seemed a gracious reward, it did not make up for the calories burned at work each day.

We had just enough time to settle in and receive another postcard to write home when the order came to move again. This time it was only a move across the city to another Lager. Again we were counted and frisked, and arranged in columns of five to say good-bye to yet another camp. Walking through the city streets in such a formation caused curious civilian spectators to line the street on both sides. The reason for the move was to concentrate and separate the Hungarians from the Germans. This effort was well received by us, for in many of the previous camps we faced discrimination from the German prisoners running the camp. For example, in mixed camps the German administrative staff would select German prisoners over Hungarians to work in easier positions such as cooks or tailors, or to serve as part of the bathhouse staff, the shoe repair brigade, or the maintenance crew. It was an understandable and accepted tradition - when the chips were down every nation ventured to save their own people, over and above any other nationality. It would be naive to expect perfect harmony among all people from different nations or races, especially when locked into a camp where survival was tested. Under situations such as these, political differences seemed to be magnified rather than minimized. So, my friend and I looked forward to living in a Hungarian Lager, run by Hungarians. Of course we would still be under Russian control and rules. After a few hours of walking, we arrived at the designated Lager on the outskirts of the city a few kilometres away. It was a warm and pleasant day in July 1946, and the smell of the summer air, the sight of the fluffy white clouds moving across the sky like a big flock of sheep, inflated my hopes of the days to come.

LAGER NO. 82/5 VORONESH

Three rows of barbed wire fences enclosed the large open field of the compound. Watchtowers stood ominously at each corner. Within, a set of old buildings became our new home. Despite the visibly tight security, this was one of the best Lagers we had encountered thus far, and the atmosphere lifted our spirits. This strictly Hungarian Lager seemed devoid of the discrimination we had experienced in the German camps. The living quarters (at one time used as hangars) provided enough room for beds. The beds were more like bunk beds and were constructed from iron pipes which supported wooden planks. Two men slept on the lower level and two above. There was sufficient walking space between them as well. Sawdust-filled mattresses and a blanket completed the unusual and, in prison terms, luxurious bedding. The kitchen was located in a separate building, surrounded by a large dining area with long tables and benches. The latrine was similar to those in the other Lagers, but was covered with a roof. The bath house even had fairly good showers, and the more frequent showering we experienced here was accompanied by a change of underwear. We now lived according to the rules and conditions set by our leaders and staff personnel of our camp. The food rations remained the same, so we were still always hungry; however, the chances to obtain extra nibbles from different sources, especially during the summertime, was possible. Within the compound, a little black market bazaar came into operation. A dozen or more prisoners sat in rows on the ground with their food items displayed to the browsing customers. Here one could bargain, buy or exchange one's soup for a piece of bread or a couple of potatoes.

A large number of officers living in the camp did not have to perform many duties, so they organized a small theatre group. Their efforts were supported by the Russians because of the positive affect such action had on the morale of the prison population. From time to time, the officers staged variety shows which lifted the spirits of the participants as well as the audience. A rumour had been circulating about a possible stage show for some time, so when the day of the first performance finally arrived, a wave of excitement rolled over the prison population. I could hardly wait for the makeshift curtain to part, revealing the prison theatre stage. The first familiar chords delivered by the unique, sometimes home-made, musical instruments brought tears not just to my own eyes but to those of all the men around me. The actors donned brilliantly colored costumes made of painted tar paper and various construction materials. Their apparel brought a standing ovation from the audience. Each prisoner's eyes, normally mirrors of struggle and hardship, suddenly were alight with anticipation and sheer delight. Faces everywhere gave way to smiles, and emotions poured from each man's heart. The performance was called "János Vitéz" and was a traditional Hungarian play. It was a story about a legendary folk figure named János and his recruitment to the army which forced him to leave behind his lover, Juliska. The Hungarian costumes and well-known old songs were like a massage to a tired wanderer's aching feet. The sights and sounds soothed my soul, lifted my spirits, and caused my Hungarian pride to well up in me until I thought I would burst. I sang out with unbridled joy. The audience became the choir, and the performance was unforgettable. These periodic stage shows and concerts, along with the playful but fiercely-fought soccer games, raised the morale of the prisoners, granting a temporary 'escape' from the here-and-now, and giving us strength to go on. For the first time, we also began to receive newspapers periodically, which allowed us to learn a bit more about what was happening in the world around us. We also organized soccer teams and played regular inter-camp matches. We began to feel a little more like humans.

In term of work, I was sent out with a large brigade to work on a burnt-out, five-storey building complex. Only the thick-brick, outer supporting walls were still standing, covered with what was once a fancy architectural facade; the rest of the building was in ruins. Our job was to clear away the ashes and rubble and rebuild the floors, rooms, and long corridors. The building itself ran 25 metres and was curved along its length to form an arc-shaped structure when viewed from overhead. To avoid the most difficult and physically most demanding work, I learned to raise my hand when the Russian engineer or foreman asked for skilled workers, such as carpenters or brick layers, etc. I denied my inexperience and ended up playing carpenter. We worked in small groups, and soon I learned the trade through experience and made only a few mistakes. The building complex was fenced and guarded, although some civilians were working beside us. The long marches from the camp and back at the day's end, not to mention the eight hours of work, exhausted us. We had one hour lunch break when we received our soup and a piece of bread. Soon after, we were sound asleep on the spot. We woke to the sound of metal banging on metal, signalling it was time to go back to work. The end of the working day was also indicated by the sound of this primitive substitute for a bell.

We spent part of the summer and the fall of 1946 on this building, progressively restoring the floors by covering them with soft wooden planks, as well as building numerous tiny rooms. The long corridors were rather undulating, but it seemed to be of little importance to the Russian engineer. Speed was the imminent concern, not quality. The building was meant to satisfy the demand for housing for workers of the nearby airplane factory. Thus there was a push to have the building completed soon, preferably before winter set in.

As soon as we completed a floor, the civilians moved in with their iron beds, mattresses and minimal belongings to occupy the tiny rooms. In two centrally-located rooms on each floor, we built stoves from brick, with metal covers and chimney pipes which ran through the window. These two stoves were to be shared by all residents of that floor for the preparation of meals. There were no sinks nor was there even running water in any part of the building, which would house hundreds of factory workers.

No bathrooms or toilets were installed in the building, whatsoever. We worked at this site to its completion, and we witnessed how the Russian workers coped with the problem of not having toilets in the building. The occupants of the first two floors went down to the yard and used the wooden-board, roofless latrine, in spite of the fact that their efforts and bare bums were clearly visible from the numerous windows of the building. The residents of the top three floors usually went up to the attic, especially in cold weather and responded to Mother Nature there. It was difficult not to step on the numerous piles of mouldy gray-haired shit in the courtyard and in the attic. Another method which was widely used by the workers, particularly lazy ones, was to shit in a newspaper and throw it out the window into the yard. It was not advisable to walk beneath the windows at any time. Without exaggeration, this was the plain truth and was part of life for these factory workers.

Over the next few months I became very disappointed in my pal, the hair dresser. A stroke of luck landed him a position in the kitchen, cutting and weighing hundreds of pieces of bread which were distributed three times each day to the prisoners. Now he had the same opportunity to help me with a few extra morsels of food as I had done, but he grew very distant. I felt I had been used, and realized that his friendly attention to me had not come from his heart; rather, it had been phony and calculated. In such a way, I learned a lot about people and the harsh realities of life.

Some of the extra-curricular activities of the camp included washing some of the prisoners' underwear by hand in the evenings in order to be awarded an extra piece of bread. It was tiring and unpleasant, but I was now nineteen and always hungry. I met numerous officers this way, and they welcomed me and accepted me as a friend, which made me feel better. I struck a new friendship with Gyula Horvath whom I respected very much, and still do to this day. He was a young soldier who had just finished his university education, was drafted into the army and ended up in the middle of the war. He turned out to be a genuine friend, who, in his later civilian life, reviewed new books for a newspaper and played jazz violin for a hobby. His values, his philosophy, and his love of our country served as a positive influence on me. He fought gallantly during the war, and I enjoyed listening to his story of how the Russians pulled him out from behind his machine gun by his legs. We shared our dreams as well as any extra food we might happen upon. We ate together on the bunk bed we shared, and reinforced our friendship with honesty and trust. It never occurred to me not to share with him any food that I managed to buy from the civilians, usually obtained in exchange for some highly-sought-after nails. In return, he always gave me an equal share of his edible earnings. The most important nourishment did not come from the extra food, though, but rather from our ability to share and our unshakable trust in each other.

During the evenings, after strenuous days of work, we sat together on our bunk beds and carried on enjoyable conversations. We planned our future, building our dream homes in our minds and furnishing each corner of them with the finest pieces. We sometimes talked for hours into the night about our hopes and wishes, and, by doing so, we managed to keep our spirits up. Many of the other prisoners had lost hope by now, and had thus made their lives even more miserable. The conversations Gyula and I shared gave us encouragement, and we met each new morning with renewed strength.

We were still working on the large housing complex when we observed the fruits of Stalin's industrialization program. Uprooting the youth of farming communities, the government herded the boys and girls into the cities, forcing them to live in common shelters and work for wages which covered only the bare requirements for their existence. I saw these children work throughout the day, carrying loads of bricks or mortar on simple carriages. When we stopped for lunch, the kids gathered and with their clear soprano voices sang folk songs to us in perfect harmony. From what I could see, they ate simple meals in the evening, after their difficult days of work. Their fate in this, their own country, seemed very similar to ours. We knew that if we did not die first, some day we would see this situation end. Still, I wondered - could these young, innocent faces envision their hardships ending? Could they remain children at heart - hopeful of what their future would bring? Finally we completed this building and, ironically, I was transferred to another brigade which was sent out to work in the airplane factory.

During the late fall of 1946, an interesting condition developed in both of my calf muscles. Toward the evening, when the temperature dropped, I could hardly walk because of a strange pain in both my legs, perhaps caused by spasm. What triggered the spasm I was never able to figure out. Most likely it was caused by prolonged exposure to the extreme weather, felt in my earlier days as a 'horse' in Bryansk. Regardless of my condition, I had to continue working. It was quite an effort to keep up with my comrades on the dreadful daily marches to the working place and back to the Lager at the end of the day. On top of the cold and hunger, this pain was a loyal companion - unrelenting and unforgiving. Eventually I reported my problem to the infirmary, and the Russian doctor painted my legs with iodine. I looked like an Indian ready for action, decorated with war paint, but this treatment did not improve my chronic condition. I struggled for many months with this strange affliction, but the warmth of the spring finally brought relief; although I had nightmares about it for many years after.

The nature of our work here was to unload trains which were filled with contraband from Germany. The occupying Russian forces systematically dismounted and removed everything, even the heating units, from the walls of the German factories. Amongst the equipment were precision Swiss, Swedish and German machines, equipment and tools. Most of the items were loaded onto flat-deck cars, and were thus exposed to a range of weather conditions without any protection. Since there were no cranes, we pushed the loaded cars beside a ramp and, using iron bars as levers, we lifted one end of each machine so we could place iron pipes beneath it. Twenty-five men played a sort of tug-of-war with the ropes, pulling the machines over the rolling pipes. Others replaced the pipes underneath to keep the machines slowly moving. Though primitive, this method worked, as it did in ancient times when the slaves transported the gigantic stones of the pyramids.

The difficulty lay in the time it took to remove each machine from the rail car. We had to unload the train within a certain period of time, but it was impossible to meet the deadline using such primitive methods. As a result, we were ordered to dump the remaining pieces off the side of the cars, and much of the costly equipment ended up lying in pieces beside the rail line in the mud and snow. We were appalled at the careless destruction that occurred. We worked all through the winter, unloading the trains. Some of the machines were somehow rescued and utilized, but most of them rusted beneath a thick blanket of snow. Some of the electronic equipment puzzled the Russians, causing a German prisoner to be brought in to explain how some of the items could be used. Among the variety of items we unloaded were some new transformers. We knew they contained oil, and after storing them in a part of the factory to which we had access, our ever-present hunger drove us to punch a hole in a bottom corner of each transformer and then quickly plug the hole with a tapered wooden plug. Out of view of the watchful guards, day after day we would drain a bit of the oil to eat with our bread. Because we had eaten a minimal amount of fat and oil and practically no meat for years, this oil we now retrieved from the transformers gave us the runs something awful; nevertheless, in spite of our troubled digestive systems, we hoped to relieve the hunger that gripped our stomachs. Our prison officers warned us about the contents of the oil, stating it was 75 percent crude oil, but the other 25 percent was extracted from squashed grasshoppers and was, thus, organic. After their warning, I refrained from eating any more of it, but some of the other prisoners continued. Just how much good or bad came of it, we never did determine.

Inevitably, another grim Christmas arrived. My friend managed to spice it up somewhat, though, by bringing home a piece of makuka[36] to share. We chewed slowly on the rock-hard substance while we reminisced about Christmases past. Despite the disappointment of having to spend another Christmas in captivity, we felt strong in our friendship, and tried to reinforce our beliefs that some day our prison life would end, and we would be free.

In the meantime, I continued to work in the factory, moving materials, unloading trains, taking the garbage out, and other similarly pleasant jobs. One day, my brigade leader took me to the Russian factory engineer. He presented me as a possible candidate to learn to work on the lathe. Having little say in the matter, I accepted the position, of course. The engineer showed me the moves on the machine,

---

[36] Russian word for a by-product pressing the oil from sunflower seeds.

the different arms, how to start and stop it, and the knife positions. I became a lathe operator. Soon I was making the first rough cut in some metal pieces which were to become the pistons for an airplane engine. Thankfully, I worked inside where I was protected from the cold. Still, the large building with its high ceiling was not heated; so the protection was rather limited. Within eight hours, I managed to complete 96 pieces, which was a respectable performance. Initially I had to concentrate hard so as not to make any mistakes, but this passed. In time, I was able to operate the machine well enough, and the work became quite monotonous. To remain in one spot for the entire day, repeatedly making the same movements, was certainly far from enjoyable. After a few weeks an opportunity arose to work with my friend Laci who operated an electric car. The task was to distribute materials to the numerous machine operators positioned throughout the large building. I grabbed at the chance with excitement and relief.

As Laci and I trucked around the building, we began to meet some of the Russian workers we served regularly. We supplied them with raw materials in exchange for their completed constructions. It was interesting to speak with some of them, and, in most cases, we managed to crumble their prejudiced thoughts of us. Eventually, most of them grew to judge us by who we were rather than where we were from.

The winter passed, and a new spring again brought new hopes. We read in the newspaper that the peace pact was signed and that war prisoners were to be sent home soon. Although the paper did not specify how 'soon' we would be released, this news made my heart leap inside my chest. I could hardly believe my eyes as the words slid in and out of view. It was written right there in black and white!

Freedom! What could it possibly be like? I had almost forgotten and now fought to imagine what it would feel like to walk freely, fearlessly down the quiet dirt roads in Felsogod. What would it feel like to wade into the cool waters of the Danube as the sun warmed my skin? What would Mama's cooking smell like, and how would it feel to fill my belly with a hot, flavourful feast? My stomach growled, and water filled my mouth just thinking about the possibilities. Most of all, I wondered what Mama and my family would look like when they first laid eyes upon me after all these years. It would certainly be an emotional homecoming and the joy would be immense. As my imagination ran like wild horses, the ache I felt to return home was overwhelming. I hoped that 'soon' really meant soon. I could not imagine spending another month in captivity. I did not want to imagine it.

So, the warm caress of the spring sunshine had provided us with more good news and a new rule. We would now receive wages for our work in the factory. Unfortunately, we found that the majority of our earnings were taken by the Lager, apparently to cover our keep. Still, we were allowed to receive a maximum of 200 rubles per month. This certainly was a joyous event for us, especially since the Russian ruble had finally stabilized and was gaining strength. We could buy a bun or a 200 gram slice of bread from the Russian civilians for three rubles. Over the course of a month, we could buy 60 extra slices of bread for 200 rubles. This bread, combined with the three pieces we received daily, helped us to survive. It did not mean that we had enough, but it was much better than having only two or three slices in a day. To calm the feeling of hunger from time to time gave us great pleasure. Up until now, our dreams were filled with warm, crusty loaves of bread and deliciously prepared meals.

Now that we managed to fill our bellies occasionally, our dream patterns changed. We began to realize that, aside from the pleasures of eating, some essential and natural needs had to be satisfied. Now we began to notice that the world was full of women, as well. We grew to look upon them with different eyes and with thoughts that had not touched the corners of our minds in years. We looked at their faces, their hair, and the gentle curves of their bodies. We began to make efforts to establish contact with them. I grew increasingly concerned about my appearance, and did everything within my means to improve my appeal.

With the money I made working, I managed to bribe the guys in the warehouse to give me better pieces of clothing and a decent pair of boots. I got rid of my wooden shoes and bought a big German army coat, and for a price, the tailors made a suitable jacket for me. Dressed in these clothes, I appeared somewhat human again, and regained some self esteem and confidence. Laci and I were like twins, zipping around the factory with the electric car, and our recognition and popularity with the Russians began to grow.

The weather turned warmer, and going to work in the morning brought a sweet feeling of excitement. I was anxious to lay eyes on the blond, blue-eyed Maria who worked in one of the offices of the factory. Laci liked Maria's friend Tamara, and the two girls seemed inseparable. While at work, we managed to see and speak with the girls once or twice during the day. It was essential that we kept our meetings discreet for we did not want to get the girls into trouble. After my experience as a 'horse' in Bryansk, it was, sure as hell, a very nice feeling to be recognized as a man, particularly by an attractive girl. The few minutes I spent with her during our daily chats were glorious, and her warm smile revealed more than just friendship. All in all, our meetings sent me for a walk on cloud nine. I was optimistic about the future, and the present felt great. With only nineteen years behind me, I knew little about life. My memories were mainly of my school years, the last few months of the war, and my last two years in captivity. Certainly, my limited experiences caused me to develop a great appetite for some living. Anything new, exciting and better, I would take - this became my philosophy. I remembered Bryansk and the times when I felt I had one foot in the grave. I had said to myself, "If I can make it through this alive, I'll take every opportunity to enjoy life's pleasures!"

So, I took a chance - with Maria - and with it a great risk of suffering some harsh consequences. Of course, such relationships were strictly forbidden for fear that prisoners would use the help of civilians to escape. The penalty was the Lager karcel,[37] and less food, if one survived the initial severe beating. Maria's actions would be judged as collaboration with the enemy, a serious crime. Knowing that one received five to seven years in the work camps for stealing a piece of bread, we feared the sentence for collaboration. Regardless, I let myself become involved with Maria. It was difficult to hold the reins on my heart. Our relationship filled my life with new color after two years of monochrome gray.

One quiet Sunday, the other prisoners and I spent the morning in the camp cleaning our barracks. When we disassembled our beds, we scrambled to kill the multitude of bed bugs which nested in the frames. Every Sunday the main attraction was an inter-camp soccer game. On a flat

---

[37] This was a cement hole in the ground covered by a lid which could only be opened from the outside. The hole was just large enough for one man to stand in it.

area just outside our camp, we erected goal posts and marked the field with lime. Civilian onlookers also enjoyed the games. When the games were over, the gates of the prison were opened and we walked back into camp. We noticed that we were not counted upon re-entry. This gave me an idea of how to steal a few hours of freedom in town. When the next soccer game was staged, my friend Laci and I were ready. We obtained a typical Russian hat. At the end of the game the next weekend, we mingled with the civilians and joined their parade as they walked down the dirt road toward the city. Meanwhile, the rest of the prisoners returned to camp. These days, the attitude of the Russian soldiers toward the prisoners had taken a turn for the better, and from time to time they would allow a small group of prisoners to attend the circus. All in all, general security was more relaxed. So Laci and I jaunted down the road without the usual guards. Our new freedom felt incredibly strange.

After a moderate hike, we reached the place where we were to meet Maria and Tamara for a secret rendezvous. The sun had set, but it had left a brilliant trail of colors - red, orange, gold - on the clouds which slept just above the horizon. It was spectacular. We waited for the girls in a little park-like area which was filled with lilac bushes. As the sweet smell surrounded us, we talked about the possible consequences of our escape. It was too late to turn back now. We agreed that everything in life had its price, so we braved it out to see what would happen. By the time the girls finally showed up, the light of the moon illuminated the park. It was the perfect setting for a romantic evening. Aside from the essence of the evening - the bright moonlight, the fresh smell of the grass and the sweet scent of the flowers - the fact that this was a forbidden meeting and that we had stolen away to have this night of freedom and passion made it all the more exciting.

Maria wore a light blue dress. Her long blonde hair shone in the moonlight. She was beautiful. The night was like a fairy tale. All the struggles and hunger seemed a million miles away now. Maria and I walked hand in hand, intoxicated by the beauty of the evening and our mutual feelings of infatuation. This was my first rendezvous with a girl, and my inexperience and overwhelming feelings for her squashed my courage to approach her in a physical sense. So, we spent a wonderful evening talking and walking. Finally I kissed her goodnight with a soft puppy kiss, and Laci and I walked back to the camp. Laci was older than I and had more experience with girls, so he tried to instruct me on what I should have done and how and why, but it was like giving me a raincoat after the storm. Thankfully, the sergeant at the gate let us in without even asking where we had been. Perhaps he thought that he had allowed us to leave, and now we were returning.

Laci and I had contemplated escaping. I mean, we had made it outside the fence of the camp quite easily. Why not continue on and try to return home? As much as we had yearned to pass through the gates to the outside world, we found ourselves returning on our own to the Lager. The difficulty in escaping was not leaving the camp; rather, it was the obstacles which followed. The incredible distance made a successful voyage home almost impossible. We would have to travel thousands of miles without any contact with Russian civilians who had been offered much-needed money by the Russian authorities for any information leading to the re-capture of escaped prisoners. Without maps, compasses, food and money, the trek would be a formidable one. Without

Russian clothing or a command of the language, our travel would lead us to almost certain death, for we would be so conspicuous, we would be like sitting ducks in hunting season. Laci and I had wrestled with the idea. Perhaps we could travel at night by foot and hide during the day. Still, this would be dangerous and difficult in the unfamiliar territory which stretched between here and Hungary. To hop a train was a certain impossibility. Aside from the train ticket, every passenger was required to carry a travelling permit, indicating his or her destination and the purpose of the trip. Police thoroughly and frequently checked the trains for unauthorized travellers. We would certainly be discovered. We had thought of sneaking aboard cargo trains; however, because we did not know our way, nor could inquire about the train's destination, we might very well end up further from home rather than closer. Even if we did manage to reach the border, crossing would likely be suicide. Fences, manned watchtowers, guard dogs and minefields fortified the Soviet borders and stood as final, possible fatal obstacles. And if we were caught and returned to the camp, the brutal beating we would receive spoke a strong voice against attempting to escape. It seemed we had no other choice but to return. Laci and I decided we would rather await our fate which might include our release, as opposed to courting death by trying to escape.

In our next meeting with the girls, Tamara brought up the subject of escape. At one time she had worked for the K. G. B. She now told Laci and me that she could obtain travel permits, fake identification papers, and Russian soldiers' uniforms for us. Onboard the train, when the police came around to check our documents, Laci and I could pretend to be asleep, and the girls could speak for us, displaying our papers. Tamara's plan sounded incredibly fool-proof. The whole thing seemed too good to be true. After much private discussion, Laci and I concluded that our relationship with the girls was relatively new. We did not know for certain if we could trust them. Perhaps, they too, were paid informants, seeking to entrap us in a web of deceit that would result in our ultimate doom. We decided not to take the risk and turned down Tamara's offer for assistance. We never did know for certain if their kind attention was sincere or not; nevertheless, we continued to visit the girls on the factory grounds. We did not meet them outside the walls of the camp again, and Laci and I were careful to keep our conversations light, away from any discussion of escape.

One morning, about 15 prisoners, including myself, were taken by truck to a nearby collective farm. When we arrived, we found ourselves surrounded by lush pasture land that was dotted with hundreds of harvested hay stacks and stretched as far as the eye could see. The dry stacks were about two metres high and smelled pleasant. The objective of our work here was to gather all the stacks into one large stack.

The method we would use was rather primitive, but proved effective. A rope approximately ten metres long was attached to each side of the saddle of the horse. My job was to throw the rope over the hay stack, positioning it near the base of the pile. I then scrambled onto the top of the haystack and lay spread eagle. The little boy who rode the horse would get the horse to pull the haystack to a central location. There, my comrades pitched the hay with forks into a large pile while I ran to the next haystack. The job was fairly easy when the haystacks were relatively close; however, the distance from the central pile to the surrounding haystacks inevitably became longer and longer. Of course, I had a chance to rest while the horse pulled me and the haystack to the central pile, but the little boy found great satisfaction in encouraging the horse to gallop to the next haystack, forcing me to run furiously to reach the next pile in time. After numerous such trips, back and forth, my burning lungs and rubber legs felt they could take no more. In desperation, I tied the rope around my waist and let the horse pull me along as I ran. This forced me to keep up. Still, I tumbled and struggled, gasping for air with every step until the next stop. This certainly was a true test of my physical and mental strength. At long last, a Russian man came to check on me. As he approached, I stopped momentarily, hopeful that he would grant me a chance to rest. Instead, I received a severe beating for stopping. He kicked the hell out of me for "not working hard enough." I will never forget this day. The sheer fact that I survived this test gave me strength in days to come.

The next day, I was assigned to the same job - the next day and the next and the next... Each day left me completely exhausted, devoid of any energy, any fuel, any life. I felt I was at the end of my rope, so to speak. I was certain that I would soon croak. One day, I collapsed in the middle of the field in a heap of tired muscles and sweat. I lay on my back in disbelief that my lungs still heaved and my blood continued to surge through my veins. I waited for my heart to retire from its endless work, but it kept its speedy rhythm. After a short while, my laboured breathing finally grew light, my heart slowed, and the sweet scent of the hay drifted lazily through the summer air and into my senses. I got up and joined the devilish little boy to continue the work.

Normally, when we were tired or uncomfortable, we

could snatch a chance to stop and catch our breath; however, this job detail allowed very little chance for recovery. After several days, though, I began to feel somewhat better, and the burning sensation in my lungs disappeared. The task never became easy or comfortable, but it seemed as though I had tapped into a new source, a new level of energy. I began to think that if a cat has nine lives, as sure as hell, I must have nine levels of energy from which to draw. Thank God, one day there was no more hay to collect, and the ten-day 'training camp' concluded. Several times over the past ten days I had experienced some of my weakest moments. I had imagined that the hayfield would be a nice place to die, to be buried in, and to eventually be blanketed with lush green grass and tiny wild flowers. Still, something inside me, some inborn fighting spirit kept me from falling. As a result, I passed yet another test without giving in to the tempting caress of the hands of death. At the end of these trying days, I felt like a winner, battling for life and competing well under the circumstances.

On the eastern edge of the Ural mountains lay the city of Uzmany. A large concentration of Japanese war prisoners were housed here among numerous Hungarian officers. The war in the east lasted a few months longer than in Europe, and it was the sixth of September, 1945, when the Japanese were forced into capitulation. One year later, the Russians planned to stage a celebration to commemorate their victory and the end of the second world war. Some of the Hungarian prisoners who were there told me of the incident. When the dark sky of early morning was broken by the rising sun, 3000 Japanese prisoners were visible in the camp yard. They sat silent and motionless, in formation by companies, with officers positioned at the head of each column. It was a dramatic display. Clearly, for them, this somber day was one of defeat - one they would not celebrate. The Russians were in their usual panic, doubling the guards and placing machine guns in the watch towers. The Russian officers ran into the camp, attempting to break the columns and disperse the prisoners, but the Japanese sat in disciplined formation for the entire day, without eating or moving. The Japanese officers were in complete control of their units, and if they had ordered their people to storm the fence, there was no question the order would have been carried out. The Russians soon realized the danger in the obedient faces of the Japanese prisoners and left them alone the rest of the day. At dusk, the prisoners finally broke their columns and quietly went to their barracks to sleep. The celebration, of course, did not take place because of the resistance from the Japanese.

One evening, shortly after our secret outing, we were required to have a checkup after work. Everyone had to fall in line in front of the Russian officers, naked from the waist up with arms overhead. The officers said they were checking for lice in our underarms. The fact was, we no longer were troubled with lice - the prison population had finally been liberated from the companionship of those little friends. The check-up was really geared to find out who had a tattoo under his arm. Tattooing was a common practice in some groups in the German army specifically the SS. The SS troops were men that had been specially selected to form an elite fighting unit that was part of the German army. Some of the troops served in the fearsome deportation forces or as guards in concentration camps, but not all. I had served in a ski-battalion and was fighting in the Russian front. Unfortunately, by being tattooed brought only one conclusion to the minds of the Russians. Instantly I was classified as a most-hated enemy and a 'fascist'. For instance, each member of the SS had his blood type tattooed under his arm so that if he ever needed a transfusion because of extensive loss of blood, his blood type was readily available. At an earlier boot camp I had received such a tattoo. Although we were part of an independent Hungarian battalion, we were still under German command and thus were marked for life.

So, the Russian officers discovered my brand. Suddenly now, when it seemed as though everything was okay, when life had finally become more bearable and the conditions were tolerable, this had to happen. It was as if a lightning bolt had struck me from a clear, blue sky. I sensed I might suffer some serious consequences. The very next day, 30 of us were gathered by the gate. We were to be transferred to another Lager. Nobody wanted to be associated with us anymore. There was no farewell from anyone - no hand shakes or well wishing. It was as if we were a group of lepers. My friend Gyula, the newspaper man, was the only one to come forward. He finally grabbed me in a firm hug and pressed a piece of paper into my hand. I quickly put it in my shirt, and we departed. I never saw him again. We were pushed into the back of a small, windowless paddy wagon. We stood, pressed together so tightly that I fainted briefly from the stifling conditions - no one even noticed. A bucket of raw beets and cucumbers was thrown around our feet on the floor of the vehicle. This was to be the food for the road. We could not bend down to pick it up though. Instead, it was stomped to mush. There was not a word about where or why we were being taken. We tried to estimate the distance, and made some wild guesses about our destination. Finally the van stopped, the back door opened, and those at the rear of the truck fell and rolled out. Once we were all out of the truck, we saw that we were at a railway station; and when we saw the special train, our thoughts turned to Siberia. We would travel in the wagons of this train with hundreds of Soviet citizens.

The train was made up of numerous dark-green wagons that had no windows. Each wagon was divided into several small compartments in which two rows of wooden benches had been installed. Sliding doors made of heavy iron grating separated the compartments from the corridor where the guards paced watchfully and endlessly. The bit of daylight we received was that which shone through a tiny chimney-like ventilation hole located in the ceiling of the car. At each end of the corridor, a sliver of light also entered through the doors of the car. Otherwise, the crowded, stuffy cubicles were as dim as our future. The weathered faces of the prisoners around me were icons of despair and fright.

Once we were herded to our designated wagon, we settled in for the ride. At last I had a chance to read the little note from Gyula. It was difficult to see in the dim light, but I will never forget his words: "Don't forget, you are a Hungarian, a soldier, and a man. Each has its honour. Guard those honours, no matter what may come! I will, with my soul, watch over you and see how you stand and fight your fight alone!" Gyula's note gave me much encouragement and direction when I really needed it. This message remains with me and continues to guide me in my life.

When the train stopped, some prisoners were escorted off while others boarded. It was surprising to see that the Soviet prisoners were not treated well even by their own people. Our compartment was located near the entrance of the wagon, allowing me to peek through the open car door to witness the exchange of prisoners. An officer called out individual names. The prisoners were to reply by shouting out their sentence: "five years", "seven years", and so on. The prisoners then ran down the corridor to exit the train, being kicked as they passed the guards. Once out of the train, they had to squat five in a row, arm in arm, and wait in that position until the rest of the prisoners were called and had debarked. Their crimes were such acts as stealing bread to eat, or firewood with which to cook their meals. These people had lost their freedom and worked for the state for years, living on three bowls of soup and 600 grams of bread per day. They had slaved on projects such as the Trans-Siberian railway or the dam in Dnyetropetrovsk. All because they had done what they felt necessary in order to survive.

Our journey ended about 355 kilometres southwest of Voronesh, in Kiev, the capital city of the Ukraine. This place was much better than what lay on the other side of the Ural mountain range. Upon the completion of our 'joyride' on the 'dream train', the usual reception committee awaited us at the railway station, including enough dogs and armed guards to make us feel important. A little army truck was on hand once again. We were pushed aboard and packed in like sardines, then transported straight to the bunker Lager. Wide rows of inmates, curious to spot a possible acquaintance, peered at us through the fence as we were counted and received by the officer at the gate.

BUNKER LAGER NO. 7062/4 KIEV

We were housed among four thousand other prisoners on the outskirts of the city in a huge area surrounded by four rows of barbed wire fence. The camp was named the 'Bunker Lager' after the physical features of the compound. Throughout the large area, rows of bunkers were dug and constructed and used mainly for accommodation. There were some barracks, as well as auxiliary facilities. The prison population consisted of people of various nationalities and ranks from a wide range of units that were active in the war. This brought an extra flavour to our prison society. There were 400 Hungarian officers that served in the gendarme, the police force, or the regular army with some ranks as high as general. There were people from the Waffen SS, the Hungarian Hunyadi volunteer division, the Spanish Blue division, General Franco's troops, and some of the Communists that had fled Spain after the civil war. This mosaic of people now shared the same territory and often exchanged ideas and beliefs when language barriers could be overcome. Within the Lager, there was a smaller Lager surrounded by yet another set of wires. This was for special prisoners, including one of the SS men who had climbed a rock wall with his group and jumped the guards to free Mussolini from the Mt. Cassino prison. There was Bela, a Hungarian who had fought in Africa with Rommel's troops.

Armed with two bazookas, he had jumped from a tank into the midst of the battle to kill two Shermans.[38] A Spanish major strolled behind the barbed wire fences, proudly displaying his rank on his uniform. There was a Hungarian baron, who had served in W.W.I on the same ship as Admiral Horthy, the leader of Hungary prior to W.W.II. The Russians called these special prisoners fascists, but the prisoners considered themselves patriots who had fought valiantly for their country.

I was soon recognized by the officers as the youngest in the camp. They often asked me, "What are you doing here? You should be in school." Sometimes they invited me to the lectures and presentations they held regularly in their bunker. I enjoyed these opportunities to be both educated and entertained, and I became a regular visitor and a welcome guest in their quarters.

The clothes which I had bought in Voronesh were confiscated and replaced by the standard issue of second-hand Russian army rags. I was assigned to a new brigade which was working at a construction site, building a huge brick factory. The work included mixing mortar and cement with a shovel, carrying bricks, digging ditches, unloading materials, and other such menial tasks. It seemed a giant step back from leading the life of a skilled factory worker to the world of the chornaja robotnik.[39] Again I was faced with more difficult work, no wages, and a hungrier stomach. The pendulum had swung back to the more dismal side, and again, hot, crusty loaves of bread filled my dreams.

While my dreams were delicious, reality sat before me

---

[38] British tanks.

[39] Unskilled workers in Russian.

in my bowl each day. Cabbage soup was on the menu regularly, and often the strange, black eye of a fish head that had been thrown in would peer back at me. The standard 600 grams of bread was the most substantial part of the meal and was, of course, gulped down in a few bites, three times daily. One never had the pleasure of feeling that he had had enough to eat, and each prisoner's brain worked overtime to discover a way to obtain more food.

Opportunities did arise from time to time for those who were devious and creative. We discovered that the civilians we worked with had their own problems. One being, they were short of soap. So, some sly prisoners collected tiny bits of soap from the floor of the bathhouse and moulded them into one piece. From the outside, the soap appeared to be one large, solid bar; however, inside the prisoners had put a chunk of wood to make the bar seem bigger. The bars of 'soap' were then sold to the Russians. Of course, this trick only worked for a short time. After receiving numerous slivers from their bars of soap, the Russians started pushing nails through the soap to check for undesirable contents.

Another trick we played was polishing brass rings and punching the gold mark into them. We then tried, sometimes successfully, to sell the rings as gold jewellery. These were the types of games we played in order to get our hands on more food - to enable us to survive.

The Russians demanded hard work and set norms which we had to fulfill daily. They also evaluated our work on a scale of percentages. I had never heard before then that one could give better than 100 percent effort. Of course, we had known nothing about the 'Soviet man'. Their party propagandist claimed that Soviet men were superior to the dirty bourgeois, capitalist men. Soviets were supposedly noble, hard-working and honest and were capable of working well above the regular 100-percent capacity. It was at this time that we met the so-called 'stahanovist'[40] Russian bricklayer. I have forgotten his name, but he was considered by Russian workers as a legend in his own right. In widely promoted work competitions, his daily output was rated as high as 1250 percent. He came to the brick factory to prove to us, in person, that he alone could lay the same number of bricks in a wall in one day as twelve men could. We were anxious to witness this demonstration.

So the work began. He started by pulling a string from the corner of an already existing wall to where he would build a wall. This was his guideline. Then he motioned to the group of Soviet workers who were assigned to help him to start supplying him with mortar and bricks at a feverish tempo throughout the day. He was handed each brick, which he quickly placed along the outside edge of the wall by the string. The rest of the two-foot-thick wall was filled with mortar and brick by the chornaja robotniks in a rather sloppy way. Any discrepancies were filled with mortar thrown onto the wall by the shovels of the helpers. They were then covered with the next row of bricks. The long stretch of wall grew in height, row upon row, with the helpers working furiously. The bricklayer's only job was to lay the one outside row of bricks along the string very speedily; nevertheless, the final outcome of the day's work, measured in cubic metres and work percentages was credited to him, and only him.

Meanwhile, the 15 weary helpers lay on the ground panting. Of course, they had to be satisfied with the fact that they were given the privilege of working with him. In return

---

[40] 'Overachiever' in Russian.

for their efforts, they received a red banner, the symbol of recognition from the party, but no extra money. In the evening, after the performance, they were busy stealing scrap pieces of lumber, so that they could cook their soup on the common stove. That demonstration finally made us understand how the superior Soviet worker produces more than 100% of the regular man's work in one day.

Life was, indeed, difficult again, and every day was a struggle as the weather changed and the fall of 1947 arrived. I lived in a big barrack with 400 other prisoners. The wooden bunk beds were loaded with bed bugs. Although we were not troubled with lice anymore, the multitude of flat red bugs that infested the cracks of our barracks made our lives miserable. At least, Sunday entertainment was guaranteed as we dismantled our beds and carried the pieces out to the yard to burn the little buggers to death with a small torch. In order to battle our bug problem, we were bathed and shaven regularly in assembly-line fashion. One by one, we each had to jump onto a chilly and rusty old operating table and lie on our backs with our legs spread apart while the barber, with quick movements of a straight razor, got rid of our body hair. It was a humiliating and terrifying experience, and our officers vehemently protested the method. Still, the Russian officers claimed it was for our own good. Frightful as the experience was, perhaps this time, they were right.

It was impossible to escape this camp, protected as it was with rows of fences, watchtowers, and guard dogs leashed to the wires of the fence. The best chance for escape was to steal away from the working places which were guarded, but not without avenues for escape. The temptation was always present. The problem was that even if one did make it back to Hungary, he would be thrown back into the hands of the Russians by the 'new' government there. Despite the problems, some German prisoners attempted a break. They did not make it. A few days later, the widespread manhunt ended and the angry guards had their satisfaction. They formed a large circle around the prisoners and allowed their dogs to attack them. If the prisoners tried to avoid the dogs by leaving the circle, the guards would beat them with their rifle butts. Between the voracious dogs and the equally wild soldiers, it was a miracle if a man could survive. Upon witnessing such torture, I knew that if I tried to escape and was not successful, I would likely face permanent physical or mental handicaps; that, or a grisly death. I told myself again, it was not worth the risk.

One late summer day, we visited a nearby kolkhoz[41] to fill our mattresses with fresh straw. We travelled in a convoy of eight guarded army trucks. The small settlement was surrounded by a vast grain field that stretched as far as the eye could see. It was harvest time, and the collective farm workers were scattered across the field. Some congregated around an old-fashioned threshing machine. It reminded me of harvest time in Hungary. I remembered it being a happy event, even though the work was demanding. It was quite different from the somber spectacle I saw here. The peasants seemed to be performing their jobs robotically, without any sign of the joy or satisfaction normally visible during this time.

I noticed that a guard stood by the grain spout of the threshing machine. He had a rifle over his shoulder, and his duty was to keep the wheat from being stolen by the workers. Still, the instant he turned away, one of the peasant women

---

[41] Collective farm.

who worked nearby stepped closer and quickly scooped a handful of grain from the bag, then walked away as though nothing had happened. Perhaps the guard deliberately looked away from time to time, so that the workers could steal a little. The irony of it all was demonstrative of the fact that the collective farm system did not work in the Soviet Union. The lack of incentive, combined with the apathetic attitude of the workers, affected agricultural production negatively. I could understand why they did not want to break their backs working hard when they received the same standard ration as everyone else, which was barely enough to survive anyhow. Clearly and understandably, they worked without enthusiasm, doing only what was absolutely necessary. They, too, constantly sought any opportunity to steal some grain to somehow better their dreadful situation. Even little children often ran beside our trucks, shouting "Pan, kleb! Pan, kleb!"[42] Apparently, even in places where grain was grown, people did not have enough to eat. It was shocking to see that even the farm workers were hungry. It was now 1948, and it seemed that the Soviet economy was under control now. From the little I had seen of the urban centres, there were adequate food supplies there; but in the smaller villages and rural settlements, the essentials were still not available.

The construction at the brick factory was nearing completion, and I was assigned to another work detail. This large brigade of 50 prisoners was ordered to work in the cable factory. The Hungarian war hero Bela was also assigned to this group. He was 6'5" tall and was a strong but soft-spoken character. He was assigned the dirtiest and most difficult job

---

[42] "Mister, bread! Mister, bread!"

in the factory. He had to carry bags of graphite and bales of raw rubber down a narrow staircase to the basement shop. The rubber bales weighed well over 100 kilograms, yet he picked them up and hugged them. Then, like Frankenstein, he stiffly descended the long staircase. The graphite bags colored him as black as could be, and we seldom saw his face its true color of white. The Russians wanted to punish him for his heroism, but with time, his extraordinary strength and tremendous appetite for work forced them to recognize his worth. Every morning when we arrived at the factory, the Russian engineer made certain that Bela was there. One time Bela did not show up for work. The engineer was so upset that he told the brigade leader, "If Bela doesn't come, don't bring the rest of the gang either." So, Bela worked every day, smiling as he did and never arguing. He accepted what fate had dealt him, but preserved his dignity and held on to his beliefs. Inevitably, the Russians too came to address him as "The Hero".

The days were now getting shorter and colder, and one morning we anxiously awaited, in the dark, the arrival of the large wooden keg which held our soup, but it did not arrive. We soon heard the terrible news that our soup carriers had been attacked, and our keg of soup was hijacked by some other prisoners. This meant we had nothing to eat for the morning. The hours until our next meal at midday were agonizingly long. From then on, a delegation of strong men, equipped with sticks, was sent to the kitchen to escort the soup and bread portions of the company to the mess hall. The rules were changing, and sometimes only the strongest would survive.

The only enjoyment I had these days was when I visited the officers in their bunker and spent time listening to their lectures or part of their conversations. They did not have to go out and work. It was not part of their assignment. Despite this, a volunteer brigade of officers was formed which went to work in the bread factory. Their rations were also limited, so they took this work with the hope that they would be able to find some more food. They definitely did. During my nightly visits to their bunker, I could hardly believe my ears. They told stories of how they could eat as much bread as they wanted. There was bread everywhere, all day long. It sounded like heaven on earth compared to the brick factory or the cable factory at which I worked. An amicable air force major, Tibor Budai, was the officers' brigade leader. I repeatedly begged him to allow me just one day in the factory. I wanted to fill my stomach just one more time. What happened to me after was of no consequence, even if it meant I would be killed. I just wanted to feel no hunger - just once.

Finally Tibor made arrangements with my barrack commandant, another Hungarian officer, and the next morning I reported to the officers' group. I was excited and very nervous until we passed through the gate and were finally on our way to the factory. I was assigned to the heaviest work with nine other officers. We had to unload bags of flour from the half dozen trucks which came at regular intervals from the mills. The bags had to be carried to a large scale, weighed, then stacked in a certain manner, ten bags high, in the warehouse. The work was demanding, and I had a hell of a time carrying 50 and 75 kg bags; nevertheless, I was pleased that they took me and that I had a chance to stuff myself with bread. To show my gratitude, I wanted live up to their expectations and work as hard as I could. The will was there, but my frail body was exhausted by the end of the day. As we left the factory, I managed to pass through the control booth, concealing a chunk of bread. I gave it to my barrack commandant to show my appreciation for letting me go with them. He thanked me and told me that I could go again the next day. So I went happily back to my barracks. I was tired, but I had a full stomach. I could not believe that I had struck luck again when I really needed it. A few days later, a new brigade leader took over the group. Thankfully, Andras Szekely, a young lieutenant now in charge, took me under his wing and allowed me to continue working in his brigade. Somehow he put me on the officers' list, and I stuck with this special brigade for a long time.

THE BREAD FACTORY

Compared to the time I spent as a 'horse', this period of my prison life was as different as day and night. Our movements were still restricted, the fences were still there, the guards were always behind us, but, at least, we ceased to feel the constant, gnawing hunger. My fellow workers were officers with good educational backgrounds and excellent attitudes. They conducted themselves very honourably. I was more than pleased when they accepted me into their fraternity, and I tried my best to show my respect for them.

One day, a brigade of approximately 60 prisoners was taken to a large automated factory which supplied the city and surrounding area with bread. Dozens of civilian workers were divided into three shifts which, altogether, worked around the clock. Fifty of the prisoners cleared the yard, unloaded boxcars of coal, and did other work outside. I fit into the second group of ten men, assigned to the warehouse. As the convoy of five-ton trucks arrived at the warehouse, our work of carrying the flour bags to the scale began. The first days on this job were incredibly difficult, and at times I could barely lift my arms or stand the pain that racked my entire body, but the thought of the alternative did not allow me to give up. I continued to work until my fingertips were raw from grabbing the corners of the rough bags. Our Russian counterparts, the Gruzchiks, who worked the night shift, soon showed us how to handle the bags in a far more efficient and less painful manner. Slowly, over time, we began to build our strength, and the work became more tolerable.

Like autumn leaves in the wind, the days chased one another down the path of time, and yet another Christmas in captivity approached. Distant hopes and broken dreams blanketed our thoughts as the thick snow of winter covered the terrain. At least our conditions had improved. I managed to play Santa Claus by giving away a few pieces of bread from the factory to people like Bela, "The Hero", and the baron who had lived in the same village where I was born. It made me feel good inside. I always felt that I was a tool in the hands of God, and when He gave me more than I needed I had better share it with others.

I was pleasantly surprised to receive an invitation to the officers' bunker for their Christmas Eve celebration. Some of my colleagues from the bread factory were also there. With excitement and anticipation, I walked through the door to receive a warm welcome. I shook hands with the officers, and we wished each other a "békés Karácsony!"[43] Bunk beds for 26 officers lined each side of the bunker. A tiny pine tree stood in the centre and was beautifully decorated with small figures cut from paper. It was a symbol of Christmas. The flickering flame of a candle painted moving shadows on the wall and gave the bunker a cozy atmosphere. We gathered around and prayed for our freedom and the safety of our loved ones. Our thoughts travelled thousands of kilometres over the Russian steppes to our families far away. We then gave way to Christmas carols. I found singing relieved the lumps in my throat and the silence of my lips. Later, we

---

43 Hungarian word meaning "Peaceful Christmas."

exchanged words and listened to stories of Christmases past. The gift I received from these officers was their camaraderie and the appreciation they had shown for the flour I had smuggled for them through the control booth of the factory. The warmth and emotion of the evening stretched far into the night and was not only a celebration of Christmas, but of the respect and admiration we had for one another. The next morning seemed to come quickly, and as usual, we had to assemble in the cold in preparation for the march to work. I was weary from lack of sleep; nevertheless, I was thankful to have spent such a pleasant evening with the officers. I had survived to celebrate another Christmas.

In the early days of the New Year, some exciting news circulated through our workplace. We learned from the civilian workers that some members of the Hungarian government were coming to visit the factory in a couple of days. The unexpected news gave us a spark of hope in a time when we felt we had been forgotten. For those days prior to the visit, we could think and speak of nothing else. A diversity of opinions was expressed by the officers, regarding the event. Some felt optimistic; some were filled with deep cynicism. Did they know we were still here? Could we see them or, perhaps, talk to them? Would they see to it that our conditions improved and that we would return home soon? Questions like these raced through my mind until my anxiety consumed me, but I remained hopeful. It seemed only logical to me that my countrymen would help us somehow. How badly I yearned to see them, even if just for a few seconds, long enough to receive some words of encouragement or promise. Even if all they could say was, "Hang on, boys! You will soon go home. We'll make sure of that!" These few words would be enough to give us hope, to give us the strength to continue our fight.

The morning sky was still dark when we began the trek to the factory. This was the first day I had felt such excitement to go to work. We worked through half the morning when, like clockwork, the guards gathered all the prisoners together in a small utility shack separate from the main building. They intended to keep us out of sight during the visit. My pal, Paul, and I managed to separate from the group by hiding in Paul's tiny electrical shop. Later we positioned ourselves in the snow close to the gate, hidden behind a pile of lumber. Sure enough, black limousines soon rolled into the factory yard, and members of the Hungarian delegation, one after the other, stepped out and were greeted by the Russian reception committee and security men. The head of the delegation was Prime Minister Rakosi. The rest, including Gero, Marosan, Tildy, and others, followed. Rakosi was involved in the short-lived Communist coup of 1919. After that, he had gone into exile in Russia, but with the end of the war, the Russians brought him back. He was but a puppet placed at the head of the Hungarian government with the boys from Moscow pulling his strings.

It was a hell of a feeling to see these government men of my country so close and not be able to shout to them, to scream, "What about us?!" With broken dreams and a sense of utter defeat, we lay on the snow in silence, watching the parade of men stroll by, unable to do anything. Rakosi was supposedly working on behalf of the thousands of Hungarian prisoners of war, trying to bring them home. By this time, according to the peace pact, we should have been home. We never knew whether the Russians deliberately hid us from the Hungarians, or whether the Hungarians simply did not want to face us in that situation. Either way, we felt betrayed and abandoned. The delegation left without consequence, and we were back to work. The day ended with blighted hope and bitter disappointment. Turbulent, black clouds rolled and rumbled across the skies of our future, erasing any patch of blue which might give us hope for better days. A somber hush fell over the brigade as we trudged at a snail's pace back to camp. There were no words which could soothe us; and listless lethargy enveloped our souls.

Since Voronesh, we had received a few copies of a Hungarian newspaper, printed in Russia and meant to provide information to war prisoners. The paper was filled with propaganda about the new democratic way of life in Hungary, the achievements of the government, and the improved standard of living. War prisoners were also promised a quick return home.

As the months passed, the work became progressively easier, for not only did I regain my normal body weight, but I also developed a fairly high level of strength. We became able to cope with the daily demand of moving six to eight hundred bags per person with relative ease. Once in awhile, during more jovial moments, we staged contests of strength to see who could carry the most weight. At first, I managed to lift a 75-kilogram bag with my comrade sitting on top of it. Later, I succeeded in carrying two 50-kilogram bags with a man on the top. Of course, there was a technique to this achievement. The weight of the bags and the man had to be distributed equally over one's shoulders and centered above the spine of the carrier. In time, I proved my superior strength by carrying three 75-kilogram bags up the ramp, then ducking the door frame to enter the scale room. No one from our group was able to match this feat, and I gained respect not only from my friends, but from our Russian colleagues as well. For two years, I had struggled with weakness and fatigue. I was barely able to walk at times, and felt that my soul simply occupied my body and rested there, rather than living and flourishing. Now I was strong. It was an extraordinary feeling. I was full of pep, and was optimistic about my future, even though it did not look very promising at present.

We eventually established a sort of friendship with our Russian counterparts, the Gruzchiks, based upon our mutual respect for one another's strength. This was an important quality which impressed the Russians; they responded negatively to any kind of weakness. Sometimes, they would invite my friends and me to their feasts of bread and oil. Ironically, we enjoyed their company and felt welcome.

With the arrival of the warm sunshine of spring, we took off our shirts, put folded flour sacks on our heads, and carried the bags with ease all day, with only short intervals of rest. The warehouse manager was very satisfied with our work, and his appreciation was shown when, on occasion, he poured some sunflower oil into a bread pan and gave it to us. Happily, we dunked our pieces of bread into it and had a good meal. We enjoyed the access we had to flour and bread at the factory. The aim, of course, was to eat as much as we could throughout the day, then take as much as possible back to the Lager at the end of the day. Obviously, such acts of self-preservation were against the rules, and an organized security system was established to halt the extra feeding. Guards worked shifts around the clock, and were positioned at strategic points in the factory. At regular intervals, replacements would turn up for duty at the gate. We knew ahead of time who would be working, and we played little games to try and outsmart those on duty. One of the stations in the factory that was closely monitored was the loading dock. There, guards stood with a rifle on their shoulder and

ensured every bag of flour made it into the warehouse. They watched us work diligently, and, over time, we gained their respect. Eventually, they turned a blind eye while we smuggled our stashes out.

My daily contraband was modest in size, which proved to be a smart tactic. In some instances, the guard would take flour from the greedy ones who loaded themselves up and give it to me. Still, I made sure that I gave it back to the original owner before we reached the Lager. My comrades, of course, appreciated my generosity. The different methods that people used to smuggle flour and bread was amazing, often times, hilarious. Thankfully, if the guards found a prisoner with any stolen food items, they would take it away, and he would get a swift kick, but he was never reported to the police. This was incredibly gracious, considering some civilians had received five to ten-year sentences in working camps for the same offence. We took advantage of their leniency, and every night there was a lot of excited babble about how we had outsmarted the guard.

Even though the weather was quite hot, one officer still dressed in his heavy winter coat. His coat became affectionately known as the 'sheep' because of its large sheepskin collar. We later discovered he regularly managed to store a few cups of flour in this collar to smuggle it into camp. Another prisoner wore a makeshift necktie which he filled with a little bit of flour each day. We tried everything, and often the methods we used to smuggle flour and bread through the gate provided us with a good source of laughter.

One day, the fierce and dreaded Olga, the only female guard, was at the gate. Sure enough, the seemingly foolproof method failed. This time the 'sheep' had been stuffed with too much flour, and the corners of the collar no longer lay flat, but rather bulged conspicuously. Olga spotted this immediately, and proceeded to rip open the freshly-sewn collar. Big clouds of flour filled the guard booth, and we realized that the 'sheep' had made its final run. It had been killed. Certainly, this did not end our smuggling attempts. Other possibilities were tested. Even the most intimate parts of one's body were used as hiding spots.

This was how the golden days in the bread factory rolled by - with hard work, good camaraderie, and plenty of laughs. Before long, preparations were underway for the first of May celebration. This was another typical communist holiday, so, a soccer game and a track meet were organized, and special stage shows were planned for the evening. The track meet hosted the 100-metre dash, long jump and shot put events. By this time, after months of carrying bags of flour, I was strong and well prepared for the throwing competition. The contest attracted 26 strong men from among the 4000 prisoners. Most were German boys who worked in the kitchen or the hospital. I was the only Hungarian. We were given only three attempts, and by the end of the second round I had the best throw under my belt. The technique I had learned during my school years was definitely more effective that those of my competitors. I was the final thrower, and in the third round, I managed to improve my distance and proclaim victory over the husky lot. It was quite an honour. The Hungarian officers hoisted me up on their shoulders and carried me around the camp. Not only did I win the event, I felt I had gained some respect for the Hungarians in the camp. It was an exhilarating experience, and I felt a great sense of satisfaction to think I had brought some pride to the hearts of my fellow Hungarians.

As we grew stronger and were able to fill our bellies

each day, our thoughts again drifted to other areas of life. We found ourselves attracted to some of the female factory workers, and, in some cases, the attraction was mutual. My Russian name, Yura, became well known among the workers within the factory because of my work, my strength and my youth. While waiting for the convoy to arrive, I had a little break which gave me time to tour the factory and flirt with the girls. It was an exciting and fascinating game to play, and I enjoyed the challenge. I got to know every good-looking girl in the factory, and some of them, to my great pleasure, were receptive to my advances. Whenever I received a smile, I smiled back, and when I was kissed, I kissed back. Because of the restrictions I had as a prisoner, and the fear the girls had of being caught with a prisoner, it was impossible to build a lasting relationship with any of the girls who showed interest in me. The consequences were rather harsh, especially for the girls. As a result, any mutual attraction manifested itself in the form of occasional short hugs and kisses stolen on the staircases or in some corner of the factory. It was a thrill. It was exciting, but it was also very dangerous. Still, it made me feel human. I gained some experience and learned to approach women, revealing my desire, but in a dignified manner and with respect. It certainly brought color to my days when one of them would run into my arms, even though I could only hold her for a brief moment.

One day, the factory engineer's wife Gaya approached me. She threw me a challenge by saying, "You are just a kid. You wouldn't know what to do if an opportunity with a woman arrived!" There was a lot of truth in her words, but they still stung. My pride was hurt. I snapped back at her, saying that I could show *her* what to do. To my great surprise she replied, "All right. I'll meet you at the noon break in Paul's shop." My friend Paul was the electrician. I did not take our conversation seriously. I thought she was only teasing me, but after the lunch break, she found me and yelled at me for not showing up for our meeting. Only then did I realize that Gaya was not joking. After some thought, I said to myself, "what the hell", and I took her up on her challenge. "Pajdyom",[44] I said, and I started walking. Gaya followed closely behind. At that moment, I did not know what I was going to do, or what would happen, but a strange desire gripped my body and I seemed to just follow my feet. I could not believe how fast a romantic dream could become a reality.

She was a husky lady, but she was very attractive and full of pep. She had sparkling brown eyes and a delicate face. She lived inside the compound in the factory's house, and she had plenty of time to browse around the factory and check on the prisoners. Her husband, a skinny fellow, was always too busy with the production to pay her any attention. I could tell that she was not concerned about the possible consequences of our meeting. She meant business. The shop was not the best place for this kind of adventure. We did not get further than hugs and kisses, for at any moment someone might walk in. We had to wait for the right occasion, which came shortly when we stayed overtime in the factory to unload boxcars of coal. This was an opportunity for us to meet in the dark to satisfy our mutual desire. We climbed a narrow staircase to the attic. It was not the most romantic setting for my first love affair. It was pitch dark. There was no moonlight, no sweet scent of lilac bushes, and instead of fresh grass, our bed was rough shale. Apart from the obvious physical attraction, there was not much emotion

---

[44] Come with me in Russian.

to this evening. Still, I was able to steal a piece of forbidden pleasure from life. After all, I was a war prisoner, and getting involved like this was not a common occurrence. It was obviously against every rule. Perhaps, this was what made it so enticing.

The next day, as I thought about this first experience, I wished I could have enjoyed such a night back in Voronesh - with Maria. We shared a genuine and special emotion. I think that my relationship with Maria deserved a better ending.

Every day, on the way to the factory, we had to walk by an old cemetery and through a large railway yard. Here, we witnessed the deportation of thousands of Ukrainians to Siberia. As we walked through the yard, we were able to count the boxcars of the train that was waiting to receive the prisoners. The windows of the wagons were covered with the familiar barbed wire. There was no mistake that the train was prepared for human cargo. Each small wagon carried 50 to 60 people, and larger cars held 90 to 100 prisoners. Two or three transports were organized weekly. On some days, we met some of the prisoners as we passed by the yard. On other days, we actually saw the prisoners being loaded. These events made a deep impression on us. We shared many commonalities with those poor people who struggled under Communist rule.

While the prisoners waited to be loaded, they had to squat, five men in a row with their arms linked. They waited in this uncomfortable position beside the train until their name was called. They were then ordered to run to the designated car. Of course, their legs were stiff from squatting, hardly allowing them to walk, let alone run. This was the typical approach used to herd large numbers of people against their will into labour camps. On one occasion, as we walked along the road, we met a group of up to a thousand people as they made their way to the railway yard. A T-34 W.W.II tank led the parade of people. Soldiers escorted the prisoners and waved red flags, stopping everything and everyone in their path. Guards with automatic weapons walked on either side of the group of people with about five metres between them. Dogs patrolled the mass, as well. It was evident from the sheepskin coats and full winter gear worn by the guards that they were not headed for the Black Sea, a favourite Soviet holiday spot. Instead, they faced many long years of exile on the frontier of the vast Siberian steppes with only a remote chance of ever returning.

The fall of 1948 brought news that trainloads of prisoners were being transported home from other locations. This was good to hear, but somehow our situation remained unaffected, although we did see a group of officers being shipped out of our camp. It was a peaceful, sunny day when they departed, most of the camp population gathered around to bid farewell to those lucky men who would pass through the gate for the very last time. I had mixed feelings as I watched the officers leave, aware that I would remain there for an undetermined length of time. As a Russian officer named off the people from a transport list, they identified themselves and walked through the gate. The officer called, "Jeso", but no one answered. A second call was made. Finally, an individual came forward and told the Russian officer that he was not "Jeso", but "Eso". Obviously, the officer reading the list had difficulty pronouncing his name. Eso vehemently protested the mistake, so the Russian motioned to him to go back to the Lager. As a result, the fellow had to stay in the camp for two more years, all because he wanted his name pronounced correctly. I was stunned to witness this incident, and I promised myself that if my time to leave the camp ever came, I would not make the same mistake. So, we said good-bye to many friends, and with heavy hearts continued our days in captivity.

The food items I managed to steal from the bread factory were well received by some of my less fortunate comrades. I never sold the food, nor did I build up any equities for leaner times. Instead, I gave it to friends. I fed Bela, the hero, regularly, because, being a big fellow he was always hungry. I also respected his unshakable character and his conduct. The other person I helped was an old man who voluntarily cleaned my shoes and did things to make things convenient for me. He did these chores with the hope that I would reward him with a piece of bread, and, of course, I did. I could not refuse him, but I found it difficult to accept his services. I liked to help others. The feeling it gave me was reward enough.

After approximately a year and a half of work here, the factory management decided they no longer required workers from the camp. Perhaps we ate too much, or maybe they really did not need our assistance anymore. Either way, the most enviable and pleasurable work we had found ceased to be open to us. When the heavenly days in the bread factory ended, I was back to the standard ration of three bowls of soup, a kasha, and 600 grams of bread. No longer were there any extra supplements. Of course, I now had my strength, which lasted a long time, and I had lots of thankful comrades whom I had helped. I was not alone.

The weather turned cold again, and the breath of the upcoming winter dressed the leafless trees with white frost. We donned our Russian winter garments again which I hated, for although they were warm, they made me look like one of them. I was sent back to the cable factory with my old brigade. From time to time, I managed to smuggle some clothing from the Lager, such as underwear or a coat, to sell to my Russian contact for rubles. I was trusted by the officers to sell their spare items and, after the sale, I received my reward from the original owner. Of course, I ran a great risk of being caught since we were frisked every morning as we left the Lager to go to work. The German Lager commandant, Jupp, recognized me from the May 1st contest. "Ah, the Kugelstosser,"[45] he said. He was one of the contestants whom I had beaten, so he just faked the frisk and let me go through, paying his respect that way.

If one was caught taking clothes out of the Lager, it meant an immediate trip to the karcel. In the wintertime, when the temperatures dropped to below -25°, it was impossible to serve a sentence without freezing one's toes. One fellow, a strong furniture mover in civilian life, was thrown into the hole for some offence. By the time he was lifted out, both his feet were frozen. They had to amputate his legs below his knees. He was part of the prison scenery right to the bitter end, pushing himself about as he perched on a crude little platform that rode on wheels. He refused to sign the papers which stated he was to blame for the loss of his legs, so the Russians kept him there. With his strong hands, he constructed a primitive violin and tried to teach himself to play. This was his way of enhancing his bleak future. It was sad to see such human injustice. There were many like him who could no longer work because they had lost their eyes, arms, or legs. Still, they were held in captivity.

---

[45] Shot putter.

Later, I was re-assigned again, this time to a brigade sent to work on a road which ran between the railway yard on one side and the bread factory on the other. Our work was to dig ditches along the road so that cables could be laid there. It took us a month to finish this work that could have been completed in a couple of days under better weather conditions. I do not know if it was the deliberate intention of the Russians to make our lives miserable, or if it was just plain stupidity on their part, but we dug ditches when the frost line was deeper than we had to dig. With dull iron bars, we chiseled the ground, piece by piece, day after day. It was a painfully slow process. A short distance away, I could see the bread factory. I remembered the good times - the exciting flirtations with the girls, and the good laughs over the events that happened in the control booth. I wished that, just for a day, I could go back there again to see the familiar faces and stuff myself with bread.

The winter days slowly rolled off the calendar during the early part of 1949 and, with their passage, the rumours about going home died out one by one. Inevitably, new rumours would surface from someone's imagination. They served their purpose, wherever they came from, and kept our hopes alive through difficult times. I am afraid to imagine what might have happened if the Russians had told us, right from the beginning, that we would not get out of this hell for years. It would be so easy to just sit down in the deep snow in -30°C weather, and go to sleep with a dream that would take me to a better place. Instead, I continued to struggle with the elements, surviving only to suffer through another day. I recalled the words of Dr. Leganyi, the lawyer who served in the medical staff in Komarichi. He said, "We will be here for at least two years, therefore, we had better start learning the language." I hated this reasoning and deliberately shook off his words. Unfortunately, his prediction became more than a reality as I began my fourth year of prison life.

Still, I prayed for my freedom, for my mother's arms around me, for happiness. I kept telling myself, "Right now, this is the role I have to play on the big stage in the theatre of life. Someday, I will have an easier and more pleasant part to play. It can't always be like this. From here on, the pendulum can only swing upwards."

In the early spring of 1949, I was transported to another Lager located in the heart of Kiev.

LAGER NO. 7062/11 KIEV

Here, in Kiev, stood a beautiful four-storey building which ran the length of a city block. Part of it had been badly damaged during the war, but what remained served as a Lager for the prisoners. Certainly, the intricate detail of the architectural facade had seen better days; apparently, the building had, at one time, served to accommodate foreign consulates. I was pleased to see a huge mural, depicting Poseidon, the mythological Greek god of sea and storms, remain intact on one wall. One section of the building enclosed a small courtyard and was used to hold the prisoners. Our task here was to restore the building for living quarters. As soon as we finished the rooms on one floor, people moved in immediately. Civilian housing was badly needed. We, as prisoners, were housed in rooms with many bunk beds, topped by mattresses filled with sawdust. Bedbugs continued to share our beds.

I was assigned to work with a 75-year-old Russian plumber named Dimitri. In spite of his age, Dimitri continued to work because his pension was not enough to provide him with a reasonable standard of living. He was amazingly agile and his chest held a youthful heart. After working together for some time, we grew to respect and enjoy one another. He taught me some of the tricks of the trade, and I became helpful to him. The heating system, a huge boiler in the basement, was installed under his leadership. I followed him like a puppy, and did my best to work hard and to learn. Eventually, I learned to thread pipe by hand and to remove the rusty and burnt heating units from the walls. I had to take them apart, clean them, and put them together again. A lack of prefabricated elbows forced us to bend six-inch pipes to form 90° angles. We did this by filling the pipes with sand, heating them over an open fire and bending them by hand. It was a primitive but effective method.

I was later introduced to another Russian man, Vasil, who had served in the navy. He now worked as a welder, and I helped him regularly as well. We shared a path in life, and developed a good relationship with each other as we travelled it together. Both Vasil and Dimitri started to open up, telling me about their financial problems. They apologized for not being able to help me with an occasional piece of bread. They could not help me, as their families did not have enough. Our lives had many similarities. We were all prisoners, only they lived in a bigger Lager.

The 1st of May celebration finally arrived. The Russians sent up a huge balloon over the main boulevard of Kiev. We had a clear view of it from the Lager. As it rose about 100 metres from us, it lifted a large red flag over the area. Army units and factory workers marched through the streets to the centre of the celebration. In the meantime, we took our bunk beds apart and carried them out into the yard so we could burn the bedbugs from them.

In the afternoon, our theatre staged a variety show and play. By this time, I had joined the group and was part of the production. Originally, I was simply a stand-in for a fellow who had taken ill and usually worked as the prompter. I was instructed to read the hand written script of the play slightly ahead of the actors as I sat in a little hole, facing the stage. I did a good job, and by request of the actors, I agreed to play this role on a regular basis. After all, I realized that this was a better way to spend the evening hours than complaining about our situation. The theatre took our minds away from our problems and pushed us to make the best of our lives under the circumstances. The Russians supported our theatre group. They recognized how the threatre improved the morale of the prisoners. This had suddenly become a concern to them. When we finished the long hours of rehearsals, we were rewarded with a bowl of soup. Although we were thankful for the extra meal, the soup was not the main reason for participating. It was the camaraderie, the unity I felt with people who had a good education and philosophy of life. It was the physical and emotional portrayal of a bit of my heritage. The Russian officers and their spouses enjoyed the theatre almost as much as our fellow prisoners. It certainly filled some of their evenings with unique and intriguing sights and stories. The whole idea was refreshingly positive for them.

One day, a young engineer approached me, and after a few questions and a bit of friendly conversation, he told me that I was to start working in his office the next day. I was to help survey and draw maps of the basements of buildings; so I wandered through the underground labyrinths measuring and drawing them. The engineer was extremely patient and understanding. By that time I was fairly fluent in Russian, and I had managed to learn the Cyrillic alphabet so that I could read and write. Certainly, this opened many doors for me, and it seemed there was no end to the variety of jobs I performed.

After a few weeks of this work, I finished the job, and

the engineer and I parted with friendly words. A new brigade was formed which started work on a building situated on one of Kiev's attractive boulevards. The street was named after Gorkij, the famous writer. We were assigned to erect a five storey structure in place of the present ruins. Other attractive apartment houses lined each side of the street. The road was divided by a promenade which was home to park benches and rows of beautiful horse chestnut trees. The blessed sunshine lured out the leaves and the flowers of these trees to dress them in their splendid spring costumes. It was a magnificent picture.

I was among the 50 or so self-proclaimed 'jack's of all trades'. Because of my ability to read, write and understand the blueprints used in construction, I became a sort of foreman; the Russians called me an engineer. My duties included assisting and supervising the tradesmen, measuring the doorways, establishing the level of the windows and staircases, and calculating the work productivity for each day. The brigade managed to meet the daily norms, and by the end of the month we were awarded a maximum of 200 rubles each.

The construction site was carefully guarded. As the building was erected, it was boarded up on the street side, and watchtowers were built at each corner of the site. By the gate was a little wooden shack which housed civilian guards who checked the workers upon entry and exit to ensure that building materials were not stolen. A Russian engineer came to inspect from time to time. In the meantime, a foreman supervised everyone each day. In the morning, I set up the transit, gathered the drawings, got the measuring tapes, and cruised the site; and when questions were asked, I tried to give useful answers. The work was rather satisfying after my long years of chornaja robot.

My prison comrades and I were considered 'undesirable elements' and were now left in the Soviet Union in accordance with agreements made with the 'puppet' government which now existed in Hungary. The prison population was now made up of people who had volunteered for military service or had served in the municipal or rural police forces and were dedicated to upholding the order of the old regime. They were a tough, reliable, and hard-working breed, and it was because of our backgrounds that we managed to meet the norms and improve our standard of living. We were able to buy some extra food, and living became bearable again.

We worked side by side with many Russian civilians - an arrangement which allowed us to get to know one another and improve our understanding of each other's situation. These people were coping with extremely harsh conditions, as were we, and it was interesting to observe their reactions and learn their attitudes and their general philosophy of life. Despite the hardships we went through, we had to recognize that our situation was not the fault of the Russian people but rather the system under which they, and we, now lived. I found the people to be quite open and warm hearted, actually. They did not want to be more than they were; they were not showy, just genuine. Their only extravagance was in their hand gestures as they spoke. Often their arms would fly wildly about while their faces lit up with delightful expressions. It was interesting and often hilarious to watch them.

When asked the question, "Kak dyela?"[46] they clenched their fist and turned their thumb up and replied,

---

[46] "How are you?"

"Karasho" which meant "good". If they felt especially fine, they would pretend to drop a pinch of salt from the finger of one hand over the thumb of the other hand - a gesture that meant "ochin karasho" or "very good." Sometimes, too, they would rotate their hand with their thumb and little finger open which signified they were feeling so-so, but not great. During those rare moments when one had had enough to eat, he would clench one fist against his stomach and hammer it repeatedly. This was definitely a good sign, indicating that they had truly stuffed their stomachs. They followed up with talk and their favourite hobby, drinking vodka, of course. They often flicked their fingers against the side of their neck to measure how many millilitres of vodka they had chopped down. After being stuffed with kasha and belting back a few glasses of vodka, what more could one desire than a little love-making to complete one's satisfaction? The sign for this was made by forming a circle with the index finger and thumb of one hand, then hitting the hole with the middle finger of the other hand. It seemed to be the universal gesture for the ultimate and most natural pleasure.

In order to survive and to cope with the harsh reality each day brought, the Russians learned to steal a little, here and there, without feeling even a slight bit of guilt about it. They called their stealing "cap-ca-rap," - a word for simply taking something when no one was watching. Everyone was guilty to some extent, depending on their position and the opportunities which presented themselves. Obviously, the important thing was not to be caught, for the consequences were serious. Stealing from the state, which claimed to own everything, resulted in a sentence in the labour camp. Using both hands, the Russians spread their fingers in front of their faces - a sign of imprisonment. They often remarked that there were only three types of Soviet people: ones who had been locked up, ones who were presently locked up, and ones who would be locked up. The possibility of losing their freedom always hung precariously over their heads like the sword of Damocles. Somehow those few signs fatefully illustrated their simple life styles - from eating to making love, from drinking to stealing, and sooner or later, from freedom to jail.

Of course, another important part of their life was the robot, or work - was a must for everyone. We saw men and women working side by side on the railroad, as well as carrying flour bags or mortar and bricks at the construction sites. There was no discrimination when it came to the robot. The work was often glorified by promoting competitions, and was forced upon the people when necessary. Everybody and everything had to work - the people, the equipment, the machines, even the sun. When the sun poked its radiant face out from behind the clouds and spread its rays over the countryside, the workers would exclaim, "solnushka robot".[47]

The lives and dreams of the Russian people were simple. The smallest things, such as a good "kurith" or smoke, brought them contentment. In previous years, when paper was not readily available, people rolled their cigarettes using the infamous Soviet newspaper "Pravda" (Truth). They folded the newspaper carefully so that when they tore a piece off, it was just the right size to make a cigarette. The mahorka, or ground stem of the tobacco plant, combined with the ink from the newspaper print, produced such a strong smoke that when I caught a whiff of the smoke, my eyes teared.

---

[47] "The sun is working" in Russian.

They carried the mahorka loose in the pockets of their pants, with the folded newspaper, ready to make cigarettes. As it was now, the authorities tried to persuade people not to use the newspaper for rolling cigarettes anymore; but after becoming accustomed to these homemade smokes, regular cigarette paper and tobacco was just too mild for them.

The Russian diet was simple, as well. They daily made soup or kasha from grains like barley or millet, or from split peas, cabbage, pig weed, or nettle. The heavy black bread they baked was hearty, without preservatives, and full of nutrients. They certainly had no worries about high cholesterol. Red or white, meat was simply not available. Occasionally, they could snag some fish which was shipped periodically from another part of the country. When a shipment arrived, everyone ate fish for days, knowing that once it was gone, it would be a long time before they would see any meat again. The people appeared relatively healthy and strong, likely from eating such a simple, healthy diet, virtually free of fat or meat.

Tamas was an amateur comedian. He often imitated the Russian political propagandist who lectured us from time to time about how well the communist system worked, and what wealth the people enjoyed, despite abundant visible evidence to the contrary. One day, Tamas began performing. "Ve imaesh,"[48] he said, and he counted on his fingers, "Soya flour, potatoes, cabbage, tomatoes, fish, bread, barley, millet, beets, and most importantly (he raised his voice), cucumbers!" Cucumbers were the most sought-after vegetable. On the food list, they were the ultimate - heaven is vegetable. "What else is there?", he questioned with a degree of sar-

---

[48] "We have" in Russian.

casm. He looked at us and said, "We have everything that our eyes and mouths could possibly desire." We just smiled silently and felt bad to think that this was all they would likely ever have.

GALINA

The spring weather dressed the trees with green leaves and colorful blossoms, and the sunshine lured the townsfolk of the neighbourhood out of their apartments. One day, as I stopped my work to catch my breath, I noticed a beautiful girl on a neighbouring apartment-house balcony. She was radiant with gleaming dark hair and deep black eyes. I sat and gazed at her for a moment, captivated by her essence, her graceful movements, her beauty so striking amidst the gray buildings and sullen faces of the prisoners with whom I worked. There I sat for a moment, gathering in her fresh loveliness. Feeling renewed and invigorated, I then returned to my work. Each day thereafter, I watched for her to re-appear. When the sun climbed over the rooftops and stretched its rays to reach her balcony, she would come out to enjoy the warmth and brilliant light. Soon she realized she had an admirer in me, and it seemed as though she positioned herself to see me while basking in the sun. After a few days of this mutual gazing, I set up my transit which brought her into closer view through the lens. Her slight smile indicated acceptance to my approach. As the days went by, her flirtations were welcoming, and with hidden waves we started a form of communication. To avoid the watchful eyes of the guards, she would step into her room but remained within my view. I often stood behind a chimney, also out of sight of the guards. Here I was able to wave to her without detection. She lived on the fourth floor in her building.

We had just completed the basement and were working to erect the walls of the first floor of the apartment we were building. It took approximately one month to build the walls before we could lay the concrete beams across to establish another floor. From this new vantage point, the beauty on the fourth floor was much closer. One morning she came out on her balcony, and when the guard was turned away she quickly threw a little parcel down to the floor where I stood. I picked it up in a flash, hid it in my shirt, and looked up to see her disappear from sight. I left my post with my precious gift to find a quiet corner where I could quench the thirst of my great curiosity. When I was certain no one was near, I reached under my shirt and brought out the little parcel. Excited as a child at Christmas, I tore open the paper to reveal the contents of my package. I was delighted to find a pack of cigarettes and a bar of chocolate with a tiny note hidden inside the chocolate wrapping. Her sweet, neatly-written words struck my heart which was as vulnerable as Achilles' heel to the poisoned arrow. It read, "Ja budu uvas lubit e nye kakda nye zabudu! Galina."[49] At last, I felt as though someone cared about me, as though someone was paying attention and watching over me. Galina was in some ways my guardian angel. Finally, I was a person who someone else found exciting, and now I knew that someone's name. The next time I saw her, I signaled that my feelings were identical, by pointing to my heart and closing my arms around my chest as though I was embracing her. She received my signs with a brimming smile.

---

[49] "I will love you and will never forget you! Galina."

I walked around all day, glowing with happiness. Back at the Lager that evening, I ate the chocolate ceremoniously, piece by piece, savouring each bite. I had not seen chocolate, let alone tasted it for the last five years. The fine quality cigarettes were encased in a fancy carton and were approximately seven centimetres long with five centimetres taken up by a long filter. On the front of the box, the name 'Kazbek' was written on a rugged silhouette of the Caucasus with a picture of a rider on a charging horse. I did not smoke, but I cherished the cigarettes, keeping them safe in my pocket. That evening I wrote a letter, telling Galina of my feelings, and expressing my appreciation for her gift and for her love. I read her note numerous times, letting my imagination fly with sweet thoughts of her before I finally fell asleep with a smile on my face.

My days were brightened by Galina and the hope she gave me. Each morning brought excitement and sweet tension as we arrived at our work area. This was quite a change from the initial dread and lethargy I felt when we first began our work in Kiev. One day, when the first opportunity came, I positioned myself so that she could see me fold a note and put it into a matchbox. With the use of hand gestures, I communicated to her that at eleven o'clock, she should walk down to the street, and I would throw the matchbox to the sidewalk. She nodded and smiled widely, seemingly understanding my charades. When eleven o'clock finally came, I stood on the wall of our building, facing the street, and lit a cigarette. When I threw down my match, I also tossed the tiny box down to the street below.

Two guards who were sitting in the control towers above the boarded fence did not detect anything. Galina, carrying a woven shopping basket, spotted the box, put down her basket and stopped for a short rest. When she lifted the basket she picked up the matchbox with it. The plan had worked. The guards did not sense what had occurred. A short time after returning home from her 'shopping trip', I could see Galina just inside the door to her balcony, kissing my letter and smiling happily.

The exchanges between Galina and me had been successful thus far, but I realized that it was dangerous to continue repeating this method as it would soon become obvious to the guards that something was going on between me and the beauty on the fourth floor. We had to find a safer delivery system. Searching my mind for a solution, the old lady at the gate who was guarding the building materials with her rusty rifle, popped into my head. She was a sweet old soul and had only kind feelings toward everyone, including the prisoners. I waited until she was alone in her control booth, approached her with trust and hope in my heart and addressed her "Mama Marusa". I explained to her that I was in love with a girl who lived in the next building and that her name was Galina. The old lady looked around in a panic and put her finger to her lips to indicate that I should not speak so loud. I told her about my plan, and asked her if she would deliver the notes between Galina and me. With a warm smile on her friendly old face, she pinched my cheek and said, "Kanyeshna, Yura, kanyeshna."[50] I was pleased to know that she would not betray my trust and would help me. I touched her arm with appreciation, saying, "Spassiva, Mama Marusa, bolshoy spassiva,"[51] and then left. I felt very good about securing a safe way to communicate with Galina in the

---

[50] "Naturally, George, naturally."

[51] "Thank you, Mama Marusa, a big thank you."

future. I encouraged her to approach Mama Marusa with trust and accept her as our friendly postman. From then on, each morning, as I walked through the gate of our working place, I eagerly made eye contact with Mama Marusa. A little smile on her face and a delicate nod of her head indicated she had a letter for me. After establishing the day's work with the Russian foreman and passing the information on to the other prisoners, I would pay a short visit to Mama Marusa. Each day she would pull out Galina's letter from under her head scarf. Each day I thanked her quickly and hurried to a corner where I could read the note which meant so much to me in those days.

Each morning, a Russian engineer and our popular foreman made their regular inspection tour around the construction site, ironing out any problems and making certain the work was up to standard. I was with them on these occasions, and I relayed their instructions to my fellow prisoners. When the time came to break for a smoke, I pulled out my cigarettes from Galina and offered one to each of them saying, "pozsa lusta."[52] They looked at me with wide ironic eyes, and replied, "Aha gospodin Yura zakurith Kazbek."[53] I simply smiled with a smugly mysterious grin, and without inhaling, puffed out the smoke from my fancy cigarette. My fellow workers smoked the Kazbek with delight, although it was much milder than their mahorka. Of course, I enjoyed their reactions far more than my cigarette.

With each exchange of letters, I felt closer and closer to Galina, but in reality, the distance between her balcony and my position behind the chimney remained unchanged. I

---

[52] "Please" in Russian.

[53] "Your worship, George, smoking Kazbek."

looked forward to the opportunity when I could meet her face to face, if it would ever come.

At five o'clock, as we finished work, we gathered and sat on the benches of the army truck parked in front of the construction site by the sidewalk. Our own inability to assemble at once, on time, was one of the most frustrating, yet typical events that made our prison life generally more miserable than it might have been. It seemed we were forever waiting for someone who was slow or failed to respond immediately to the call. This recurring event placed an extra burden on the group, especially on frigid winter evenings. There were always late arrivals - prisoners who would hide in a sheltered spot and watch the main group assemble. Then, when almost everyone was there, they would come to join the angry prisoners. Sometimes, impatience would cause tempers to flare more than usual, and those people notorious for being late would meet the fists of their comrades.

This routine waiting process gave me an idea. In my next letter, I asked Galina to come down to the street and walk casually by the parked trucks so that I could see her more closely. That very day while we assembled she did as I requested. It was an exciting, yet difficult time for both of us. Coming so close, we were able to see each other for a short moment, but were unable to say a word or crack a smile as this might reveal our connection. After work, I would hurry to occupy the seat on the bench closest to the sidewalk, and excitedly watch her stroll toward us. It was incredibly difficult to sit still and remain calm when I felt like my heart would jump out of my chest at any minute. When she lifted her delicately cut face and looked at me, I could see her high cheek bones, characteristic of her Gruz origin, and her black diamond-like eyes. Her stunning beauty was even more than

I had imagined. Although she was just a few steps away - so close I could almost touch her - she seemed so far away. I was overwhelmed with a feeling of frustration, as one of the most fulfilling human feelings could not be expressed freely between us, and was, instead, forbidden for fear of our lives. After all the brutalities and pains that had been injected into our lives, now the craving for love was also denied; nevertheless, her daily stroll was cherished. She seemed relaxed despite being watched by fifty pairs of prisoner's eyes.

Through our correspondence, she urged me to set up a plan which would enable us to meet somehow. It was as impossible for me to sneak away from my work place as it was for her to come into our building. Our meeting had to take place somewhere else. The idea struck me that it might be possible for her to come and pretend that she lived in the same place where I had worked earlier with the old plumber and Vasil. This was the place where we hardly completed a floor and made it liveable before the civilians moved in. So I asked the Hungarian prison officer, whom I knew very well, to dispatch me to the apartment structure just for a day. He agreed to assign me there, and so, with a joyous heart, I began to see my plan fall into place. I wrote a letter to Galina to let her know the details of my plan, and I drew a map with instructions for her to follow.

The address of the place was Krasne Armyskaya ulica 25.[54] I described the splendid archway through which she had to enter, and instructed her to ignore the guards as they would not question her if they thought that she lived there. I told her that as she passed through the archway she would be able to see me in the distance, and without saying any-

---

[54] Red Army Street 25.

thing, she should just follow me. With some apprehension, she agreed to carry out my plan. We set a day, and my close friends eagerly promised to assist me by watching the area in case anyone should wander through the place of our rendezvous, including the patrolling guards. According to the plan, they would also purposely blow the electrical fuse serving that part of the floor so as to provide the safety of darkness for our meeting. I hardly slept at all the night before our meeting was to take place.

The morning of our meeting brought extreme nervousness and anticipation which heightened as I marched through the gate toward our rendezvous place. After the brigade leader explained our task, we dispersed to our work areas. I noticed my friends were acting busy, but, following the plan, kept close contact and were alert. Every minute seemed like eternity as I waited for Galina to appear. At one point, I thought she might decide not to take such a risk and would cancel the plan, but alas, I finally spotted her. She was wearing a black dress, high heels and stockings, and as she floated past the guards at the entrance, my heart seemed to be beating in my throat. We made visual contact, and I started to stroll down the street, leading her to one of the entrances to the building. When we were inside the corridor out of everyone's sight, she flew into my arms, whispering, "Yura, Yura" ("George, George"). As we embraced, I felt her trembling body close to me. I tried to calm her by reassuring her and instructing her that if something should go wrong, she should act like she was lost and looking for her friend who lived somewhere in the compound.

She seemed a bit relieved and followed me into a partially finished tiny room on the second floor. I took her in my arms and instantly showered her with kisses. Without inhibition, I fell over myself to express my feelings and thank her for coming to me. It was such an extraordinary feeling to have all of my earlier fantasies turn into reality, to hold her, to feel her sensuality and tenderness. I smelled her perfume and enjoyed touching her delicate, feminine clothes. Her graceful movements met my highest expectations. In that world, where you saw the women working as part of the railway gang, carrying bags of flour, and bundled up in the same heavy clothes as the men wore, it was refreshing to see and feel a girl who managed to preserve her grace, poise, and womanliness. Our ecstasy ended with tears running down our faces. They were tears of joy and perhaps of sadness in the realization that as much as this was the beginning of our simple and honest relationship, it was also the end. I imagined how wonderful it would have been to dance together, arm in arm, out of the compound, ignoring the guards, the people and the whole world. With smiles on our faces, we would simply enjoy being in love. Instead, as I looked into her tearful, sad eyes, I was forced to bid her farewell; and with a heavy heart, I watched her delicate steps as she walked through the arch and out of sight. I walked back to the little room, leaned against the wall and slowly slid down, until I sat with my head on my arms as they rested on my knees. I wept. Such extremes of emotions had filled my heart, then shattered it in but a few minutes. The lingering scent of her perfume was the only evidence of that sweet and beautiful moment which would never be repeated, except in my memories.

The next day I was ordered to go back to the Gorkij boulevard with my brigade. My efforts to arrange another rendezvous did not meet with success since my Hungarian friend who arranged my change of work place was transferred

GalinaGalina

to another Lager. So the relationship between the fourth-floor beauty and me fizzled into only seeing each other daily when she came out on her balcony or when she walked by us as we waited in the army truck. We still kept up our correspondence with each other, and this served as small medicine for our aching desire to meet again; however, our mutual admiration would be manifested only in words and longing glances.

FALL OF 1949

A quiet Sunday turned into a day of anger, frustration and turmoil in the Lager. We had been kept inside the compound all day, performing the usual rituals of killing the bedbugs and cleaning the rooms. Later in the evening, we had finally settled down to relax when the mood of the Lager suddenly changed. News that an escaped prisoner from another Lager had been caught and brought into our Lager for interrogation travelled with amazing speed from one room to another. Word spread like wildfire that he had a Russian girlfriend, and she had aided him in his unsuccessful attempt to escape. As the Russians interrogated the prisoner, they exercised their usual brutality. We could hear his cries as they beat him, until finally it stopped. Miraculously, he had managed to break out of the room and was running down the corridor, shouting for protection. Doors flew open, and prisoners swarmed out of their rooms to see what was causing the commotion. Within minutes, the once-quiet Lager resembled a disturbed beehive. An angry crowd formed a protective wall around the bleeding, frightened comrade, and despite the demands of the Russian officers to give him up, the prisoners refused to turn him over. They moved out into the courtyard in a tight bunch, aiding and comforting the beaten prisoner along the way. Gradually, the numbers around him swelled, and soon the entire population of the Lager had congregated in the yard. The compound became like a keg of gun powder, and any false move by the Russian officers would set a spark to it. Someone began shouting that our rights as prisoners did not allow for beatings even after attempts to escape. Words were exchanged between our 'spokesman' and the Russian officers, and the discussion became progressively hostile. Questions of why we were being kept here still, and why they were violating the peace pact of 1946 which had guaranteed our return home, came up again and again. We knew very well that the local officers did not have the answers, so we demanded to speak with a higher authority.

Through our spokesman, we took a stand against the Russians. We refused to eat or move until a delegation from Moscow arrived. In response to our sudden courage, the Russians doubled the guards and positioned more machine guns in the watchtowers. The small incident had quickly and unexpectedly grown into a full-scale riot.

The possibility of an uprising within a Lager in the heart of Kiev immediately drove the Russian guards and officers into a panic. We did not know what the future held, but we had suddenly been charged with such energy, such courage, and such belligerence that we intended not to abandon our new-found position without a fight. I sensed the silent pleasure we now took in knowing we had stirred a fear into the hearts of the officers and guards.

The majority of the prisoners remained in the yard throughout the night without eating. We knew very well that we could not refuse to work, but we could always refuse to eat, and the officers were not supposed to send us to work unless we had eaten. For the first time, they had unwillingly relinquished their authority and control. We now held the power. The tables had turned, and it was they, who, perhaps, now feared for their lives. After all, here stood hundreds of hungry, angry prisoners. What did we really have to lose? Our lives? Likely, most would not mind such an exit, and the Russians knew it. We knew our chances of any action toward our release were slim to none, but we revelled in the temporary strength we had suddenly found.

The sun fell behind the buildings, black rain clouds covered the sky, and the rumbling of the prisoners quieted. As the darkness of evening enveloped the yard, only the periodic cry of some disgruntled prisoners disturbed the uneasy calm. As I listened, I recognized the voice of one of my pals. I got up and waded as inconspicuously as possible through the crowd to try to get to him. There were people everywhere, sitting, lying, talking, snoring. Finally, when I reached him, I begged him not to shout. He would attract attention to himself, and once this was all over, he would suffer some harsh consequences. I tried to convince him that the best thing was just to stay in the yard with everyone and keep silent. He did not have to do more than that. He was angry with me, and as I left him, he continued his outbursts with great zeal.

Unfortunately, a slow, drizzling rain began to fall. This made our situation uncomfortable, and we huddled together in small groups to try to keep warm and dry. Some of the prisoners went up to their rooms for more clothes. Many did not return. They were seduced by the warmth of a dry bed. Nevertheless, the next morning broke, wet and gloomy, to find about two-thirds of the Lager's population, about 800 men, still in the yard standing strong. Even though we had not eaten our evening nor our morning meal; the officers deliberately ignored the rules and sent us out to work, but not until after they had confronted those prisoners who had abandoned the main group during the night. One brigade after another slowly began to move toward the gate and out to their working area. As we passed through the gate in the usual five-abreast formation, the officers busily picked out the spokesmen from the lines of people. They called the names of those people who had noticeably and verbally fuelled the events of the previous night. In order to identity all those involved, the Russians called upon their informants. Unfortunately, the prison society also had its share of slimy characters - people who would disclose the names of their comrades for an extra soup or for an easier working position. Twelve individuals were stopped at the gate and extracted from their brigade. Their punishment was inevitable and unavoidable. We feared what they had coming.

After an extra long day of work without any food, we discovered that a three-man tribunal, comprised of a sergeant, a lieutenant and a second-lieutenant, had tried and convicted these people of organizing a strike and they were sentenced to 25 years in a labour camp. Of course, we felt the whole exercise was unfair. There was no defense; one was simply charged and sentenced without question, but where was one to file a complaint? Who could one appeal to? The Latin words, "Wae victis,"[55] stuck in my mind.

The 12 sentenced men, as well as the young boy who had escaped and had innocently triggered the unrest, were hustled away in a truck. We never saw them again. We were deeply disheartened and now felt even more helpless than before. We had lost the battle and had not accomplished anything with our disorganized, impromptu uprising.

The often foggy and rain-drenched autumn was a fore-

---

[55] Wail for the defeated one.

runner to another harsh winter, and our unsuccessful attempt to change our situation cast an apathetic melancholy over the prison population. Like a flock of sheep, we performed our duties and lived our lives with minimal reward or enjoyment. The annual celebration of the Bolshevik Revolution found us in a despondent state. Four huge balloons were anchored to the ground and were in plain view of our building. As they were inflated, it became evident that each supported a large red flag emblazoned with a portrait of Marx, Engels, Lenin or Stalin. The balloons drifted upward and floated over us every day for an entire week. They were grim reminders of the omniscient or omnipresent evils which hovered over this part of the world. I began to believe with more and more certainty that as long as those balloons were allowed to fly, millions would remain oppressed. This included us, the prisoners, as well as the Soviet people. The Lord's words to Adam, in Madacs' 'The Tragedy of Man" came to mind. He said, "Man, strive on, trust. Have faith." This was my destiny. For how long or why, I did not know.

My work with the brigade at the Gorkij boulevard continued. Our hard work met the approval of the Russian engineer and our foreman Vanya, and a good working relationship was established with them. They treated us with respect, and we showed our appreciation by working hard; the fruits of which became evident. We completed the fourth level ahead of schedule, and with one floor to go, the building's superstructure was near completion.

As the floors went up, I was pleased to see Galina's smiling face closer up. In these uncertain times, our relationship seemed to be the only reassuring and stable entity in my life. The love she expressed in her letters made my heart dance. I felt incredibly lucky to be on the receiving end of her affection. Through our written correspondence, we tried to arrange another rendezvous, something we both desired immensely. One evening after work, I was playing out a variety of scenarios in my mind when I was interrupted by a call for an urgent meeting. The Russian Lager commandant wanted to make an important announcement which apparently would affect our lives. Rumours had been sweeping through the Lager, stating we would be going home. These rumours were always good to hear, even though we never really expected them to come true. After five years of prison life and many such promises which had not materialized, the response to the commandant's call was very poor. With some reluctance, only one-third of the Lager's population showed up to listen to his speech, including myself. Of course, the brigade leaders and support staff were obligated to be present. With great reservation, we listened to the commandant's announcement of our departure. He told us that, in a few days, we would be leaving to join others at the central Lager, and from there we would be travelling home. We were incredibly pessimistic, of course, and we did not want to raise our hopes only to have them dashed again. Certainly, I would only believe I was going home when I was pushed from a train in Budapest. This news came when we had least expected it. I always believed that the time would come when I would go home, but I found it difficult to fathom the time might be now. Besides, my mind had been so preoccupied with plans to meet with Galina again that I had no time to entertain thoughts of going home.

Now, I was awake half the night, thinking of the possibility of finally going home, but, invariably, my thoughts kept returning to Galina. Sometimes life seemed so unfair. Why had this possibility not come when I needed to return home the most - when my lice-ridden, filthy body needed to be cleansed, when my growling stomach was starved, and my lonely soul ached for attention? Why now, when conditions were so much better than during my days as a 'horse' in Bryansk? Why now, when I had Galina?

During those last few days in the Lager, a little old man set up a small bazaar where we could buy a few items, such as cologne or printed material. This had never been allowed before, and the whole thing began to pick away at our ever-present skepticism. Suddenly we could buy and keep items. We actually had personal possessions for the first time in five years. Until now, everything had been confiscated, including the wedding bands of the married men. As these events unfolded, we began to recognize that the time had indeed finally come to return home.

Our last day of work, as well as the departure date was set. I relayed the message to Galina by letter, and I could see the bright smile of her face fade into a visage of melancholy and despair. My heart ached as I watched her, unable to do or say anything to comfort her. Our separation was inevitable. I could promise her nothing, because I was not sure where I was going either. The only thing that I could write was that I would never forget her.

The last working day at the construction site on Gorkij boulevard began without sunshine. Its face was hidden behind the gray clouds stretched across the morning sky. Regardless, all of the prisoners were jovial, exploding with anticipation - all, except me. I was confused and saddened by my thoughts. I had survived five years in the camps. One more week or two would not kill me, and this would enable me to meet with Galina one more time. Suddenly I felt I would not mind staying just a little longer.

Just before five o'clock, the end of the working day, an amazing thing happened. Without fear of the consequences, and disregarding the guards, Galina stormed through the gate to find me. Down in the yard, I stood, watching her in disbelief. I felt like my feet grew roots and anchored me to the ground from the surprise. She rushed toward me, carrying a small farewell gift. She flew into my arms and kissed me, not paying any attention to anyone. Before I could say anything, she ran just as quickly out through the gate, tears streaming down her face. I stood there dumbfounded and confused. I felt like saying "to hell with the world and to anyone who did not approve of what just happened". I looked around to see who had witnessed this emotional event. Vanya was but a short distance away. He just smiled, winked at me and did not say a word. I put the parcel under my jacket as the workers started gathering in the yard. Our work in this place was finished. Our work in this country was finished. I shook hands with the civilian workers as they wished all of us a safe journey home. I approached Vanya to greet him and thank him for his help and his fairness. He asked me, "Were the Kazbek cigarettes from the lady?" I nodded my head and replied "Da."[56] He smiled and said, "Yuri Molodyets."[57] It made me feel good to receive his approval of Galina.

I was anxious to pay one last visit to Mama Marusa. She was at her post in the control booth and greeted me as I entered. "Drastvuijte, Yura" she said softly. I hugged the friendly old soul, and thanked her for her understanding and for the postal service she provided between Galina and me.

---

[56] Yes.

[57] George, good man.

After I released her, she stepped closer to me again, smelling the perfume on me. With a sly and knowing grin she asked, "It's Galina?" I blushed and replied, "Yes, Mama Marusa, it is hers." Even though the guards must have seen Galina pass them and rush into the yard, they never said a word to me about it. I was relieved. I prayed she would suffer no consequences. I suddenly felt tremendously drained after the emotional and unexpected farewell to Galina. We had been called for the last time to climb on board the trucks, but my knees were weakened, and I had a sick feeling in my stomach. Eventually, I found the strength to board the truck, and as I sat in my usual spot, I wondered if Galina would come. Then I spotted her on the sidewalk in the distance. I fought back my tears. This time she did not walk by as she usually did, but rather stood there crying. The engines rumbled, and as the trucks began to pull away, she waved to me frantically and did not stop until the trucks had turned the corner and we lost visual contact. With tear-filled eyes, I took one last look at the beautiful chestnut trees dressed in their autumn colors. The falling leaves signalled the twilight of summer's splendour as well as the end of our romance.

The next morning we were transported, again by truck, from Lager 85/11 back to the bunker Lager where the final preparations for our departure were taking place. We were allowed to bath, and received clean underwear and decent clothes. We were quite happy with the events that had taken place thus far, but we did not get overly excited. We still found it difficult to believe the Russians. Who knew where we might end up in spite of all these preparations? After all, it was possible these events were designed to keep us under control during a Lager transfer. If they made us believe we were going home, when we were really destined to go elsewhere, they would find no resistance. The thought of this possibility made us very apprehensive.

A few days prior to our scheduled transport, I found out my name was actually on a list to go home. This information seemed too incredible, and my skepticism tempered my excitement.

The autumn sun burned the morning fog off to reveal hundreds of prisoners gathering at the gates, hours before the scheduled departure time. This was the day we had dreamt about so many times during the past five years. An officer began the slow process of reading out an alphabetical list of all the names of the prisoners who would be leaving. As I stood there, anxious and impatient, I recalled the incident with Eso, two years earlier. Knowing that the Russians never pronounced my name correctly, I decided not to argue with them about how they should say it. Anything close would be good enough for me. So, I listened eagerly for my name.

Suddenly, I realized the officer had passed through the names that started with the letter 'G' without calling mine. I could not believe it. It felt like my heart stopped and my stomach felt sick. What had gone wrong? Had they changed the list after all, or was it merely a mistake? A thousand questions were racing through my mind when I heard the officer call "Himmler." I immediately shouted "DA!" and moved briskly toward the gate. The officer did not know who the hell Himmler was, but Colonel Romanchuk, who stood by overseeing the procedure, did. Himmler was the highest ranking SS leader, one of Hitler's close associates.

Just as I was about to pass through the gate, he shouted, "Stoj, stoj, stoj!" and lifted his arm in front of me. He must have been thinking, "We're not going to let Himmler walk out of here just like that." I stopped. He looked at me and looked at the list then asked my age. I replied, "Dvacet-dva."[58] He realized that I could not possibly be Hitler's friend, and motioned me to go. My comrades inside and outside the gate had a great chuckle over the incident, and from then on, the nickname of 'Himmler' stuck with me, even though I did not like it very much.

Once we passed through the gate, we sat outside the barbed wire fence, five in a row, until the rest of the names were called. There were more than a thousand names, altogether. After what seemed to be hours of torturous waiting, the large group of prisoners finally began to move down the familiar road with guards on either side. We hiked past the cemetery to the industrial railway yard, the same spot we once passed daily on our way to the bread factory; the same spot where we had seen the many transport trains prepare for the journey to Siberia with their human cargo. I could not help but think that, perhaps, we were headed for a similar unwanted journey, in spite of what they had told us. My anxiety increased when I saw there were no flags or signs decorating the train. This had been the standard formality in the past for homeward-bound transports. While waiting for our turn to board the prepared boxcars, I gazed dreamily at the sun as it dipped below the horizon and painted the clouds with vivid orange and red colors. A more magnificent sunset I had never seen.

After settling into our places in the wagons, the guards pulled the heavy doors shut and locked the latches on them, further increasing my doubts that I would return home. I sat on the hay-covered floor of the wagon and tried to imagine all

---

58 Twenty-two.

the possible paths my future could take. Why did they have to close the doors? If we intended to jump from the train, where else did they think we would go but home? It was late at night, and we had been sitting and dozing in the boxcars for hours when we finally started moving. As the train gained momentum and rolled through the darkness, an occasional distant light flashed through the window, illuminating faces filled with anxiety and fear. We were unsure of which direction we were travelling, and this definitely added to our tension. A large loaf of black bread that we had received earlier was the only positive thing from our point of view.

The night was long in the slow-moving train. We sometimes stopped for what seemed to be hours, and then would continue on to an unknown destination. The excitement and uncertainty of the day's events finally got the best of me, and I collapsed into a restless sleep. I slept through the night and awoke before the first welcome light of morning shone through the small window. The terrain I could see through the little hole gave no indication of our whereabouts. We pulled through a few tiny stations, but their names were unfamiliar and provided no clues. Sometimes, the train stopped for hours to wait for nightfall before moving through larger cities. It seemed almost as though they were trying to keep our destination a secret.

Finally, we managed to make out a sign at a railway station. It read 'Lvow', which meant we were indeed travelling toward Hungary. This incredible discovery instantly destroyed all my doubts and I felt vindicated. I was ecstatic, elated, overjoyed, and relieved to realize the long journey was, at last, coming to an end. I was going home!

I suddenly remembered the words of the fortune teller, and I believed that the long journey she referred to was the one I had been taking throughout my prison years. Now the journey would soon be over. The thought of it restored my energy, and swept away my anxieties and the aches and pains of my body and soul. It had been years since I felt such vitality and hope. It was as though my heart began to beat again after years of silence. If I had ever wondered how it felt to be born again, to discover the world and behold the treasures of the earth for the first time, I knew now. My eyes were opened to the beauty and wonder which surrounded me. My lungs drew in the autumn air, and as I gazed out the window to watch the vast terrain roll by, I looked forward to the moment when we would finally reach Hungarian soil. My imagination flew high as all sorts of pictures of the welcome home flashed into my mind. My impatience was nearly unbearable.

ONE BUCKET TO ANOTHER

It was late afternoon when we reached Csap, a town on the border between the Soviet Union and Hungary. As the train inched slowly across the border, we left behind the barbed wire fences and watchtowers, signalling our entry into Hungary. We had made it! We were back in our homeland at last. Our jubilation brought handshakes and hugs, as well as tears. We instinctively began to sing our national anthem. As we sang the words, "We have been punished for our past as well as our future," we were reminded of the many times our country was nearly swallowed by the waves of the wars in the great sea of nations. Now, as we sang, fate and our history moulded this group together.

When the full length of the train had reached Hungarian soil, it stopped. Russian border guards checked the underside of every section of the train in search of any Soviet citizens who might be trying to escape from their country. When they were satisfied their search was complete, they yanked open the door of the boxcar and said to us, "Dos vidania, washi pridot."[59] They meant the Hungarian guards were coming. After a few minutes of silent anticipation, we were greeted by two Hungarian soldiers who jumped into our wagon, pointed submachine guns at us and ordered us to

---

[59] "Farewell, yours are coming" in Russian.

shut up. They stood, back to back, in the middle of the wagon, alert and watching us like hawks. We sat on the floor of the wagon in shock. This was not the welcome I had envisioned upon returning home after five years in captivity. The soldiers were wearing rounded hats, decorated with blue ribbon and the red star in the middle. Later, we learned that the soldiers were members of the infamous A.V.H. political police, the government protective force. If this new republic was the 'People's Republic', as they called it, then why would they have to set up special forces to protect the government? This question remained unanswered for many years, but we now knew why we had to travel home in closed boxcars. In the new People's Republic of Hungary, we, as prisoners of war, were regarded as undesirable enemies of the country. The Russians had sent us home in response to pressure from the American government, but the Hungarians did not know what they should do with us. They were afraid to set us free. This was my country's welcome-home reception - the country for which I was willing to die. I felt the same rage and anger possess me that I had felt in 1945 when the newspaper reported the 'first free May in Budapest'. As the train began to roll again, the door of the boxcars remained locked, and the two soldiers continued their watch glaring at us with blank, unfeeling eyes. It did not seem I had a bright future ahead in this, my homeland. It was just as the fortune teller had predicted.

It was dusk by the time the train stopped on the outskirts of Sostofurdo, once a lovely resort area. We disembarked to find ourselves surrounded by officers, dogs, and hundreds of armed soldiers. Flashing lights of army cars threw blinding lights into our eyes. We were immediately rounded up into the familiar Russian-style lineup, and as the soldiers barked orders, the line of twelve hundred men was herded down the road. Two rows of beautiful old poplars stood along each side of the road. The tall trees had likely weathered many storms and survived two wars, but I imagined their branches had never stretched over anything like this parade. While guards were spaced at five metre intervals on either side of the mass of people, more soldiers kept watch from behind the trees. No words were spoken amongst the prisoners. The only sounds were soldiers yelling, and the heavy footsteps of the gloomy group of men. We had not been accompanied by such a fortified escort for a long time, and it spoke grimly of our future. Part of the large group, including myself, was herded into an empty swimming pool. A layer of straw covered the bottom and would serve as a place for us to sleep.

Before we went to bed, though, we were called into a room to eat. Considering that we had travelled all the way from Kiev on only bread and water, we looked forward to receiving a cooked meal. A dozen ladies worked diligently to serve the food. They were curious, but only smiled a little and did not strike up any conversations, even though it was apparent they wanted to. Perhaps they had been instructed not to speak with the 'enemy'. Compared to the cabbage, millet or nettle soup I had eaten for the past five years, the Hungarian gulyas soup and the crusty white bread which was now placed before me was superb. The meal was delicious - fit for a king. I had forgotten how good a well-prepared meal could taste, so the soup I now inhaled seemed a genuine feast. After filling my stomach, my optimism returned, and I believed that, no matter what fate dealt me now, it could not be worse than the years I had just spent in captivity. I got rid of my remaining piece of Russian bread, naively thinking that I would never be hungry again.

That night, we were put through a medical checkup. We lined up in single file, and as I reached the sympathetic and distinguished-looking doctor, he asked, "Do you have any problems?" I told him that I was all right. He then asked me my age and where I had served during the war. I replied that I was 22, and that I had served in the Hunyady division. He patted my shoulder and in a soft whisper told me that his son had also served there. He seemed to want to help somehow, but knew he was unable to do anything. He wished me good luck and smiled at me with warmth and understanding: then took the stethoscope off my chest and let me go.

After the emotionally exhausting day, I settled on the hay, put my plywood suitcase under my head and tried to go to sleep. This first night on Hungarian soil did not allow me a good rest. The day's events left me agonizing for long hours over my uncertain future. I tried to transform my mind into a crystal ball that might bring into view a picture of my days to come. When that failed to work, I tried to interpret the fortune teller's warning. It was in the wee hours of the morning when I was finally escorted into the world of sleep by the unpleasant concert of my snoring comrades.

I awoke the next morning to the bright face of a cheery sun, however, it brought me little to smile about. My spirits were dampened by the realization that, after all I had survived, all the distance I had travelled, all the battles I had fought to stay alive and return home, I still had awakened in captivity. I slowly stretched and got up to walk about when I noticed the dozens of soldiers positioned in the distance about the perimeter of the resort. Still, I walked on. I came across a beautiful, natural lake. Its glassy surface was disturbed only by the graceful gliding of swans. The golden sun-shine danced on the lake, beckoning me. I pulled off my shirt, waded into the cool lake, and splashed the refreshing water on myself. It was most invigorating. My comrades soon caught up with me and told me we had been called to eat. Breakfast consisted of a cup of black, lukewarm liquid called coffee and a piece of bread - remnant's of the previous evening's supper. This was disappointing, especially after the delicious supper we had enjoyed last night. It was not the last disappointment we would experience. The most frus-trating thing was the silence of the authorities. No explana-tion or reason was given for our continued captivity, nor was any information provided regarding our future. Uncertainty seemed to remain an integral part of our life. I could only think of what form the misfortune would manifest itself in my life. Midday passed without a bit of nourishment for our souls nor for our very hungry stomachs. The aimless, news-less, uncertain time suddenly changed when we were given orders to get ready to move out. The sun was about to leave the sky and fall behind the horizon when we were assembled into a long column. We were surrounded by hundreds of sol-diers and escorted back to the train. This would be the final leg of our journey to Budapest. The trip was well timed, so that darkness would mask our faces as we peeked through the boxcar windows at the people in the railway stations. We were seasoned prisoners and were able to read the signs which indicated, with more and more certainty, that we would not be going home to our families. Our educated guesses did not fail us.

As the train pulled into the Eastern Railway station in Budapest, we found it completely empty - no civilians or rail-way workers. The area had been blocked off, and what was normally a bustling, busy place was still and quiet. The only people around were the heavily armed A.V.H.[60] men from the special forces. They lined up alongside the train, and when they opened the doors of the boxcars, we tumbled out almost into their arms. Within minutes, the empty platform between the two railway lines was packed with prisoners. The hostile soldiers shouted and used the butts of their sub-machine guns to knock the stiff prisoners into the usual five-in-a-row formation. The wide rows counted twelve hundred men and stretched the length of the train. Soon we began to shuffle toward the street, avoiding the station's main hall. The streets were blocked off, traffic halted, and not a bystander was visible.

Evening's stillness enveloped the gray four-storey buildings which lined the narrow, dimly lit streets and empty sidewalks. The silence was disturbed only by the rhythmic thumping of prisoners' footsteps as we marched across the cobblestones, sending echoes between the buildings and through alleyways. Our destination was the nearby jail which normally housed the thieves, the pickpockets and other petty criminals. Now, it would become our home. The cells were already overloaded with war prisoners just returned from the Soviet Union. Straw covered the concrete floor, and we had but a shoulder-width of space to lie in for the long, restless night. One wriggle or movement sent a ripple of tossing and turning down the row of squished bodies. The iron grill doors and windows, and the heavy sliding bars which blocked the corridors, made this imprisonment unique from our past experiences. At least in the Lagers we had the freedom and space to move about, but now we were jammed

---

[60] Allam Vedelmi Hatosag - Government Protective Agency.

in tiny barred cells with dozens of other inmates. It was a sure test of our tolerance and self control. Looking out the window, I saw the tall building of what was once the National Medicare office. On its side, a huge red star was lit up by neon tubes. I came to the somber conclusion that as long as that star shone brightly overhead, my future here would be anything but bright.

Imprisoned now, within my own country, I had plenty of time to think, to review the past, and contemplate the future. The grave words of the old fortune teller echoed in my head. "You won't have a good future at home", she had warned. Fear had crept over my skin since we had entered Hungary, for time after time, her predictions had become reality.

Via the established communication system, we were informed of the arrival of still more prisoners. Later on, I learned that due to pressure from the American government, the Russians were forced to release twelve thousand unwanted Hungarian prisoners. Of course, these prisoners also had to be locked up, although the jails could hardly accommodate such numbers.

Our only escape from the smothering stench of the cell was the few minutes we spent each morning washing ourselves in a stone basin in the corridor. The few strides to the sink, the cold water and some quick arm movements refreshed my body and left me feeling somewhat invigorated. I often tried to slip back into line and repeat the 'walk of the life' to the sink, but the attentive guards usually caught me and chased me back to my cell. This excitement had to last for the rest of the day, for only when we received our food rations did the painful boredom of the passing time break. The food itself was no better than what we had received in

Russia. Hunger took our hands again with a faithful grip. I now cursed myself for carelessly tossing away the pieces of bread I had brought with me from Russia.

The door of the cell rattled, and opened to the silhouette of the guard. His voice shot in. "Sorakozo"[61] he said. Instantly, the quiet cells became like beehives. "Bring your stuff," he included in the order. In no time, we stood in the corridor ready to go. We rushed down the narrow concrete staircases to assemble in the yard. The small cobblestone courtyard was surrounded by the four-storey prison building. Its simple inner facade was broken by the rows of barred windows. Only a small patch of gray sky was visible, but it was enough to lift my spirits as I took deep 'schlucks' of the fresh November air. Soon all I could smell was the exhaust from the army trucks as they rolled in and lined up, waiting for us to board. We were hurriedly packed into the guarded canvas-covered trucks and began to roll through the streets of Budapest. Hidden beneath the canvas, our presence was unknown to the street goers, perhaps even to relatives who might be walking close by. I listened to the familiar ring of the streetcar bells, and the squeals and roars of the traffic. Only the thickness of the canvas separated us from the outside world, the real world, but it might as well have been a stone wall. The truck travelled only a short distance it seemed, when it halted and lurched backward to stop again. A guard lifted the canvas cover and opened the tailgate to let us out. I jumped off the truck to find myself in a huge building filled with noisy people. They were the overflow prisoners, recently released by the Russians. When I looked up at the curious faces, I spotted my dear childhood friends from

---

[61] Hungarian word meaning "assemble."

Felsogod. There they stood before me like pictures in a book - awestruck, their faces masks of surprise and relief. I was in complete shock. Coincidence? Perhaps, but I suddenly felt as though some Higher Being was toying with me. To find one another in this crowded place after five long years and thousands of kilometres had fallen between us, seemed impossible. We had no hope of ever meeting again, but now, I stood in front of my friends once more stunned, dumbfounded and deep down, a bit proud because somehow, with God's help, I had made it also. We looked at each other for a moment, paralyzed by the amazement when Szani, my pal, said, "Gyuri, What the hell are you doing here? You should have croaked in Bryansk!" We had been separated in Komarichi in the fall of 1945. At that time, I was in poor physical condition. They were certain I had been buried somewhere with thousands of others in unmarked graves in Russia. But I had promised myself that even if no one else made it home, I would. Now, here I was and so were they. Certainly, we had seen better days in Budapest, but at last, we were home, together again after five years of separation.

The building we were in normally housed hundreds of domestic animals during the annual agricultural exhibition staged each spring. The cement floor was covered with straw, the same as it would be for the animals, and we were herded about and packed in just the same. We nudged and pushed to gain a little more elbow room. One didn't want the breath of his neighbour in his face any longer than necessary. The noise, the crowd, everything was secondary, though. Tamas, Szani, Paul and I were too anxious to tell one another our stories from the past five years to notice anyone but the four bright and weathered faces which now gleamed united. We laughed and talked, stretching stories and truths into the wee hours of the morning until we could finally chatter no more.

In the morning, we received a bun weighing about half a kilogram and the first of three bowls of Russian-style corn-meal soup that we would be given throughout the day. We huddled together as if to ward off any chance of separation again, and succumbed to a weary slumber. There was no word as to why or how long we would be held in this place. The A.V.H. men continued to keep us under heavy surveillance. From time to time, an officer would come in, accompanied by several guards. He would call out someone's name. The named individual was forced to gather his belongings, and without a single word to anyone, he was whisked away to an unknown place. Much later, I learned that the new Communist regime was quick to learn the methods of their big brothers - anyone who was suspected as a potential threat to the new order was sent to a labour camp once again.

Day after day, some of our comrades would vanish in such a way. We discovered that they were transported to Hungarian work camps such as Kazincbarcika, Inota, or Recsk. They served another five to six years of forced labour without a sentence or even a trial. Some welcome home!

Two months went by, and we lived out the last days of 1950 in this hell-hole. Yet another uneventful and rather sad Christmas drifted by as quietly as a snowflake in a winter breeze. Naturally, the Communists discouraged any form of religious activity, so it was out of the question to celebrate Christmas in the traditional manner. I was a mere 27 kilometres from my family - such a short distance - but they might as well have been on another planet under the circumstances. They did not even know I was back in Hungary. This most important of religious holidays was completely ignored, never mind celebrated, but the authorities did do a terrific job of promoting brotherhood and equality. The bathroom facilities were located outside. There was always a long lineup of men who had to go. We had to wait inside the building, for only ten at a time were allowed to go outside to the latrine. The guards were forever watchful. Severe constipation added to our agony as we waited for our turn to race outside. When finished, we were escorted back to the building, and the next ten were on their way. The lineup was constant throughout the day, so we had to plan ahead for our urges - there was no room for a last-minute call.

The officers recognized we had not had an opportunity to wash ourselves. Water was not readily available though, so they organized a bath which was as primitive as those in Russia and, to some extent, worse. Again, we lined up and stood for what seemed like hours. When we finally reached the front of the line, we were each given one army dish full of water to take a bath. In the middle of the room sat a wooden keg, half-full of gray, murky water. We had to step into the knee deep, soupy water and, with some help from our comrades, bathe ourselves, using the clean water sparingly and carefully. Starting with my head, I washed myself section by section. I did not particularly enjoy this 'communist' style of bathing! It was ironic, in a sense, to have to squish myself into a keg of dirty water to bathe in this, in a city famous for its wonderful and numerous therapeutic mineral baths.

One day, at meal time, I watched with familiar anxiety as two prisoners approached, carrying the big tin kettle which held the corn soup. Everyone watched their every step, as they waited impatiently for the dinner. Suddenly, before our eyes, one of them slipped, lost his balance, dragging the other prisoner and the heavy load of soup down to the straw-covered floor. The thick cornmeal soup flowed out of the pot like hot lava. Thankfully, most of it oozed over someone's blanket rather than onto the straw floor. It was a fraction of a second before the frozen panic of the hungry prisoners erupted in a wild fight for every drop of the soup. Within minutes, the prisoners cleaned the floor and the blanket, lapping up the soup like dogs and using fingers as spoons. By the time the frenzy had died out, not one speck of corn was visible anywhere. It was a sad sight to witness such animal behaviour in Hungary, a country where agriculture had always abounded and food had been plentiful.

In the days that I spent here, I tried to keep the days interesting by getting to know some of the other members of the prison population. My friends introduced me to two individuals. One was D.M., a Jewish boy who was taken by the Russians during the liberation of Hungary. I found his story fascinating. He was watching a movie in a theatre one night. When it was finished, he got up to leave. As he opened the door to the theatre, he saw that about a dozen Russian army trucks waited outside. Every man was grabbed as he departed the theatre and taken for a 'malinki robot'. D.M. tried to show the officers his papers and his Swedish passport. His passport, granted to him by Raoul Wallenberg, was supposed to protect him from the Germans, but the Russian soldier tore his papers to pieces and shoved him into the truck. The 'malinki robot' turned into five years of labour in the prison camps in Russia. In the camp, D.M. vehemently protested, but in vain; and when he started a hunger strike, the Russians increased his sentence to ten years in a hard-labour camp. He had to live his life among the thieves, murderers and other misfits of Russian society. He spent only a few years here, though, before he was sent back to the war prison camp where he became a well-liked brigade leader of an SS group. The people worked under his leadership in perfect harmony. When he finally arrived home with the rest of us, he should have been released immediately, but instead, the A.V.H. kept him and treated him as an enemy of the system. Eventually, we lost contact with him in prison. We never did learn what became of him. It was discouraging to hear of his struggles and trials he had faced for no apparent reason. Sure as hell, he was no Nazi, but it didn't matter to the Red Army who took people indiscriminately from the street. There was nothing anyone could do.

The other individual was a seventy-five-year-old retired army officer. When the Russians occupied Budapest, he decided to put on his old army uniform and take a walk on the promenade. They took him too, and he was placed in captivity for five years. Some retirement! His uniform was confiscated during his prison years, but he still made an effort to mark his rank with pencil on the ragged clothes the Russians gave him. He was proud of his past as an officer and his rank of colonel. Every morning, he lined up to go to the latrine, but as soon as he was outside, he made a break, running around the large building with the guards chasing him. After completing a lap of the building, running, dodging, jumping and grinning all the while, he would triumphantly announce that he had completed his morning exercises. He seemed a bit looney, but after five years of captivity and hunger, who could blame him? It was a miracle he was still alive.

Another high ranking officer, who was from my home town, had survived the camps and had returned home from Russia, but the Hungarian Communists refused to release him. He was a well-respected leader in our small community, but because he was a Baron, the Communists found him undesirable. I later told his wife the news that he was in Budapest, but there was nothing we could do. He died in that jail only miles from his home.

Still another officer, a doctor, managed to smuggle a list of the names of dead prisoners home in his boot. One would think such an effort would deserve commendation, but he, too, never made it outside the walls of that jail in Budapest. For five years, we had all dreamt of returning home to Hungary. Now, we faced elimination by our own people in our own country. If we would have known what fate would bring to us in Communist Hungary, we would have found it easier and more dignified to die in Russia a long time ago. The temptation to give up had always been with us. It would not have been difficult, especially in the winter time, to just lie down and go to sleep in the cold. We would have frozen within a short time without any pain.

Throughout the fall and the early winter of 1950, we remained hidden in the agricultural complex. In late February of the following year, we were transported back to the jail. Here I patiently awaited the dealer's next card, which at that time, could have been another year of labour camp or freedom. My comrades, Tamas and Paul, had already been released, and I clung to the hope that I, too, would soon be able to go home.

For a short time each morning, the curious spring sun peeked directly into our cell through the barred window, splashing lines across the floor and walls. It always found us waiting. Our rows were picked by that time. Some of the prisoners were released; others were transferred to concentration camps.

The morning of the eighth of March came, and I decided not to shave. I would leave it for the next day, I thought, which would be my 24th birthday. Before noon, a few prisoners were taken out of our cell. That would be it for the day, we thought, so we lay back to wait for yet another day.

In the late afternoon, our cell door opened again. A guard stood by as an officer called a few names again. "Kovács Józef, Bartha Károly, Rigó István, Gemer, Gyorgy ..." When I heard my name, my stomach flipped. I jumped into my boots in a panic and gathered my belongings with shaking hands. Within a minute, I stood trembling, ready to go - where to, I did not know. Two other prisoners and I followed the young officer down the long corridors, the guard behind us.

An eternity seemed to pass as we waited outside the officers' office, while he prepared some papers. Finally he called me into his office. He handed me a piece of paper to fill out. My hands were still shaking. I scribbled in the information as best I could and returned it to him. He signed it, and handed it back to me stating gruffly, "This is yours." It was "The Document" - the ticket to freedom - that piece of paper the Russians had dangled like a carrot before us five years ago while they led us to the train that would take us to captivity. That elusive document was what had kept us in line when we had a chance to leave the line and just go home. What I had gone through - all for a few precious lines that contained only my personal data and the words of my release!

The officer gave me a twenty forint[62] bill which was enough to purchase a train ticket to Felsogod. Before I left his office, he looked into my eyes, hatred all over his face, and said, "If you don't want to come back here, you'd better keep

---

[62] Hungarian currency.

your mouth shut!" I looked at him for a moment, turned and left without a word. As I walked down the hall, the heels of the guard's boots echoing behind me, I thought of the officer and wondered how the hell he had been transformed into the uniformed animal he now was. The guard opened the heavy door at the end of the corridor, and I found myself standing in the street. The door slammed shut behind me, and I was alone.

HOMEWARD BOUND

I stood for a few seconds in disbelief. The guards were gone. There were no bayonets or gun barrels pointing at me. No orders were being shouted at me. I was suddenly free to walk away, to disappear in the shadow of the gray wall and the quiet of the street. My steps were hesitant, and I was afraid to disturb the late afternoon hush with the sound of my boots on the cobblestones. Perhaps, subconsciously I was afraid to step into this strange and different world with its 'new freedom'. I should have been dancing down the street with the joy of being free, but a new fear now gripped my heart. Rumours had abounded in the prison of the ruling regime that silences its people with the threat of death. I was wary and uncertain of what danger my steps might lead me to. The only ray of light that guided me through the darkest of shadows, was the hope that within a few hours I would see my dear mother again.

It was a strange feeling, not being followed, but deep down I still did not feel free. I walked away from the prison walls until I passed by the Eastern Railway Station. I slowed to lose myself in the crowd of people that bustled up and down the street.

I followed the main street toward the Western Railway Station, gazing down the familiar streets at the buildings, the people, the colors. There was my old school, standing tall as ever. I remembered the first anxious steps I took toward this building, accompanied by my dear mother. For four years after that, I had walked the same way until I finished high school. The street names had changed. This was now Lenin Ring Road, and the square that I had once passed daily was now called November 7 Square. I felt strange, uneasy, and worried about the future that lay ahead. It was hard enough to be oppressed, humiliated, and forced to submit to the enemy, but to also witness the obliteration of the heritage of my country, to have to accept the Russian's rules was too much for me to take. What link did I have to these Russian names printed on the signs, except the five years that I had just been through. How could I not feel angry as I walked down a street named after the Red Army? - the same Red Army that had raped my country and herded me, along with thousands of others, to captivity under the guise of liberation. My anger and bitter hatred toward the Russians and what they had done to my country, welled up inside me as I strode down the sidewalk toward the train station.

I wore black pants, a white cotton shirt and a three quarter length khaki officer's coat, with a black hat atop my head. It certainly was not the everyday attire of any man on the sidewalks of Budapest, and I felt like a conspicuous outsider, some sort of outlandish tourist that attracted attention despite efforts to blend in. I carried a small wooden box in which was some cheap Russian cologne and presents for my mother and sisters. I was presented with the box when I had won the shot put competition. I also carried a metal discus which I had taken from the sports field. People in the street stared at me, but no one said a word. I must have looked like a ghost from the past. In the railway station, I bought a one-way ticket to Felsogod. The final stage of this five-year journey over thousands of kilometres, was about to be concluded with a 27-kilometre train ride. I boarded and sat down, waiting for the final trek to begin. Again, memories of my high school years and vivid pictures of those pleasant days danced before my eyes. I saw myself dressed in the traditional navy blue school uniform, complete with hat with an emblem on it. I was full of hope then and confident about my future. After sometime, the train finally began to move, and I watched with curiosity each building in each little station along the way. When the conductor came, I noticed a red star on his hat, instead of the red, white and green Hungarian emblem. I had seen enough red stars in my time in the camps, and now, in my own country, again set eyes on that dreadful symbol which appeared hand in hand with the hardship and suffering of millions of people.

The train stopped. It was Felsogod. My heart pounded in my chest until I thought I would faint. I could barely contain myself. I was so nervous and excited to get off the train. Immediately, I noticed that the rows of well-groomed acacia trees which had shaded the station were gone. In their place was trampled, brown grass. I wanted to take it all in though. I stepped off the train to the asphalt pad below. It was nearly dark, and I walked slowly down the street where I used to run barefoot with my friends. The dirt roads were in bad shape, and I could see no signs of construction or improvements since the war. It looked as though time had stood still under the Communist curse. As I turned the corner, I could barely make out my house down the street. My legs felt weak, and my stomach twisted and turned with such anxiety that I thought I would fall down in a heap on the street, but I kept walking. That house had stored so much warmth and happiness for me in the past, but now, I could see that our home was deteriorating. The stucco was falling off the walls, and the roof had been repaired with several different types of tiles until it looked like a patchwork quilt. The appearances of the homes usually gave an indication of the owner's financial situation. Now, not only our home, but the whole village reflected the poor state the country was in.

The front gate was latched inside, so I jumped the fence and approached the entrance of the house. I peered through the glass door to see my dear mother, working in the kitchen. My heart was beating in my throat as I pushed the door open and entered the house. I had hoped to happily surprise her, and I expected some sort of welcoming ovation, but instead I received a long silence. My mother's face held a curious look. I suddenly realized she did not know who I was. I said, "Mama, it's me". She kept looking at me and said, "Tibor?" "No," I replied, "it is Gyuri, your son!". Instantly she broke into tears. Opening her arms, we met in a tight embrace. "I am home, home for good, Mama," I whispered. "No more tears." She felt terrible that she had not recognized me, and hurried to explain that the authorities had notified her of my death. I was supposedly hit by a train.

The past five years of struggle and despair had left their imprint on her face. She appeared tired and aged, and her eyes revealed a sadness that only a woman who felt the pain she had, could understand. Her voice was soft. She spoke to me in a tone that reminded me that, these days, the walls had ears. She showed me the heel print of the Soviet soldier's boot on the white door of our pantry. It was a lasting sign of the days of their liberation. Not much more was said of our experiences of the past years. There was no reason to tear open the healing wounds of the past, but I did tell her that I had been locked up less than 30 kilometres away for the last few months prior to my release. There are no words for the expression which swept over her face.

The Russian authorities had lied to the relatives of the soldiers so that they would not search for their loved ones who had failed to return after the war. Thanks to the Americans, who kept good records of our whereabouts, and investigated discrepancies in numbers. They pressured the Russians to respect the points of the peace treaty which ordered the return of war prisoners.

For an instant, a flash of the agent who questioned me in Kiev crossed my mind. He approached me with questions, seemingly to verify his extensive knowledge of our Lager, our numbers and our nationalities.

Later on in the evening, my sister Eszter came home. She lived just a few houses down the street, so she popped over several times a day to visit mother. As she opened the door, I caught her eye. She looked at me, but didn't seem to have any clue as to who I was. She told my mother that she would be back later, then turned and left. Mama winked at me and let her go without saying a thing. When she got to the gate, Mama called her back and said, "Don't you recognize this man?" Eszter shook her head and just looked at me. "This is your brother Gyuri!" Mama shouted with delight. Eszter looked like someone had slapped her. Then, doubt washed over her face. She kept looking at me, examining me. The last time she had seen me was in December of 1944. I had changed somewhat from the seventeen-year-old school kid I once was. I was now a frail and weathered man with a total of six years of prison life behind me. I would later find that everyone who knew me would comment on the strange expression on my face. Finally, I passed Eszter's test and she drew me into a warm hug. It was certainly good to be home at last.

FALSE FREEDOM

Despite the soft pillow, the clean white sheets, and the warm cozy comfort of my bed, my sleep was disturbed by wild dreams of my prison life. Many years would pass before these recurring nightmares would finally cease. I tossed and turned that night until finally I sat up, wide awake. I spent the remainder of my first night at home sitting, staring at the walls which now enclosed me in a welcome warmth.

The next morning, I celebrated my birthday by waltzing up and down the quiet, familiar streets of Felsogod, savouring my freedom. It felt incredibly strange to walk alone - almost naked somehow. No guards followed me, no other prisoners lined up all around me. I was able to turn at the street corner and go whichever direction I pleased. It would have seemed so basic, so simple to anyone else, but to me, it was the most incredible birthday gift I could or would ever receive. With slow, easy strides, I wandered down to the river to greet my old friend, the beloved Danube. On the way, I sucked in huge breaths of the spring air. A mixture of flowers and green grass with the distant scent of the river floated under my nose. Across the water, the bluish profile of the Pilis mountain range stood looming in the distance. I found myself back in the place of my fondest childhood memories, discovering what it was like to be content and carefree once more. After a most glorious walk, I returned home to find my mother preparing my favourite meal - noodles with poppy seeds and sugar. Mama and I enjoyed the meal together, laughing and reminiscing. We talked for hours, sharing news of old friends, but I spared her the stories of my years in captivity. I did not want to spoil the bliss of the peaceful and sentimental evening. In the days that followed, Mama was careful to prepare simple meals, avoiding the traditionally rich and heavy Hungarian foods until I could tolerate such a diet again. We heard incidents of prisoners returning home, only to die from the good food that ecstatic relatives prepared for them. After all, throughout my prison life, I hardly ever ate any meat. Even then, it was in minute quantities. On rare occasions, I was given small bits of salted fish, but it seemed barely enough to be felt as I swallowed. I was more accustomed to tasteless, watery soups. The famous chicken paprikas or goulash dishes were certainly not on the menu, except in our dreams.

I was eager to return to school or work so I could begin to melt back into the life of a regular civilian. Uncle Gyula was still supporting Mama, and it was high time I took on that responsibility. Upon returning to the Tungsram factory where I had worked during my summer vacation in 1944, I was surprised to learn that my contract had not been officially cancelled; therefore, I retained the right to continue to work there. When I stepped through the doors of the factory once again, I was given an ecstatic greeting by my old colleagues, many of whom had survived the Nazi concentration camps. No doubt we had shared some common experiences, but I had not forgotten the officer's warning when I was freed from the jail, and I did not discuss the time I spent in the camps. The daily train ride from Felsogod to Budapest and back again was tiresome, but was a welcome change from my journeys pulling the sleighs in Bryansk, so I travelled back and forth happily each day. At the factory, I produced blueprints of mechanical drawings, and although the work was rather monotonous, it was easy. I looked forward to earning enough money to help Mama, and to buy some decent clothes for myself.

My next wish was to return to my track and field club where I had spent many a day training under the guidance of professional coaches. With great enthusiasm, I tore open the door to the dressing room only to find rows upon rows of uniforms and hats decorated with red stars. I felt as though I would be sick, and sat down on the hard bench before my knees could buckle beneath me. I soon learned that the club now served the needs of the Internal Ministry workers of the new regime. The young athletes were physically trained by the new regime, then given administrative jobs in either the police force or the fire department. I was not wanted there anymore, but I continued to attend the training sessions simply because I enjoyed training. It did not take very long to find out that my physical capabilities were at an all-time low. The years in the camps had taken their toll on my body. I was weak and lacked endurance, I felt tired and run down.

My Olympic dreams faded, and I realized that my chances of making it to the Games as a competitor were slim to none. Despite my disappointment, I continued to crave the training atmosphere and the magic of competition. Track and field was like a vitamin to me. Exerting my body nourished my spirit, and brought fulfillment and satisfaction into my life. The best years of my youth had been spent in the prison camp, though, and this was certainly not the ideal preparation for realizing an Olympic dream; therefore, I redirected my energies to pursue the field of coaching. I kept telling myself that although I would be unable to excel to the level that would allow me to achieve my ultimate goal - to compete in the Olympics - as a coach I might be able to inspire and help someone else to achieve their goals. This would be my reward. With renewed enthusiasm, I attended every training session, eagerly listening and learning from the other coaches. This goal gave substance and direction to my life, and counterbalanced my most unsatisfying work in the factory.

A few days had passed before I was able to arrange to meet with my childhood friends, Tamas and Csibo at Tamas' grandmother's home. Csibo was the first to arrive at her house and was sitting in the living room when I arrived. Tamas' grandmother greeted me at the door, showed me into the living room and left. Csibo did not recognize me, and so, as I had with my mother and sister a few days earlier, I simply said "Good morning," and sat down across from him in the small room. With some hesitation, he acknowledged my greeting. We sat for a few long minutes in complete silence before he finally stated with purpose, "Gyuri will come shortly. He has just come home from the prison camp. We are supposed to meet him here." I nodded my head, barely able to contain my laughter.

Tamas arrived moments later. His face instantly exploded into a huge smile. "Dear Gyuri!" he cried loudly, and he grabbed me up in a rough bear hug. I watched Csibo carefully as Tamas crushed me in his strong arms and repeatedly slapped me on the back. Csibo's eyes grew as big as saucers, and his mouth dropped open. He was astonished that he had not recognized me and ran over to join the embrace. We all had a big laugh, and began to reminisce about the times we had spent together up until the last day of the war, and discussed what we had encountered while we were separated for so many years. Csibo had managed to reach the American side and was taken into an American prison camp about the same time as Tamas and I fell into Russian hands. Despite the warning of the officer to not discuss our backgrounds, we were close and trusting friends, and felt secure in sharing our memories and comparing experiences of our prison lives from both the American and the Russian sides.

Three weeks after my return to Felsogod, I arrived home after the day's work and training to be greeted by Mama. She wore a concerned look on her face and held a letter in her hand. I took the envelope, and a strange numbness gripped me as I realized it was from the A.V.H. authorities. The words of the fortune teller rang through my head again: "You will return from the long journey, but you won't have a good future in your homeland." My hands trembled as I struggled to open the envelope. I finally managed to extract the contents. I unfolded what appeared to be a standard form letter, but the heading leapt out at me. "Police Order" it said, and typed below was my name, birth date, place of birth, and my mother's name and address. The form continued:

You are being placed under police surveillance and are to adhere to the points which follow. These conditions take effect and must be met immediately upon receipt of this police order.

The person under police surveillance:

Must not leave, without permission of the local police, the community which is designated by the authorities as his permanent address.

Must report to the local police station on the Sunday of each week at 09:00 hours.

Must not leave the premises of his home between the hours of 22:00 and 05:00.

Must not visit any public places, or government houses, and may not participate in meetings, public gatherings or demonstrations.

Must not walk on main streets or in squares which are used by the general public, nor may he use any type of vehicle.

Must not send telegrams or use the telephone. Mail and parcels received or sent are subject to police inspection.

Is forbidden to communicate with people outside his immediate family or living environment unless in the presence of a designated person to be named by the police.

Must not have any printed banners, documents, or illustrations in his possession which, in the case of circulation, might disturb or be dangerous to the public order.

Should the named subject violate the above points, he shall be jailed for a period of two months, unless during a time of war when he shall be jailed for a period of six months; however, one does have the option of paying a fine, to be determined by the police, as an alternative to serving the second six-month sentence.

This police surveillance is necessary for the protection and security of the country. With the understanding, your presence without these

restrictions, in the view of the public order, public security and vital government interests,
would be a threat and, for economical reasons,
undesirable, I order the police surveillance over
you and the connected restrictions which affect
your personal freedom.

Dated in Budapest on this 27th day of
March, 1951.

Signed: S. K. R. Major

Pest Province Police Office

It came like lightning from a blue sky. The freedom I
had found at last survived no more than three weeks. I was
devastated. I now looked hopelessly into a future which I had
once dreamily envisioned during my walks and before sleep
draped over me at night.

Reality struck me with a stiff hand, and I realized that
I could no longer saunter down the main street of my beloved
village, nor could I cheer at the soccer games or see a movie
at the local theatre. I couldn't even jump on my bicycle and
peddle down to the Danube. Here, in my own village, in my
own country, I had suddenly become an undesirable, a threat
to the country. Only a short while ago, in my naive innocence, I had been prepared to die for this country. Now, I felt
trapped within its borders. My release from the prisons in
the Soviet Union had set me free from one place of misery,
only to land in yet another. Hungary was now a Soviet-con-
trolled satellite state which exercised strict Communist rules.
I found myself in the midst of a camp fenced in by its international borders.

From this point on, I was watched and informed of
what I could and could not do. I had to request police per-

mission to travel from Felsogod to Budapest so I could work. At least once every other night, at varying times between 10:00 p.m. and 5:00 a.m., the police would rap furiously at the door of our house to ensure I was not breaking curfew. The policemen always travelled in pairs with rifles slung over their shoulders. It was not enough that they set their piercing eyes upon my sleepy face when I appeared at the door. On the contrary, they would routinely push their way in, sit down uninvited, only to fire a multitude of accusing questions at me. They hung on my every word, looking for any morsel of doubt or hesitation like ravenous dogs waiting for a scrap to fall from the table, but I knew better than to break the rules. It took supreme concentration to answer the prodding, calculative questions without giving the men the slightest chance to accuse me of disobeying the rules. I was extremely cautious not to incriminate myself with careless responses. I remained one play ahead of them in these nightly mental chess battles, and I answered all the questions with a cheerful disposition even though I despised these regular invasions of my home.

At the factory, I was demoted from my position in the printing room to performing the most menial tasks in the machine shop. I repeatedly loaded, pushed and unloaded a wagon, delivering various supplies to work stations around the huge plant. I worked with a multitude of distinguished, well educated people who had previously held leading positions in ministries, businesses, educational institutes and various public offices. Now, they too, pushed wagons with me. The operation in the factory was run by trusted party members and opportunists, while the actual physical labour was assigned to the intellectuals, the educated people. They had been stamped as 'undesirable' and, because of their independence and knowledge, were considered enemies, threats to the new order. Their university degrees and high ranks meant nothing now. Their fate was in the hands of the rulers of the new regime.

I went to work each day with a 'Rakosi Sandwich' in my lunch pail, which consisted of bread spread with lard and onion. This lunch-time delight was named sarcastically after Prime Minister Rakosi, the new despised Communist head of Hungary's government. I worked at the factory for two forints 88 fillers an hour. This was barely enough to survive on. My monthly wages would buy a pair of cheap shoes, but only if I could sacrifice my groceries for the month. Life continued to be a struggle, a new battle for food and freedom. The only things that gave me pleasure were my family and my love for athletics.

One day, when I returned home from work, I found Mama sitting at the kitchen table, her head in her hands. She seemed terribly distraught. Without stopping to remove my coat or boots, I knelt beside her and wrapped my arm about her shoulders. "What's wrong Mama?" I asked. A tear streamed down her cheek as she produced a draft notice from the army. I thought I had served my time. Now this?! I read it over and over again until the sickness I felt in my stomach overwhelmed me. The message was clear. Within thirty-six hours, I was to report to the nearest army unit in Vac, ten kilometres from Felsogod. My service would not be for more than three months I thought. This was the usual tour length for soldiers who had already served time in the army. Mama was sobbing now, and I tried to calm her. "Mama" I said, "If I am trusted enough to serve in the army, the police surveillance will have to end." I believed this and hoped that this call to service would finally wipe my slate clean so that I could live freely in my own country.

The next day, after an affectionate and heart-wrenching farewell, I left. Mama stood in front of our house by the gate and waved her tear-soaked handkerchief until I turned the corner. After a short train ride to Vac, I walked to the army post. Under my arms I packed a small parcel of food that Mama had prepared for me. Many other people had already congregated in small groups in the yard and were talking excitedly to one another.

I studied the people's faces as I waded through the crowd until I finally laid eyes on a familiar face. It was Paul from the bread factory in Kiev. I continued to glance about me, and soon I met Tamas and Csibo. After jubilant handshakes and bear hugs, I grew more comfortable knowing that whatever happened now, at least I would not be alone. It was amazing to think that since our early childhood soccer games, Tamas, Csibo and I had served in the army, survived the prison camps, been put in jail, and now we were once again drawn together here. It seemed we were like magnets to one another.

We stuck together and began to ask questions, trying to find out more about what had brought us together with all these people. Most of the other men were younger kids who had just reached the minimum age to be drafted into the army. Some were the sons of high ranking officers of the old army. Others were the boys of wealthy farmers, more commonly known as Kulaks. Still others had parents who were landowners or who held influential positions, serving the old regime. We concluded that since all of us had been declared 'undesirable elements' we were, in fact, not being drafted into the regular army. The next thought was terrifying - if we were not destined for army service after all, what did the authorities have planned for us? What could possibly be next? I sensed the 'bucket' was about to tip over again. After about an hour of torturous waiting, a corporal ordered us to march to the railway station to board a train headed for Budapest via Felsogod.

When the train rolled into the quiet station of my home town, I fiercely fought my urge to jump off and run home, for I knew that I would be hunted down and would face severe consequences. I could not believe that I found myself in such a situation again. After a brief stop, the train rolled again, and I gazed out the window at the familiar sites and the rows of beautiful trees.

As the train cleared the station, a moving picture began to roll in my mind. There was me, as a child, playing with my brothers and sisters, running barefoot with my friends, staging mini-Olympics in the nearby empty lot. I visualized the theatrical productions we had staged in our backyard. Blankets draped over ropes that had been slung between the fruit trees of our backyard served as curtains, and any clothes or towels we could sneak from Mama's cupboards served as costumes. The character roles were distributed among the eager actors and actresses. Of course, no one ever wanted to be the audience, so we coerced one of our little girl-friends who was unable to speak, into playing that role. Although she was reluctant, she watched our performances patiently as the only member of our audience, and rewarded our brilliant acting with enthusiastic applause.

Suddenly the train squealed and lurched to a halt in the Western Railway Station in Budapest. My daydreams faded away as I stepped off the train. From here, we marched down the street toward the Eastern Railway station - the same station at which I had arrived from the Soviet Union less than a year ago. A thousand thoughts seemed to race through my head. What the hell was wrong with this stupid world? Why did I have to go through this again?! We boarded the train, and as it began pulling out of the station, we were certain we were heading east. A rumour that we were being taken back to the Soviet Union to the labour camps spread quickly among the people, and desperate fear and panic gripped us all. My world seemed to collapse around me as I realized that this might, indeed, be the end for me. I could not go back to face another unknown number of years in forced labour. I would jump from the train first, even if it cost me my life. The events of my life flooded my mind until they ran into one another in a blurry watercolor of memories and emotions. Soon it would all be over, I thought.

THE HUNGARIAN LABOUR CAMP

Once the train cleared the city limits, it turned south, and we realized we could not be travelling to Zahony - a city on the Hungarian-Soviet border. It was as if an incredible weight had suddenly been lifted from my shoulders. We were not heading back to Russia. The relief this knowledge brought was accompanied by a new trepidation, though.

After approximately a two-hour voyage, the train pulled into the station in the city of Hodmezovasarhely. We were ordered to disembark. We then marched to another huge army camp. The first 'treat' was to have our heads shaven - a deliberate form of humiliation. Since we were labelled as the 'enemy', we were treated like enemies and handled with hostility from the moment we arrived.

At six o'clock each morning we started with an hour's marching drill followed by a breakfast of a black hot liquid called coffee, and a chunk of bread. The work began at eight o'clock and finished at 8 p.m., interrupted only by a half-hour break. The work included unloading trainloads of cement, gravel, and sand; mixing concrete with shovels, and pushing wheelbarrows loaded with building materials. All work was done at a feverish tempo, as dictated by the officers. At the closing of each exhausting day, we gathered in the mess hall to listen to lectures of political doctrines from uneducated superiors. Before curfew, the officers completed an inspection, rummaging through our barracks and tossing things about. The whole process was really a final opportunity each day for the officers to express their hatred for us. When the lieutenant came in each night, we stood at attention by our bunk beds. He would stride with painful slowness down the length of the barrack. Invariably, he would haul off and slam someone in the stomach with his fist and shout, "Why don't you stand still?!" Of course, there was no room for retaliation and no complaint could ever be voiced - the world of an officer went unquestioned in such cases, especially considering we were 'enemies'. We were at the mercy of the turbulent moods and violent whims of the officers, and they seemed to delight in waking us in the dead of night to unload a train that had just arrived. We worked like fools, swinging picks and shovels in the frigid night air. The usual task was to break chunks of frozen sand and gravel free from the towering heaps that sat aboard the wagons of the trains. The longer it took us to complete the job, the less time we had to sleep, so we rushed to gain as many minutes of rest as possible. After all, the alarms was always set for 6:00 the next morning, regardless of whatever work was done in the night. Three months went by. There was not even a whisper of any change in the situation or when this ordeal might possibly end.

As the harsh days rolled off the calendar, Csibo, Tamas, and I found that the hard work cemented us together. It manifested in the growing respect we had for one another. We enjoyed great admiration from the younger people as well, for our ability to maintain a solid stance under the pressure. The authorities made an effort to distinguish us from the regular army units by clothing us in the old Hungarian army uniforms. We were rather proud to wear these uniforms which bore the thousand-year-old symbol of the Hungarian crown on the buttons. The regular army had to sport the despised Russian uniform complete with red stars. We were soldiers, to be sure, but instead of rifles, we carried shovels on our shoulders.

Being around Tamas and Csibo, whose genuine humour never succumbed to the hardships, would always lift my spirits. We chuckled to imagine what we might do in a confrontation. Since we had no gun, we couldn't shout "stop or I'll shoot!" We decided we would have to settle with "stop, or I'll bury you!"

The month of December was characterized by heavy, wet snow, which also brought mud and a fresh dump of misery. Still, I held hope that the approaching Christmas holiday might bring a few days rest from this torturous prison life. Word was out that half of the battalion would be allowed to go home for three days at Christmas, while the other half would have their holidays around New Year's. Some of the young guys were crushed to learn they had only a 50:50 chance of being with their families at Christmas. They sulked and dragged themselves about, disheartened and hopeless; however, when they discovered that Tamas, Csibo and I had not been home for seven consecutive Christmases, they felt a little less sorry for themselves. Some of them even went so far as to tell the officers that they would not fuss if they could not go home for the holidays as long as we three would be allowed to spend Christmas with our families this year.

When the officers caught wind of our situation and the day came to let us go, they could not resist playing games with us. An icy easterly wind blew in our faces as we stood in formation, motionless, in the courtyard awaiting the officer's announcement concerning our Christmas leave. Having previously been selected to shout commands for the regular morning marching drills, I stood at the front of my company. The officer was but a few steps away from me when he began to shout out the names of the people who had been selected to go home. After he called each name, he glanced up at me and flashed me a curious look. I remained stone-faced, staring at him coldly and trying desperately to mask any twinge of emotion.

He had read off most of the names when I commenced convincing myself that I had survived seven Christmases away from home - certainly, I could struggle through the eighth. Sure as hell, I would not crumble now. As I consumed myself with such spirited thoughts, the voice of the officer faded away until his bellowing was barely audible. As I thought about what I would do to keep myself going this Christmas, a whisper of a name floated in my ear and tickled my brain for attention. "Nagyreti, Tamas" it was saying softly. The voice grew louder. "Bartha, Csibo" it called. The voice grew stronger yet again. "Gemer, Gyuri!" it shouted, and I realized the officer had purposely left our names for the last. It took a moment for it to register. Was I really going home for Christmas? My heart filled with joy at the news of my incredible luck! We were ecstatic about the break.

The next day the three of us travelled home to Felsogod. With our travel permits in our pockets and joy in our hearts, we laughed at Tamas' antics throughout the journey. It was late in the afternoon when I arrived only to find my dear mother busy decorating the tree. I had been unable to let her know I was coming, and so again, she was shocked when she saw me standing in the doorway. When I embraced her, I could feel her trembling in my arms. I do not know how the hell Mama survived so many of the surprises in her life, but the rest of that evening she smiled radiantly and we spoke of happier times.

The kitchen was warm and smelled of freshly baked poppy seed rolls - a traditional Hungarian Christmas treat. She had hoped there would be a good reason for her to go to all the trouble of preparing a Christmas feast, and now there was. I had come home. I quickly shed my uniform to take a hot bath. As I soaked in the steaming tub, I tried to forget the past few months. I was ready to celebrate. It was such a joy to leave behind the shouting officers and the crowds of 'soldiers' who for so long had been my bed partners in the stinking barracks. There was such peace and love within these walls, and the lingering aroma of Mama's hearty cook-ing and delicate baking made me believe I must be in heav-en. How I enjoyed the tranquillity of this house, the distinct smell of fresh pine from the Christmas tree, and most of all, the company and love of my mother. The next morning, Christmas Day, Tamas and Csibo came over, and we spent a delightful time together. Tamas was always eager to imitate the speech and mannerisms of the officers. His humour always added color to our unpleasant time in the camp and elsewhere. Unfortunately, the three-day visit flew by like snowflakes in a winter storm, and I was soon in my uniform again, travelling back to camp.

The break seemed like a blink of an eye before I was back, spending New Year's Eve unloading gravel. The stroke of midnight was signalled by the whistle of the steam engine. Instead of lifting a champagne glass to greet the New Year, I lifted my shovel rhythmically, barely missing a stroke.

Like in many of the camps in Russia, getting to know people helped to pass the time and diminish one's sense of loneliness. Many of the friendships we made would last a lifetime. Three men I met, Karoly, Istvan and Nandor were jailed because their fathers had been high-ranking officers in the old army of Hungary. The latter two were also fine musicians; therefore, they did their best to preserve their hands and protect them from injury. They continued to hope they could some day pursue a future in the world of music.

Our safety was of no concern to our officers, nor did they every display a hint of sympathy. Someone once dropped a heavy concrete beam on his foot and crushed it. Not a bit of concern or compassion was shown to him by the officers. Another one of our comrades accidentally backed into a live electric wire exposed from a wall. He was electrocuted immediately. There was no investigation, let alone any sort of funeral.

For people like myself who were in the reserve, this ordeal in the working camp finally came to an end in February of 1952. The younger soldiers, who were serving the compulsory time of two or three years, spent the years of their service in this working unit, instead of in the regular army. They were assigned to work in construction companies, mines, or road construction without any earnings. It was the youth of our country who were again classified undesirables and enemies of the new regime. But for Tamas, Csibo and me, our time in this Hungarian hell-hole finally ended after six months and we headed home once more. Another hurdle had been overcome; I had passed one more test. Instead of starvation - humiliation and degradation were causing me pain. Nevertheless, I came out of it healthy, and I adjusted to that kind of treatment without sacrificing my ideals.

My mother was beside herself to have me back at home

again. The day after my return, I reported to the factory. At the department of payroll and personnel the man asked, "Where have you been?" When I tried to explain the events of the past six months, he said, "The assignment is supposed to be a three-month service, not six!" Because they refused to stamp my soldier book in the unit where I had served, I could not prove my whereabouts for those months. "If you don't believe me, ask the army unit when it was that I reported to them for the first time," I stammered. To this day, I still have no documented proof of my six-month stay in the forced labour camp in my own country; nevertheless, the factory eventually let me back to work, and at the same time, my police surveillance was lifted. I regained a little freedom. Perhaps my involvement in sport helped as well, for this was regarded as positive work by the authorities. At any rate, another battle was won.

BACK TO THE 'BIGGER' CAMP!

Although I was no longer under surveillance, I was still not free to voice my opinions or express my thoughts about the situation in my country. Extreme political pressure fell over everyone, suppressing rebellion and the spread of hatred for the new Communist government. The hatred still filled the hearts of the people, but since no one dared to whisper a word about it, everyone lived in their own silent and passive imprisonment. Instead of focusing on this, though, I concentrated on those aspects of my life which were positive and provided me with enjoyment and fulfillment. Athletics was definitely one of them. In my spare time, I voluntarily formed a track and field section to complement the soccer, handball and gymnastics activities of the sports club in Felsogod. I found coaching young athletes incredibly rewarding. Their fresh innocent faces and unbridled enthusiasm were a bright light in the darkness. We did not have proper track and field facilities in the village; nevertheless, I organized regular competitions, which included a few events that we could stage on the soccer field. Our excitement overrode the difficulties that we faced, and we always found spots around the village where we could run freely across the scenic countryside and share our friendship. These competitions seemed a shadow of my earlier efforts as a boy to organize the little Olympics in my neighbourhood.

I took advantage of numerous regional track and field clinics so that I could expand my knowledge and become more effective as a coach. Aside from my coaching duties on Monday evenings, I went to the Provincial Athletics Association in Budapest for meetings where, along with my colleagues, I planned and discussed matters that concerned our sport. It gave me a sense of worth and purpose, and gave meaning and direction to my life. I felt my contributions were appreciated and welcomed by my fellow coaches. I told them a bit about my life in the camps and about my desire to finish my education. They encouraged me to take some positive steps, and I did.

Eventually, I wrote a letter to Prime Minister Rakosi requesting to know why I could not go back to school to finish my education, since I now held a recognized place in society. The reply came. I showed the letter to an acquaintance who was in the communist party. His eyes slid quickly across the pages before he exclaimed with great excitement, "This is tremendous! You have a reply!" "Yes!" I cried, "Read it!" He continued reading aloud, "When you are worthy of the trust of the people, you will be able to continue your schooling."

Time went by. I watched the new school year begin and eventually end once more. All the while, I could do nothing but sit tight and pray for the trust of the people. I was disappointed, but I would not give up hope. I stuck to athletics. A hard practice with my athletes always made things seem a bit better. I sought information about the National Coaching School, and with a glimmer of hope in my heart, I directed my attention to gaining enrollment. In order to apply, I first had to work as an apprentice under the guidance of a master coach for a two-year period. I was also required to attend numerous clinics and workshops. I began my program under the direction of Hires Laszlo, a master coach who was the Hungarian champion in middle distance running many times over in his competitive days. He was also the man who took me under his wing and helped me land a summer job at the athletics club when I was younger. I now found pleasure coaching in a club in the nearby town of Dunakeszi, where practices were conducted on a well-maintained, red shale track, complete with up-to-date field event facilities. Here I learned the tricks of the trade, and the nitty gritties of athletics; and as I became more effective as a coach, the satisfaction I gained from the sport swelled. Eventually, I began to receive official recognition for my coaching abilities. After years of humiliation in the prison camps, it was sweet to receive some praise for my efforts. Time rolled by while I worked to complete my apprenticeship, kept up my job in the factory, and continued to volunteer as a coach in Felsogod. The days were long and tiring, but it was a happy kind of tiredness.

By May 1953, I had completed the criteria and was ready to apply to the National Coaching School, but I discovered that a new obstacle now stood in my way. Aside from completing my apprenticeship, and of course, providing a list of my credentials, it was also demanded that I submit an autobiography. Well, I knew very well that if I mentioned my army experience, the time spent in prison camps, the police surveillance, the working battalion, and all the other political events of my short life, I would disqualify myself from any possibility of gaining entry to the school. One of my colleagues in the athletics office advised me to make my autobiography short, avoiding mention of those details which might work against me. So, I sent in a brief autobiography with my application. After two weeks, I was notified - to my great surprise and joy - that I had been accepted.

The school was set up in a colloquium system which allowed each participant to study after working hours; and for two days each month, we sat before a board for oral exams. It seemed the pendulum was swinging high on the positive side now. I was now surrounded by opportunities to learn and to coach - a position I had craved to be in for so long.

THE FALL OF THE TYRANT

The autumn of 1953 was marked by the death of Josef Stalin. I couldn't help but feel relieved to hear the news. When I arrived at the factory the next morning, I was sucked into a hurricane of commotion as party functionaries ran feverishly about, attempting to organize the factory workers who were talking and strolling between the rows of silent machines. We did not start work this shift but were, instead, instructed to assemble in the courtyard. It was a slow process, but once we had lined up outside, we were told that on this day we would be participating in a nationwide mourning for Stalin. We, as workers, were happy only because this meant we would have a paid holiday.

After some instruction, the procession from Ujpest, a suburb of Budapest, to Hero's Square in central Budapest, began. The march took hours as rows of people filled the street. On either side of the river of people, party members kept a watchful eye for trouble. We were given posters with a huge picture of Stalin to carry as we were led down the street. I was furious because, sure as hell, after my experiences in the Soviet Union, I was not sorry he was dead; rather I was elated, but I knew I was being watched. My name was already on the black list, so I had no choice but to hoist Stalin's picture over my head. Inside, I felt an overwhelming joy at the thought of his death and the end of an era. I could only hope that wherever he was now, he felt as much disgrace to have someone like me, someone who found his death a reason to celebrate, carry his poster as I did in the pretense of mourning for him.

Once the swarms of people had joined in one mass, the thousands of factory workers, uniformed police, army units and communist youth organizations were ordered to bow their heads for the man who had caused so much suffering, agony and death. Above our heads, hundreds of red flags, decorated with black ribbons, blew in the sharp autumn wind. I was quite a distance from the centre of the ceremony and could only make out what was happening by the boom of the loudspeakers. I listened as someone rhymed off a lengthy lament, then listed the somber achievements which affected not only the Soviet people but the rest of the world. As I stood there, I speculated on how this event would affect my life, along with millions of others. My thoughts were interrupted by the clamour of a military band, playing the Soviet hymn. The wailing sound of it reminded me that I was still under the Russian thumb. The Soviet Union's hold on Hungary had been greater in the last few months than it had ever been, but now, in our hearts we hoped that the new leader of the Soviet Union would take a more humanitarian approach to his rule than Stalin had. Although the faces were masks of sadness, inside the people rejoiced with the hope that the empire so long ruled by Stalin's iron hand might soon crumble, and Hungary would regain a new freedom.

When the ceremony ended, the masses of people broke, quickly dropping the signs to the ground to be trampled by the sea of people rushing home after the long day. The next morning everything returned to normal. The empire stood strong, and yet another hard-handed dictator followed in Stalin's footsteps. Life went on without much hope for change. My days within this bigger camp called Hungary were not yet over. The iron curtain was reinforced, and the 'peace camp' was established. The words of the fortune teller, like a re-occurring nightmare, whispered to me again.

The winter was busy, and aside from being with my mother, the most enjoyable time I spent was with my dear athletes. We constructed a makeshift indoor training facility in which we could hold our practices through the winter. We gathered regularly for exhilarating workouts which boosted us physically and spiritually. We found in one another mutual trust, strong friendship and understanding. Our relationships were rare and precious in these dreadful times when sons sold fathers, and one did not dare to speak out about any political situation for fear of getting into trouble with the authorities. People were silent, and socializing was minimal.

In ten months, I had finished the academic component of the National Coaching School program and was ready to begin the practicum. This was conducted at the National Olympic Training Centre located in a beautiful and secluded setting on the outskirts of Tata. Aside from the sports field, track, gymnasium and indoor arena, the centre was equipped with housing units and recreation facilities. It was a privilege to enroll in this camp which was established by the state specifically for the preparation of the various national sports teams. I was extremely excited and proud to be accepted into the program.

Before we could continue with our practicum, we had to pass an oral exam. Of course, I danced my way through the track and field portion of the exam with flying colors, but the unit on Marxism gave me trouble. I found it difficult to swallow this ideology, for it was contrary to everything I had been brought up to believe in; nevertheless, when my attention was directed to the various track and field techniques, I was an eager and willing student. This camp was quite different from the earlier camps I had been in. This time, I was truly enjoying the experience. I was pleased to share a room with some retired athletes whom I had admired during my high school years, and who were now turning to coaching careers as well. We had to perform a number of preparatory exercises and specific drills that were related to each individual event. We were taught the approach to instructing the various techniques from steeplechase to hammer throwing. Each day was filled with thrills, laughs and learning, as well as a good physical workout. I felt like I was on cloud nine. When May 1st, the final day of the camp arrived, I remembered my small triumph five years earlier when I won the shot put competition. Now I had finally received my coaching diploma and could look forward to the days ahead with renewed optimism. I wished my colleagues good luck and bid them farewell. I was now ready to return to Felsogod. My heart was light, and I was quite pleased with my accomplishments.

Shortly after I returned home, Lajos, my friend at the Athletic office, found me a part-time coaching position at the Military Academy. "Not there!" I exclaimed, but he insisted. He encouraged me to simply go and coach. "Just don't say a word about your background, and keep your mouth shut regarding anything political," he warned. "The pay is good, and they have first-class facilities."

I took heed of his warning and went for the job. My duties included conducting three practice sessions per week for the students, and then organizing and coaching a month-long training camp. I was also in charge of preparing athletes from other schools, as well as this one, for the National Army Track and Field Championships.

In order to conduct practices at four o'clock, I had to leave the factory by two. I approached the young engineer in the factory and explained that I was working at the factory doing menial tasks for the lowest of wages and did not have much hope of advancement. My productivity was far from satisfactory only because it was such a boring, dead-end job. Now I had an opportunity to earn extra money in a coaching position. If he would consider allowing me to leave work early twice a week, I would be sure to work up to capacity when I was on the job. He reached out, shook my hand and replied, "All right. Let it be. You may go." I was extremely happy and I thanked him for his understanding. From that point on, I worked very hard and took responsibility for my performance at the factory. I also coached at the Military Academy and at the club in Felsogod. My days were extremely long, beginning at five in the morning and concluding at midnight.

In the Military Academy, sport was an integral part of the program to develop the officers of the future. The school only hired highly qualified coaches from sport organizations outside the military. The boxing, handball, gymnastics and soccer coaches were the only other civilians in the compound. Every time I came to the secured gate, I had to show my pass and say the password for the week. I never shook the uneasiness I felt walking into the camp, but I contended with it because I loved the coaching; and the hourly wage of 15.75 forints put my factory earnings to shame.

More than a hundred students gathered from various schools and clubs to attend the month-long training camp I was hosting. It was a true test of my organizational skills. I did my best to ensure all the participants were working hard and receiving the best value from the training sessions. Prior to each session, the officers presented their groups to me, saluting and greeting me with the typical army greeting - "Strength and health!" It was ironic how, at the factory, only a short distance away, I was treated as an undesirable element - an enemy - tolerated and watched constantly. Here, at the Academy, the officers saluted me. Little did they know that just two years ago, I stood motionless in front of the officers of the working battalion, awaiting their orders which I executed without hesitation.

Because I was on the go all the time, I was better off financially. I was able to give my mother more money, and buy myself some new clothes. The provincial athletic office eventually appointed me the head coach for the Pest Province Track and Field Team. Once a month, I had to conduct a practice or competition for the team, and visit one of the clubs that had athletes on the team. I consulted with the local coach, assisting him with training plans and offering my advice. I took the provincial team to the national 'Spartakiad', a ten-day competition. It was a satisfying and enjoyable experience to see my athletes perform well. I had made the right decision in choosing coaching. It not only improved my economical situation, but more importantly, it provided me with a sense of achievement and many opportunities to make new friends and to travel. The practices and competitions provided a milieu within which I felt comfortable, secure and content.

Still, no matter how I felt or how hard I worked, in the eyes of authorities, I did not belong to the working class. They did not permit me to travel with my Provincial Track

Team just a few kilometres over the Czechoslovak border for a dual competition. My spirits were dashed, and it seemed as though I would never regain my freedom. On the surface my life seemed better. I was allowed to work and to coach, but beneath it all, I was still considered an enemy and was kept under close watch. I was still waiting for the 'people's trust,' and I was not allowed to finish teaching college until I had it. Perhaps the fortune teller had goofed when she said I would cross the ocean. I could not imagine myself getting within 50 kilometres of the Iron Curtain without being stopped by the A.V.H., let alone travelling to the other side of the "big water" as she had predicted. It was during this time of hopelessness, political pressure and misery, that the Hungarian Revolution broke out.

REVOLUTION!

On the evening of October 23, 1956, I was invited to a national sports meeting. I left the factory after lunch and travelled by streetcar to Budapest where I decided to visit the Athletic Office before proceeding to the gathering. By about 2:00 p.m. my colleagues at the sport office were returning from their lunch break and chattering excitedly. They reported that a demonstration, organized by the students, was taking place in the square where the statue of Sandor Petofi, one of our country's greatest poets and revolutionaries, stood. The oppression of the masses was at its strongest, and the people were frightened. Political terror was rampant, so it was hard to imagine any type of resistance or demonstration; nevertheless, it was happening. After my visit, I left the office and strolled slowly down the street to the main thoroughfare of Bajcsy Zsilinszky. What I saw there was unbelievable. Thousands of people had swarmed into the streets, wearing radiant smiles and shouting cries of freedom. They carried Hungarian flags with a gaping hole in the centre where the Communist emblem normally was. The electrifying atmosphere drew me, and I found myself accompanying the jubilant people through the streets. My heart was beating in my throat, and tears welled up in my eyes. It was an emotional experience to be part of the people's quest for freedom, and to share their determination to obtain it. People from all walks of life wore red, white and green ribbons across their chests. I gazed at the hopeful faces of the people all around me and noticed several policemen who had joined the march - the Communist star torn from their caps. As I marched with the crowd, I felt drunk with joy, convinced that we were in the midst of regaining our national independence. I was unaware that nearly four decades would pass before Hungary would ever achieve this goal.

As the parade wound its way across the Margaret bridge to the Buda side of the city, I slipped away from the peaceful but lively demonstration, and ventured on to my meeting. I could hardly sit still in the quiet meeting room as I strained to listen to the boring reports being presented. I was still electrified by the march for freedom which continued to take the streets of Budapest.

I did not say a word to my colleagues about what I had seen and been part of. By now, I had learned it was sometimes best to keep quiet. Besides, it would have been too difficult to tell them about the parade without revealing my joy. Instead, I stifled myself and endured the lengthy gathering which only became interesting when the recommendations for participant recognition were presented. To my great surprise, I had been nominated for a national award which was approved by the meeting. In the end, I never did receive the award because of the events that were unfolding in the streets of Budapest as we spoke. When we left the hall, we found the peaceful demonstration outside begin to turn into a violent revolt. As I hiked toward the Western Railway station, truckloads of armed civilians waving flags roared through the streets. It seemed these young revolutionaries were ready to take more aggressive action. I walked hurriedly into the railway station to catch the train back to Felsogod.

Just before I climbed aboard, a freshly printed flyer was shoved in my hand. People on the train were saying that demonstrators had gathered at the parliament buildings with a list of sixteen demands they wanted addressed; but instead of negotiating diplomatically, Minister Gero's 'bloodhounds' - the infamous A.V.H. - had opened fire on the people.

Later that same evening, an angry crowd toppled a giant bronze statue of Stalin. A church had been demolished to make room for the statue, and now, it had finally crumbled. The students and the workers, disillusioned by their own government, had taken up arms against their oppressor. This revival of Hungarian pride and the raising of voices in the quest for freedom, was a fresh breath of air, a new hope for a better life.

At home, Mama was frightened when I told her the news. She despised violence and the disturbance of peace, but I knew in her heart she, also, was eager to see some changes.

The next morning, I made the voyage to the factory as usual; but instead of being greeted by the regular hum of busy machines, I heard only the people buzz of discussions about the events of the previous evening. I was only at work a short time before an announcement was made that we were all being sent home. This was a common occurrence in uncertain times, for it was an accepted and unspoken rule that large numbers of people were not allowed to congregate for any reason during troubled times, even for work.

I left the factory with one of my friends and we decided to look around. The public transportation system had halted operation throughout the city since the night before, so we walked down the main street through the industrial section until we reached the square adjacent to the city hall. Here, we found an organized gathering around a stone statue of a Soviet soldier. At the foot of the figure lay the body of a seventeen-year-old boy, covered with the Hungarian flag and dozens of flowers. He was killed on the first evening of the uprising. To my astonishment, I saw angry young boys climbing the statue with sledgehammers, intending to knock off the head. The people broke out in a spontaneous ovation when the head of the soldier broke free and tumbled to the ground. Shortly after, a worker pulled up in a horse-drawn wagon. He threw a heavy chain around the torso of the statue, jumped up on his wagon again, and started the horses pulling. The people pushed and the horses strained, until finally the figure broke off its foundation. The people let out a thunderous roar as they watched the hated figure fall to the ground. The young worker made a short speech, then led the people in the singing of the national anthem. It was a magnificent celebration of the patriotism and hope which lived in every Hungarian's heart.

The statue was replaced by the body of the young Hungarian freedom fighter, showered with flowers. During this event, I noticed the blade of a kitchen knife sticking out from the purse of an elderly lady who was standing in front of me. She was ready for the revolution. My friend and I chuckled at the sight, but we understood her possible reasons.

After awhile, we headed toward the street. As we crossed the road, we broke into a sprint to avoid being struck by armoured Russian vehicles which sped down the street. Eventually, we reached the Lenin Ring Road in the heart of Budapest. On one side of the street, the Russian soldiers' machine guns were set up on the empty sidewalk; on the other side, people like us were looking for action. Dead bodies lay by the walls of the apartment houses.

As the days went by, the fighting spread across the country. The news over the radio was frustratingly controversial and confusing. One day, I was enjoying the freedom I had to ride my bicycle in Felsogod with a friend and some of my athletes, when we happened upon a Russian convoy transporting gas to supply their tanks. We tried to hold them up, with little success.

After the apprehension of Prime Minister Nagy and his delegates by the Russians, the end was inevitable. We sensed that retaliation was in the works. Upon receiving the sad news, our hope for a free Hungary disappeared in minutes. I realized the dreadful times of the A.V.H. arrests, tortures, and jail sentences without trials would return, backed by the power of Soviet tanks.

My athletes visited me that night for a final discussion about what actions we should take. "I am leaving tomorrow morning to escape to the West. If you wish to join me, you are welcome." "We will be fed beets, and we will wear muzzles," I told them. "I have no choice." I was on the Communists' list as an enemy and would be a target if I remained in Hungary.

ESCAPE

Early the next day, November 8, 1956, three of us climbed on our bikes and began the 200-kilometre trek to the Austrian border. The morning shrouded the countryside in a milky fog that shielded us from watchful eyes, but could not hide the sadness we felt for leaving everything and everyone behind. For so many years, my heart had ached to be home with my family and to enjoy the house which had harboured contentment and peace in my life. Now, after five short years at home, I was leaving for good. I kept looking back, tears welling up in my eyes, to say a silent farewell to the familiar streets as they disappeared from site, but my thirst for freedom drove me on. I did not say good-bye to Mama or anyone in my family. That was the toughest decision I had ever made, but I convinced myself it would be easier for everyone. Perhaps I secretly hoped that this would not be a long separation. Thoughts and prayers consumed me as we rolled silently toward the highway. Would this journey be successful? Where would we end up? How far would we have to go before we found a place to build our nests in freedom and tranquillity? With nothing but the clothes on my back and a piece of bread in a shopping bag, I tried to appear nonchalant as we reached the highway.

The plan was that, if we were stopped or questioned, we would say that we were on our way to visit my grandmother in the next village. Sure enough, as we rode further up the road, we spotted some Russian soldiers controlling a major intersection. Thinking quickly, I rode ahead, put on a pleasant face, and greeted them in Russian, asking how they were. They were quite receptive, seemingly relieved to be shown such friendliness, and they allowed us to continue without incident. As we rode away, we all breathed huge sighs of relief. No words were needed. We knew exactly how each other was feeling.

The ferry that crossed the Danube at Vac was no longer running, so we continued on to Visegrad where we hoped we could cross the river. When we arrived in Visegrad, I spotted the ferry gliding across the water. Lady Luck must have been on our side. We were anxious to load our bikes and board the boat. A distinguished looking, sympathetic lady was the only other passenger on the ferry boat that trip. We sat in silence for awhile, beholding the breathtaking view of the mountain range which provided a scenic backdrop for the approaching shoreline. The trees were bare now, and their spindly arms seemed to shrivel in the cool air. The scene was peaceful and the gentle hum of the ferry was soothing somehow, but it failed to calm my anxiety which was perhaps more visible than I realized. Breaking the painful silence, the lady finally asked, "Are you going to the West?" I could not lie and responded with a simple nod. Her eyes twinkled. "Just go," she said softly, "I wish I could go too. God be with you." I sensed her sadness and her own helplessness. No other words were said except a short thank-you and good-bye as we disembarked on the other side. We took one more glance at our old friend, the Danube, before we jumped onto our bikes to follow the road once again. The disappearance of the fog and the lady's kind wishes lifted my spirits, and with renewed energy, I led our little expedition throughout the day.

It was dusk before we finally decided to stop and look for overnight accommodation. Peddling through the quiet streets of a small village, we searched unsuccessfully for a place to bed down. Thankfully, the third place we approached housed friendly faces. They opened their door and gave us a warm meal and comfortable beds. They were Kulaks, so their understanding went without question and their encouragement was sincere. We trusted them enough to reveal our plan to them. They were incredibly supportive, and assured us that our secret was safe with them.

The day's ride had worn us out; upon turning in, we instantly fell into a much-needed sleep. It was sweet relief to enjoy such warm hospitality from complete strangers. Their assistance was a shining example of how difficult times brought out the best in people.

After an affectionate farewell at day break, we were on our way. The forecast was a repeat of the previous day - foggy and damp - a typical November day, but our spirits were high for we had travelled half the intended distance without a hitch.

In the late afternoon, after a gruelling day, we reached Gyor, a large industrial city where we met the relatives of one of my travelling companions. They were extremely helpful, and we had a chance to rest and eat before continuing our journey. They advised us to leave our bicycles behind, though, and make the remaining 50 kilometres by train.

The railway station was like an ant hill, jammed with noisy, busy passengers, bumping into one another at every turn. The train we finally boarded was filled with people, fleeing the country, just as we were, to seek freedom elsewhere in the world. Normally, any individual travelling within 50 kilometres of the border was required to produce a document to the A.V.H. men who patrolled the border. The document declared one's destination, thus preventing anyone from escaping to the West, but the entire country was now in chaos. With the absence of the A.V.H., we were able to reach the last village before the border town of Hegyeshalom. The train stopped on the open line just before the little station of Level to allow escaping passengers to avoid the Russian soldiers who would be waiting at the next station. We jumped off the train, and followed the instructions we were given in Gyor. The little piece of paper I held in my hand was a rough sketch of the route we should take, and was the only guide we had to carry us across this unknown terrain. Beneath the darkening sky, we approached and passed by a large, white house. We had been warned not to seek guidance here, so we marched on looking for large haystacks. I soon noticed that our little trio had swelled to seven, as people had joined us in the dark. They pleaded with us, saying they had no idea where they were or which direction they should go, so I invited them to stay on with us, but they had to accept that I was in charge, and they could not argue. Also, if we failed to make it to freedom, they were not to blame me. Accepting my terms, the seven of us continued on our way. We tumbled through rough terrain, but managed to keep our concentration on our task. Only the sounds of our steps and our heavy breathing were heard in the stillness of the evening.

After a two-day journey, we found ourselves hiking the last few kilometres which separated us from the free world. It was important not to make any mistakes now, and to maintain our cool despite our overwhelming anxiety. The Iron Curtain, the infamous wall of barbed wire, watchtowers and trip mines, which separated the free world from the eastern block, was down; nevertheless, we expected some form of resistance at any time.

After what seemed a long hike, I finally spotted our reference point, the towering haystacks just ahead of us. We passed by them cautiously, hesitantly, before we noticed two lights in the distance. The faint rumble of engines could be heard before we saw two vehicles rolling back and forth across the field. I quickly concluded that those damned vehicles were Russian tanks patrolling the border.

Everyone drew back in fear. "We have to go on", I announced to the group. I relayed to them the lessons of my wartime experience. "They won't see us in the dark unless we move directly in the beam of their lights," I told them. "Just keep your eyes on the lights, and before the turning beam hits you, throw yourself on the ground and be still."

After they worked through their hesitation, we advanced through the freshly-plowed field, moving closer and closer to the roaring vehicles. The rumbling noise from the engines certainly resembled that of a tank. We became more convinced of this when we fell to our stomachs to avoid the lights, bringing our ears closer to the ground. From here, we crawled on our elbows, breaking into a sweat from the effort and tension. The smell of the earth was soon overtaken by the exhaust fumes of the vehicles which now passed mere metres ahead of us. I peered through the darkness and found the vehicle did not appear to be a tank after all. I jumped up and took a few strides toward it to realize it was, in fact, a tractor plowing the field! We had made it to Austrian soil! All at once, I was overcome with joy, relief, exhilaration and a touch of sadness. I looked up to the sky and lost myself for a moment in the twinkling stars. After eleven years of captivity, control and humiliation, that stage of my life ended abruptly. I was truly a free man! My friends and I hugged and danced jubilantly in celebration of our successful voyage to freedom. Soon we continued on our way, and as I walked through the field, I took a huge breath of the sweet and free evening air. Tears welled up in my eyes and spilled down my cheeks. I thanked God in a silent prayer for leading me to my freedom.

Relieved of tension, we chuckled about our close encounter with the imaginary tanks, and headed toward the nearest concentration of lights - a settlement in the distance. As we approached the lights, though, our apprehension returned, and I went ahead to find some clue as to our location. I felt incredibly uncomfortable to step out of the protection of the darkness as I neared the first street light. I scanned the small area illuminated by the street lamp for any evidence of our whereabouts. Finally, there it was - on the wall of one house, there was written the name of the street - in German! We were in Austria! My fear and uncertainty melted away, and I called the others out of the dark, shouting, "We made it! We are in Austria." They ran toward me hooting and hollering, to hug me and to praise my leadership, while I, in my thoughts, praised God.

It was after nine o'clock on the evening of November 9, 1956, when I finally relaxed after the long ordeal. We walked down the street, chattering and laughing until we met some people from the village who escorted us to the Gasthaus. They treated us with sandwiches, hot chocolate and radiant smiles. I will be forever thankful to the village folk of Nickelsdorf for their warm welcome and genuine friendliness. They touched our hearts.

In the midst of their care, I couldn't help but reflect

upon my life - the past, the present and now, the future. Although I had successfully escaped from an uncertain and oppressed life in Hungary, I had also cut the umbilical cord which had always drawn me back to my family, my dear mother and my friends. It was an incredible price to pay, but one I was willing to accept to know the feeling of freedom. I felt like a bird whose broken wing had finally mended, enabling me to fly again. Now I soared about, looking for a place to build my nest. It hit me that there would be no more stinking boxcars, crowded jail cells, barbed wire fences, nor barking guards. I would no longer have to endure the filth, the crawling lice, and the hunger pains in my stomach which were once a part of everyday life for me. My worth would be decided not by my political views, but by my productivity, my personality, and my self worth. I would be given a fair chance to make the best of my life. The gates of the free world were suddenly opened to me. I could go almost anywhere! A hell of a feeling filed my heart as I imagined the possibilities. I could have burst from joy at that moment, but instead I stood and danced.

JOURNEY'S END

The giant silver bird began its descent and was soon swallowed by the fluffy, milk-white clouds. In preparation for landing, the flight attendants began collecting the earphones and gave the usual order to fasten seat belts. As the plane drifted lower, my thoughts, which had wandered thousands of miles away and many years back to Bryansk and beyond, now returned to the present. My youth and the memories of a life of hardship and struggle had whirled before me like a movie. After a smooth landing at the Montreal airport, I rushed to collect my luggage in a land of peace, security and promise.

ZENITH

MY LIFE THEREAFTER

As I near the dusk of my life and look back over the events of my past, I thank the Lord for giving me the strength and courage to face the hard times in my life. My life's journey has led me through sunshine and darkness, happiness and despair, fulfillment and misery, but somehow, all the good and bad are drawn together to form a life that is, what I consider, balanced and complete. Sometimes, I feel I have seen one-and-a-half lifetimes, and I have often fought to understand the irrationality and irony of my fate; nevertheless, I feel everything I have experienced was for a reason, if only so that I would appreciate when my dreams did come true. Indeed, my dreams did come true, I reached my goals, and I was triumphant after a tough fight. I have been able to continue to enjoy those things that were always dear to me. Predictions became reality.

ACROSS THE 'BIG WATER'

Just a few short months after my escape from Communist Hungary in the spring of 1957, I was on my way to fulfill my destiny in the new world when I boarded a plane for an agonizingly long flight which was transporting Hungarian refugees from England to Gander, Newfoundland, in Canada. As I bounced in my seat on the rickety convert- ed W.W.II bomber, I had plenty of time to think. We were soon flying over the Atlantic Ocean, and I again found myself living out the fortune teller's predictions - predictions which, only a few months ago, seemed utterly impossible. The 'Big Water' stretched out beneath the fluffy clouds over which our plane flew as I travelled toward my new life. Filled with hope and nearly unbearable anticipation, I dreamt of building my new home in Canada. I landed in Winnipeg, and from there, I continued my journey by train across the prairie - the land of 'cowboys and Indians', the land I envisioned in my child- hood games. I gazed out the window, and my eyes ran over the gentle curves of the vast, green wheat fields which flowed like a calm ocean to meet the blue sky on the horizon. I was travelling over the land which at one time only existed in my imagination.

After many hours, we arrived in a place called Medicine Hat where we transferred to a dayliner to continue our jour- ney toward a city called Lethbridge. I and fifteen other jolly refugees, led by a accordion player, sang Hungarian folk songs - a traditional custom for expressing happiness. The other passengers were taken aback by such a display, and listened with disdain to the strange, incomprehensible lyrics. One man, who sat across the aisle from me, peered at me with a look of disgust. Little did I know that this man who sat before me would be my future father-in-law. I would become the husband of his only daughter Carole. A number of years later, Cecil and I would laugh about this, realizing that fate had brought us together seven years earlier on the train to Lethbridge.

ROME

It was 1960, and the August sun seemed to shine brighter than usual upon the thousands of happy faces that had gathered here in Rome to celebrate the XVII Olympiad. Prior to the opening of the Games, the Olympic Village was the centre of attention. Here, athletes, coaches, visitors, media and enthusiasts mingled in a colorful bubbling cavalcade. I was in heaven as I strolled amongst them. This was my first visit to the Olympic Games. I glowed with excitement and pride as I walked around the compound, looking for familiar faces. Suddenly, two hands shot up from behind me and covered my eyes. A voice whispered into my ear, "Guess who?" it said. I had no idea who it could be, and I stood there in a numb silence. The voice continued, this time crying, "I made it! I made it! You told me to work hard, stay with it, and someday, I would make it to the Olympics!"

"Csaba," I shouted, and I reeled around to meet the beaming face of my former athletes from the Pest provincial team. I could hardly control the joy I felt at this surprise. What great satisfaction I felt to embrace that young athlete who, years ago, despite his talent, had been on the verge of quitting athletics. He lived in a small village then, without proper facilities, and training by himself was a difficult task for him. I sent him training plans and letters to inspire him to stick with athletics. I visited him once a month, as well, and met with him at competitions and during our monthly training sessions. When I left Hungary in 1956, I did not realize that my absence contributed to many of my athletes giving up track and field, but not Csaba. He found a club and a coach to train with, and he continued to run. Now, here he was a member of the Hungarian National Team.

Those glorious days in Rome brought unforgettable moments to my life. It seemed fate was now compensating me for my earlier years of pain and torment. From the moment the torch was lit and the Olympic flag raised during the opening ceremonies, I struggled with tears. I thanked God again and again for saving me and giving me the opportunity to witness this magnificent event. I thought back to the time I spent in Bryansk fourteen years earlier, and remembered the officer who told me of his experiences at the Berlin Olympics. How I had envied him then, and how I wished I could experience even one Olympics. Now, I savoured the moment and basked in my pleasure at being in the middle of these Games.

When the athletics competition began, I positioned myself under the bright sun and carefully eyed Csaba's every move through my binoculars. He ran well against the best sprinters in the world, and succeeded in advancing to three-quarter finals. The prime years of my own youth had been spent in a different field, engaged in a different form of competition - a battle not for medals, but survival. I never would be a competitor in such a spectacular event, but I now drew satisfaction from encouraging and helping someone else to achieve his best.

Later on, during a stroll through the Olympic Village, I accidentally bumped into Jesse Owens, my childhood hero. This was truly a moment worth waiting 24 years for, and after exchanging handshakes and a few words, he gave me his autograph. I had come a long way since that first mini-Olympic festival I had organized in my neighbourhood more than two decades earlier. Then I had pretended to be Jesse Owens. Now he stood before me - an icon of athletic greatness. In my wildest dreams, I had never thought I would come face to face with this man. I was selfishly glad that, of all my friends at that first Olympics, it was I who met my hero.

BLUE HAWAII

The sunrise over the Pacific Ocean painted a spectacular picture for the passengers as we completed our night flight from Vancouver to Honolulu. It was February 1961, and I was one of many happy people who had left the Canadian winter behind in search of the sun, sand, and beauty of this tropical island paradise. During the flight, a young fellow traveller offered me the use of his electric shaver, which I accepted with appreciation. As we enjoyed each other's company, his wife inquired about my origin. Apparently my thick accent was impossible to miss. I explained that I had fled my native Hungary and was now residing happily in Canada. They wished me good luck in a tone that revealed some skepticism about my days in Hawaii; nevertheless, I was anxious to leave the plane and pursue the dreams which had kept me alive through the cold winter in Bryansk. Finally we landed, and I hurriedly disembarked. By the time the couple I had met on the plane caught up with me, I was embracing two lovely girls and was wearing the welcoming lei of orchids, not to mention a wide grin on my face. As the couple passed, the woman said with a smile, "I guess you didn't need more luck after all." I just stood there smiling. Their remark boosted my ego and left me with a feeling of satisfaction. After we left the airport, we stopped at a small church where a wonderful Sunday morning service was taking place with many young people in attendance. I was deeply touched at the sight of so many beautiful faces of this golden race, shining and smiling as the choir floated down the aisle dressed in purple gowns and singing a familiar hymn. The scene brought a fulfilling sense of joy and peace to my heart. Once the service was over, I wandered outside, admired the exotic flowers and drank in the fresh ocean air. I felt I must be in a place that God had created when he was in an extremely good mood.

Finally, in the early afternoon, I strolled down to the crystal clear waters of the ocean to "wash my filthy body and warm my buns on the soft sand". Tears rolled down my face but went undetected as I splashed in the warm, salty, ocean water. Although it was easy to hide my tears, it was much more difficult to suppress my emotions. I remembered my poor comrades who were left behind on the steppes of Russia, and I shouted to the heavens above, "I made it!"

As evening fell over the city, the twinkling lights of Honolulu blinked like stars, and a gentle breeze blew in from the ocean. The palm trees swayed gracefully in the wind, and the leaves looked like giant fingers waving at me. Finally, I could hide my tears no longer, and they streamed freely down my sunburnt cheeks. As we sat on the balcony in the bright moonlight, my girlfriend asked, "What is the matter with you? This should be a happy occasion."

"Do you know where I came from?" I asked. "I was a 'horse' in Bryansk, hungry and cold, with a lice-infested body; still, prison bars, police surveillance, forced labour camps, the Iron Curtain, and years of discrimination could not wash my dreams from my heart. Now, sixteen years after it all began, I am here. These tears I cry are in celebration of the end of many years of pain, and for the realization of a dream."

RETURN

Ten years had gone by since I left Hungary before an unbelievable turn of politics opened up the Hungarian borders to refugees, like myself, who had been condemned and sentenced in 1956. Up until now those who had escaped from Hungary during the Revolution were automatically sentenced to five years should they ever return; but after spending ten years out of the country, these refugees were granted amnesty to return to Hungary. This opened the door for me to arrange a visit to see my dear mother and family once again. Just a few short years ago this seemed an impossible dream. I was filled with apprehension and fear of returning to the country I had fled, but I was also driven by an overpowering yearning to return. I flew with my wife and some of my Canadian athletes to Vienna. From there we travelled by hydrofoil on my beloved Danube to Budapest.

It seemed like a fairy tale to be back in Felsogod in my sweet home, surrounded by the love of Mama, my sisters and their families. The thrill and excitement of being reunited with my loved ones was surpassed only by my relief that I could be with all of them once again. Nothing could hinder my joy - not the fact that police would watch our every move, not the fact that some of my friends would be too afraid to be seen with me in public places, not the fact that Hungary was still living in silence and fear.

WINNIPEG

The pouring rain did not dampen the enthusiasm of the full capacity crowd during the opening ceremonies of the

1967 Pan American Games in Winnipeg. Prince Philip, the Duke of Edinburgh, stood with the crowd, soaking wet, and waved as the uniformed athletes from various nations marched in. By the time the team of the host nation, Canada, marched into the stadium, the rain had eased, but there was enough drizzle to mask my tears as I marched along with the team. I had been selected to the Canadian Track and Field Team as a field events head coach, fulfilling another dream of mine.

When I came to Canada ten years prior to this, I spoke not a word of English, but still managed to find work in a greenhouse. My fellow worker and former athlete from Hungary would often pass by me, pushing a wheel barrow and announcing, "Gemer, Gyuri - Head Coach, Pest province; now, Head Dirt Mover." He loved to tease me. After a few times, I retorted, "We have to be patient and learn the language. Then we will show our value. Mark my word, someday I will be the coach of the Canadian National Team." He smiled at me with skepticism as we continued to work.

Over the next years, my love for track and field never weakened. I organized and coached a small team in Lethbridge, hosted competitions and worked for the sport endlessly and happily. My happiness was topped by the fact that one of my protégés from the small group was selected to compete for the Canadian team at the Pan American Games. My encouragement and expertise, combined with his hard work, won him the honour of representing his country, and gave me gratification as well.

Recognition and rewards for my coaching began to become a regular occurrence as I pursued my dreams in the field of athletics. In addition to numerous invitations to instruct at provincial, national and international clinics -

which provided new challenges and great satisfaction - I was invited to teach track and field at the newly established university in Lethbridge. It was 1967 when I accepted my first yearly contract with the Department of Physical Education. Later on, fencing was introduced into the curriculum, and I began teaching this activity as well. To this day, I continue to fulfill my role as teacher - a dream which I hoped would be my life.

MONTREAL

Exactly forty years had passed since the time I had organized my first little neighbourhood Olympics in Felsogod, when I was asked to help organize a much bigger track and field event at the 1976 Montreal Olympic Games. I was awarded the position of Technical Manager for the throwing events which, needless to say, was a great pleasure for me. I was extremely proud to be part of this world event. I considered it a tremendous reward - one I was given in return for my long years of volunteer work, my love for the sport. My work began in May and was finished after the Games ended in July. The entire experience gave me a natural high that lasted for many months after the event. By that time, I had experienced the Olympic Games in Rome, Mexico City, Tokyo and Munich, and had a thorough understanding and appreciation of the needs and presentation of each track and field event. My enjoyment was topped when my wife Carole joined me. She also worked for the Games and was placed in charge of information and protests for Athletics. I was elated to be so closely associated with the Olympics, and to share my dreams with the one I loved.

EDMONTON

Two years later, another world event came to be staged on Canadian soil - the Commonwealth Games. I was asked to make a contribution to the cause, and I was more than happy to attend the numerous meetings held in early preparation for the Games. I picked up my family and moved to Edmonton months before the Games began, to work as Technical Manager for athletics. My experiences to this point served me well, and I believed I was useful to the athletics organizing committee. When the spectacular opening ceremony finally took place under a bright Alberta sun, and hundreds of young athletes and dancers formed a splendid display of color and movement, I was again overwhelmed with emotion and was grateful that I, the 'horse' from Bryansk, had made it this far to be part of this magnificent event. As the drama and excitement of the competitions unfolded, another unforgettable event happened to me. I was presented with a coaching award by Prince Philip, the Duke of Edinburgh! I wondered then how many prisoners had received a warm handshake and a reward from him. Regardless of the irony of the situation, it was a moment I'll never forget.

Less than one year after that, I was named Chief of Throwing events at the second World Cup in Athletics held in Montreal. This was yet another opportunity for me to serve my new country and my old friend, athletics.

RETURN TO SCHLOSS HAINFELD

In the summer of 1981, five good friends and I packed our panniers with a few items of clothing, strapped them on our bikes and flew from Calgary to Frankfurt. That night we stayed with some friends in a nearby village, and early the next morning, we embarked on a three-week bicycle trip through Germany, Switzerland, Austria and Yugoslavia, to Budapest. Travelling on secondary roads and bike paths toward Lake Constance (Boden-See) was a great thrill, and fulfilled yet another dream. We rolled through the heart of the Rhine valley, past beautiful, well-cultivated vineyards; and through small villages with cobblestone streets, friendly 'Gasthauses', and fine wines. This unforgettable, carefree and exuberant journey led us over green alpine slopes dotted with wild flowers. The bells of grazing cows, and the singing of the birds were truly a tranquil concert. As we neared the Austrian border, I began to recall 1945 when I was held in the prison camp near Feldbach. As I pedalled on, my urge to visit the place where I was once a prisoner became overwhelming, and with the agreement of the other members of the group, we headed toward the city. A silver-haired policeman responded with some surprise to my inquiry about the prison camp, left his post and led us on his bike to the outskirts of the city and toward Schloss Hainfeld.

I instantly recognized the castle as it came into view. Painful memories swam through my head until I was dizzy with emotion.

The baroness who owned the castle, opened the heavy door and welcomed us to stroll through the huge inner courtyard which, at one time, had housed thousands of prisoners. She showed us what was left of the library - a single, partly torn book, a slashed painting, and a pile of broken Baroque furniture. A small card was propped near one window. On it was printed "Das is Krieg."[63] The room was left untouched

---

[63] That is war.

as a solemn reminder of the senseless destruction that occurred during the liberation by the Soviets. I had mixed feelings; but now, with my Canadian passport in my pocket, I was able to pass through five countries with ease. At one time, such travels could cost people their lives. I now savoured my new privileges and freedom.

ANSWER TO FORCED LABOUR

In the fall of 1992, I received copies of three articles written by Dr. Karoly Csonkareti and published that year in 'Zalai Hirlap', a weekly provincial news periodical distributed in Hungary. These articles gave detailed information of the Hungarian forced labour camps in which thousands of victims, including myself, had been held. Since the withdrawal of Soviet troops from Hungary, and the establishment of a new democratic system earlier that year, events such as those which took place before the Revolution have been brought into the open and spoken of freely without fear of suffering harsh consequences. In the following, I would like to summarize the articles which explained why the political forces of that time felt justified in altering the lives of thousands of people, disregarding basic human rights, and why they herded so many young people into slavery.

On June 27, 1950, an important meeting took place in Budapest at the Ministry of Defense. In attendance were ten Hungarian and three Russian high ranking army officers. The decisions made at this meeting would affect the future of thousands of young Hungarian men. Szergejev, a Russian officer, stated that, "The sons of the Kulaks should be drafted into the army, but through a strong education process, they should be kept separate from the others."[64]   Karoly Janza, a Hungarian officer, agreed with the Russian suggestion and promoted the idea further, stating, "The Kulaks, their sons and other undesirable subjects should be drafted, but they should not be armed. They should be forced to do hard labour."[65] The results of this meeting, endorsed by the Hungarian Workers Party at the July 12, 1950 Congress, sealed the fate of Hungarians. They lost their freedom and were forced to serve years of their life in organized labour camps spread out across the country. Between the years of 1951 and 1956, 12,500 young Hungarians were drafted into these working battalions. The living and working conditions were incredibly harsh, and with the acceleration of the Cold War, the working tempo was stepped up. There was a desperate need for army barracks, not only for the Hungarian Army, but for the Russian Army as well.   Officers and sergeants were hand-picked by the Party and assigned to battalions because of their faithfulness to the system, rather than for their skills. They were instructed to treat Hungarian prisoners as enemies; and their personal conduct was a clear reflection of their hatred, manifested in acts which aimed to destroy any shred of one's dignity.

Since that time, such discrimination and mistreatment have eased, the Iron Curtain has come down, the Berlin Wall was demolished, and the Soviet Union has crumbled. The day finally came when the last Soviet soldier left Hungary, and the church bells rang throughout the country for an entire hour to signal the joy of all Hungarians. People who were herded into camps, within or outside the country, were

---

64 Zalai Hirlap. (Nov. 14, 1992). "Az," "a," "b," "c" hadmuvelet."

65 Csonkaréti, Károly, p. 5.

---

released, pardoned and compensated. At least, the Communists admitted that what happened in the past was wrong, and that they had violated every rule in the book with regard to human rights.

I travelled a great distance, and a number of years passed, but the words of the wrinkled and mysterious fortune teller always whispered in my mind. I had never been superstitious, and had always held faith in God, so I found it difficult to believe predictions until they had come true. Only then did I realize that, indeed, I had completed the "long journey" she spoke of. I, too, returned home to find no future for myself in my country, forcing me to cross the "big waters". For many years, though, one of her predictions remained to materialize - her belief that I would become rich. It wasn't until 1993 when I was notified that I would be compensated monetarily for my prison years that I felt her final prediction had come true. By Hungarian standards, the money was quite substantial. Still, could I possibly feel that money would replace the years of my youth? Could any dollar figure negate the hunger and cold and misery I had struggled with for years? The questions need no answers. Perhaps, all along, though, I had enjoyed the wealth the fortune teller spoke of fifty years ago. Perhaps my wealth is in my experience. Truly, I am a rich man.

EPILOGUE

I have happily spent the last four decades in freedom in my new country, Canada, but the years of comfort and contentment I have enjoyed of late have not swallowed my memories of my prison experiences. When I gather with family and friends, I continue to refer to some of the episodes of the time I spent in captivity. I also cannot help but regularly draw parallels between the days I spent under oppression and hunger, and now in freedom and comfort. It was a colorful, interesting and rich life, made up of events that led me sky high in one moment, and saw me hit rock bottom in another. My endurance and strength were tested, as well as my soul, but I lived "a helluva life!". Indeed, I went from playing games with lice and rats, to shaking 'paws' with royalty.